The long journey

**South Africa's quest for a
negotiated settlement**

The long journey

South Africa's quest for a
negotiated settlement

Edited by Steven Friedman

Researched by the
Centre for Policy Studies

RAVAN PRESS
Johannesburg

Published by Ravan Press (Pty) Ltd
Standard House, 40 De Korte Street, Braamfontein
P O Box 31134, Braamfontein 2017, South Africa

First published 1993

ISBN 0 869754 444 0

Project co-ordinator
Thaven Naidoo

Designed and produced by
Riaan de Villiers and Margie Edwards

Printed by Whitnall Simonsen
Batavia House
15 End Street
City & Suburban

Research funded by
the Liberty Life Foundation

Printing funded by
the governments of
The Netherlands and Canada

Cover: ANC supporters march to the Union Buildings
in Pretoria, 5 August 1992
Photograph: Paul Weinberg, Southlight

Contents

Preface

Since February 1990, when the country's quest for a negotiated settlement formally began, a bewildered society has had little chance to reflect on the political events unfolding in its midst. Our attempted transition to democracy has produced much journalism, and almost as much analysis. But in the midst of the maelstrom there have been few, if any, attempts to offer a detailed history and analysis of the events of the past three years.

This study is a modest attempt partly to fill that gap. It does not claim to offer an exhaustive account of the entire transition, but concentrates only on an aspect of it – the Convention for a Democratic South Africa, or Codesa, which sat from December 1991 to May 1992. It also attempts, briefly, to draw from that experience some of the challenges which face our divided society as it seeks to create a workable future.

Simply to record events through the life of Codesa is itself important: much of what happened at the convention remains a mystery even to South Africans who take a keen interest in politics. But, for at least two reasons, an unadorned narrative is not enough.

Firstly, to those outside the inner circle of negotiators and party advisors, events at Codesa were often arcane and confusing, not only because the convention worked primarily behind closed doors. Important clashes of interest were often concealed behind 'technical' submissions and counterproposals. If the citizenry whose future is to be decided by the negotiations is to understand what was being agreed – or not agreed – in its name, these require explanation. Secondly, Codesa's experience should have something to say about our prospects of reaching and sustaining a workable settlement. Analysis is needed to link the events at the convention with the pitfalls and possibilities facing our society.

When, therefore, the Centre for Policy Studies was approached to undertake a study of Codesa, it seemed a task suited to CPS's team of analysts, but also one which could be enriched by the contribution of skilled journalists. This is reflected both in the way in which we have approached the topic, and in the team chosen to research and write this book.

Alan Fine of *Business Day* and Patrick Bulger, who covered Codesa for that newspaper but has since left journalism, were invited to join a small CPS research team. So too was Kathy Eales, a researcher with a deserved reputation for accuracy and insight, who has since left research for journalism. The CPS team, headed by Louise Stack, also comprised Richard Humphries and Steven Friedman, who contented himself with editing the work from the comfort of his desk. Khehla

Shubane, while not a member of the original team, contributed some vital interviews to the final chapter.

While co-operation between analysts and journalists is not unknown, it is rarer than it perhaps should be. Journalists must approach their task with an eye to the immediate, while analysts seek to bring a longer-term perspective to a study of contemporary events. If good journalists can offer a 'feel' for – and a closeness to – the history unfolding about us which often eludes the analyst, the latter can help to place the immediate in a context and, if only tentatively, point to its likely future impact.

Whether this attempt to combine the two skills succeeds, is for others to judge. But our experience during this study convinces us that the attempt to combine journalism and political analysis, and to produce a study which attempts to combine the best elements of both, can provide readers with a better rounded understanding of events than either reporters or academics could produce on their own.

For the most part we worked as a team. We met regularly, pooled information and insights, and tried to reach agreement on our interpretation of what we had learned. Usually we succeeded, although at times team members accepted with good grace a majority view with which they disagreed. This explains why sections of this book are not signed by particular members. Nevertheless, labour was divided and team members accepted primary responsibility for researching and writing the first drafts of each section – 'primary', because each researcher relied to some extent on information gathered by other members of the team.

Patrick Bulger was primarily responsible for the runup to Codesa, the discussion of Working Group 2 and, with Alan Fine, the account of events after Codesa 2.

Alan Fine took responsibility for Working Group 1 and, with Bulger, post-Codesa events.

Kathy Eales, with Richard Humphries, provided the account of Working Group 4 and the Gender Advisory Committee.

Richard Humphries, a specialist on regionalism, worked exclusively on Working Group 4.

Louise Stack, besides co-ordinating the study, is primarily responsible for Working Group 3 and, with help from Khehla Shubane, the final chapter.

Steven Friedman was responsible for the final version of the book.

Thaven Naidoo acted as project co-ordinator.

Riaan de Villiers joined the team to copy-edit and produce the study.

Margie Edwards assisted with design and production

Ultimately, however, this attempt to record and understand Codesa should be seen as a collective effort.

In the limited time available to prepare the book we inevitably became aware of inquiries we could have pursued, people we could have interviewed, and analyses we could have developed more fully. We brace ourselves for the inevitable criticism of Codesa participants and fellow analysts. In time, no doubt, hindsight will become clearer; new information and insights may add to our understanding of Codesa and the process of which it is part. But if this first record provides a basis for new inquiries – and, equally importantly, if it adds to the knowledge of both analysts and lay people who seek to understand our society's attempt to forge a future out of our unhappy past – the team's work will have been richly rewarded.

Particular thanks are due to the **Liberty Life Foundation**, whose generous grant made the research possible, and the governments of **The Netherlands** and **Canada**, which helped to fund publication.

Steven Friedman
March 1993

Acronyms and abbreviations

ANC	African National Congress
Apla	Azanian People's Liberation Army
AVU	Afrikaner Volksunie
CA	constituent assembly
CBM	Consultative Business Movement
CDF	Ciskei Defence Force
CMB	constitution-making body
Codesa	Convention for a Democratic South Africa
COM	Campaign for Open Media
Contralesa	Congress of Traditional Leaders of South Africa
Cosag	Concerned South Africans Group
Cosatu	Congress of South African Trade Unions
CPS	Centre for Policy Studies
DMC	daily management committee
DP	Democratic Party
EPG	Eminent Persons Group
GAC	Gender Advisory Committee
IEC	independent election commission
IFP	Inkatha Freedom Party
IGC	interim government council
ISA	Internal Security Act
LDRC	local dispute resolution committee
LHR	Lawyers for Human Rights
LP	Labour Party
MC	management committee
MK	Umkhonto we Sizwe
MPs	members of parliament
NA	national assembly
NEC	national executive committee
NIC/TIC	Natal Indian Congress/Transvaal Indian Congress
NIS	National Intelligence Service
NP	National Party
NPA	National Peace Accord
NPC	national peace committee
NPP	National People's Party
NPS	national peace secretariat
PAC	Pan-Africanist Congress
PF	Patriotic Front
PSA	Public Safety Act
PWV	Pretoria-Witwatersrand-Vereeniging
RDRC	regional dispute resolution committee
RSA	Republic of South Africa
Saccola	South African Employers' Consultative Committee on Labour Affairs
Sacob	South African Chamber of Business
SACP	South African Communist Party

SADF   South African Defence Force
Saita   South African Independent Telecommunications Authority
SAP   South African Police
Secosaf   Secretariat of the Economic Community of
          Southern African States
SG   subgroup of Codesa working groups
SGT   self-governing territory
TBVC   Transkei, Bophuthatswana, Venda, Ciskei
TC   technical committee
TEC   transitional executive council
TGOR   transitional government of reconciliation
UDF   United Democratic Front
WG   Codesa working group

Photographers

Andrew Bannister: 145.
Andrew Mohamed, Department of Information and Publicity,
African National Congress: 79, 101, 113, 133, 184.
Brian Givens, Southlight: 147.
Brian Hendler, *Business Day*: 89.
Cecil Sols, Dynamic Images: 108, 158.
Elmond Jiyane, Dynamic Images: 44, 140.
Eric Miller, Southlight: 11, 56.
Graeme Williams, Southlight: 8, 181.
Guy Tillim: 168.
Kevin Carter, *Weekly Mail*: 155, 160.
Mbuzeni Zulu, *Sowetan*: 177.
Nigel Dennis, DIP, ANC: 64, 137, 165.
Paul Velasco, Southlight: 151.
Peter Magubane, Codesa archives: 61, 68.
Phumla Radu, DIP, ANC: 119.
Robert Botha, *Business Day*: 18, 23, 24, 27, 29, 31, 32, 35, 37,
41, 51, 73, 131, 143, 166.
Rodger Bosch, Southlight: 2, 12, 15.
Steve Hilton-Barber, Southlight: 7.
William Matlala, Southlight: 191.

PART 1

The road
to Codesa

The reluctant reconcilers

For much of the 1980s, South Africa seemed doomed to join the Middle East and Northern Ireland on a short list of countries whose intractable conflicts attract academics and journalists, not tourists and investors.

Conventional wisdom – and strategists on both sides of the political divide – assumed that the country could settle the conflict between minority rule and majority demands in only two ways: reform or revolution. The first meant that the minority would continue to rule, while adapting to the economic and demographic changes which threatened classical apartheid; the second, that the 'liberation' forces would overthrow the apartheid state.[1] Since the second seemed highly unlikely, and the first promised lengthy conflict, only a long and debilitating war of attrition seemed possible. In sum, South Africa did not seem, through the 1980s, a likely candidate for peaceful constitutional change.

To be sure, in 1986 the country had purportedly hovered on the brink of a settlement. Shocked by violent revolt in the black townships, the government had – rhetorically at least – acknowledged that apartheid had failed by acknowledging that the black majority could not be denied a say in central government. The British Commonwealth had assembled an Eminent Persons Group which had appeared to secure an agreement from Pretoria to negotiate a new order with African nationalist leadership. The talks did not begin: the government, convinced that the price it was asked to pay was far too high, ordered a military attack on its neighbours, purportedly aimed at camps housing cadres of the nationalist movement, the African National Congress. A state of emergency followed soon afterwards; it was to last through the rest of the 1980s. The quick solution promised by the EPG was replaced by that far more familiar South African phenomenon – the protracted struggle.

Through the barrel of a gun: parties to conflict

The government's chief adversary was the ANC, formed in 1912 in protest against a law which declared more than four fifths of the country's land surface the sole property of whites. It began life as a vehicle for dignified and educated gentlemen who believed that the petition and the eloquent argument would be enough to secure black participation in national political and economic life. In the early 1950s it turned to mass mobilisation in the hope that non-violent pressure would succeed where argument had failed. It did not; in 1960 the ANC was outlawed and, in a formal alliance with the South African Communist Party, it sought from exile to overthrow the system which neither pleas nor mass protest had been able to move.

Despite some highly visible (and at times extremely bloody) urban guerrilla actions, the exiled ANC's 'armed struggle' did little to weaken the white-ruled state. A far more substantial challenge emerged from within the country's borders. In 1973 a strike wave in the industrial port city of Durban triggered a resurgence of black worker organisation which, a decade later, had produced a militant and growing trade union movement, armed now with legally recognised bargaining rights which ensured its permanence. In 1976 conflict in the country's largest township, Soweto, prompted more than a year of nation-wide township turmoil. It petered out, but not for long. By the early 1980s grassroots resistance organisations began to emerge in the townships and, in mid-decade, student protests followed by township resistance triggered a new wave of turmoil whose stated aim was to render black areas – and, presumably, the country – 'ungovernable'. The exiled ANC had little role in these events; the United Democratic Front, formed in 1983 in reaction to a new constitution which confirmed black African exclusion from parliament, led the protest. But, as later events were to show, the resistance was led by activists who identified strongly with the ANC even if they could not publicly join or support it.

This conflict, more organised and durable than its predecessors, sparked an almost tangible euphoria among local activists and the exiled ANC. The latter saw it as the beginning of a 'people's war' which, together with an increasingly successful campaign to isolate the 'regime' politically and economically from the world community, would soon bring the system to its knees. The 1986 emergency was greeted as 'the last kick of a dying horse', the final authoritarian spasm before the system's collapse. They soon learned that the horse was healthier than they had believed – militarily, at any rate. Armed with emergency powers, the government detained thousands of activists and the military put an end to the turmoil. The ANC and its internal sympathisers sought ways of retaining small pockets of organisation among the ruins, and looked ahead to a 'struggle' which had no visible end.

The ruling National Party seemed equally willing to see that battle through to its distant end. To be sure, since the 1970s the NP had been forced to concede that the 'classical' apartheid which it had imposed during the 1960s – built on the assumption that a very low ceiling could be placed on black economic and political participation in the 87 per cent of the country deemed 'white' – was no longer workable. The 1973 strikes had forced it to accept that black workers were permanent and indispensable participants in an industrial economy; by 1979, it had recognised the right of black unions to bargain.

The 1976 conflict had forced it to recognise that black people were an equally inevitable and indispensable feature of urban life in 'white' South

Africa. And the conflict of the mid-1980s had forced it to acknowledge that people whose labour and presence in the 'white' 87 per cent would always be needed, would have to enjoy political rights.

But the government remained convinced that these unpleasant realities could be accommodated without conceding its hold on power. Each reform which sought to adapt to black indispensability was designed to prevent the need for further change. Initially, it hoped to avoid black political participation at the centre altogether; when it conceded it could not, it sought to extend it in ways which would guarantee white supremacy. The 1980s were not only a decade of conflict but also of constitutional tinkering in which ever more elaborate and exotic plans were unveiled, all of which had a common theme: whites and their political representatives would have the final say in decisions or, at the very least, a veto over anything which blacks decided.

Frederik Willem de Klerk takes the salute during his inauguration as state president, 20 September l989.

The Commonwealth mission failed because it insisted that the government concede a non-racial state. This, the NP believed, would mean the political extinction of it and those it represented. If the choice was between that and a long battle against foreign sanctions and local 'radicals', the government believed it had no choice but to resign itself to the latter. Armed with an American book on counter-insurgency[2] and the largest security capacity on the continent, it determined to ward off the 'total onslaught' of its enemies with force and resourcefulness.

That the battle lines were irrevocably drawn seemed to be confirmed both by a heightened bellicosity on both sides, and the grim realities of daily life. Military strategists repeatedly warned that the country was at war with a deadly enemy, and that the township activist or white suburban anti-conscription campaigner was as much a part of the 'onslaught' as the guerrilla. In 1987, on the occasion of the 25th anniversary of its armed wing, Umkhonto weSizwe (MK), the ANC declared: 'Our history has taught us that people's power cannot come through a change of heart from the rulers.' Its military strategists suggested that it could no

Nelson Mandela
greets supporters
upon his release
from Victor
Verster prison,
11 February 1990.

longer restrict itself to attacks on military targets, and that civilians would find themselves in the crossfire.[3] The rhetoric on both sides translated into a military occupation of the townships and isolated, but traumatic, urban terrorism in the 'white' areas.

And yet, four years after the 1986 emergency was declared, the NP and ANC met at Groote Schuur, the presidential residence in Cape Town, and signed a pact meant to be the first step in a negotiation process leading to a non-racial political order.

The odd couple: parties to compromise

If that seemed odd, at first glance the identities of the leaders in both camps who had led the adversaries into this historic compromise seemed to make it stranger still. The NP's leader, state president Frederik Willem de Klerk, was the scion of a family of prominent Afrikaner Nationalist politicians, a man steeped in the politics and lore of the movement and party which had imposed apartheid on the country.[4] While he was the first NP leader who had not personally experienced

the indignities of British colonial rule, which had shaped the vision of his predecessors, he was as firmly within the main stream as any leader of his generation could be.

Nor was he a reformist maverick. To be sure, De Klerk had, as he was later to point out repeatedly, stumped the country in the 1987 white election campaign as Transvaal leader of the NP, warning voters in the most conservative reaches of the white heartland that change was inevitable. But his brand of change was NP-led reform, not accommodation with 'the enemy': in 1987 he led the government condemnation of Afrikaners who had flown to Dakar, Senegal, to meet the exiled ANC leadership for the first time. Throughout the second half of the decade he was regarded, with justification, as one of the cabinet conservatives.

Indeed, his vision was in some ways more uncompromising than that of many of his colleagues. De Klerk was the chief zealot of 'group rights', which implied that racial groups, not people, were the primary and permanent elements of a workable political order: one implication was that people would continue to live in separate suburbs and send their children to separate schools. 'Group rights' was not a slogan designed to soothe his constituency: to those who discussed the concept with him during the late 1980s, he appeared to see it as an article of faith.

The ANC's chief protagonist, Nelson Rohihlala Mandela, was not even the titular leader of the movement at the time of the Groote Schuur meeting. As a young lawyer in the 1940s he had been a key figure in the ANC Youth League which had steered the movement towards militancy in the 1950s. After the banning of the ANC it was Mandela, labelled the 'Black Pimpernel', who had organised the military underground as a member of the high command of MK.[5] In 27 years of imprisonment he had become a symbol of unremitting opposition to white rule.

Both De Klerk and Mandela are more complex figures than this brief description implies. Nor was their joint commitment to negotiated constitutional change quite the bolt from the blue which it seemed. It stemmed from a joint realisation that the (very different) visions which had informed most of their political lives were unattainable. And this, in turn, was rooted in realities which had begun to impel the adversaries towards an attempt to negotiate the future even while they seemed to be preparing for interminable battle.

On the surface, the seeds were sown in 1988 when Mandela, in a letter from prison, extended an invitation to the government to negotiate a political settlement. Mandela, a sophisticated strategist, sensed both that the overthrow of the white state was a chimera and that an unprecedented opportunity existed to secure through negotiation at least a large part of that which 'people's war' had failed to achieve. This was the first public indication that there might be an alternative to civil war (although a government intelligence source says that contact between it and the ANC began in 1984 in Geneva) and it triggered a series of negotiations between Mandela and senior government ministers and intelligence strategists. Some say a 'secret deal' was hammered out; more prosaically, the contact appears to have persuaded some key government figures that a settlement with the ANC need not mean the demise of white South Africa – or, indeed, of the NP itself as an influential political force.

As long as P W Botha remained state president, this was not enough to secure a breakthrough. Botha relied on different advisors to those who were meeting Mandela; he and those on whom he relied were too steeped in the ethos of the 'total onslaught' to countenance so new a course. But by August 1989 he was no longer president. De Klerk, whose easy manner and bemused smile had led one NP member of parliament to describe him as the Noel Coward of the party, was a conservative, but he was also a pragmatist. And, precisely because he was a creature of the NP, he was more ready to listen to political advisers and to respond to a pragmatism within the party caucus, rather than – as his predecessor did – a small group of senior military officers. In sum, De Klerk's accession to the presidency opened the way for the NP to seek a compromise which its strategists had concluded was inevitable, but which Botha's presence had, in the last two years of his presidency, prevented it from pursuing.

Settling for second best: the roots of compromise

This description begs a question: why did De Klerk and Mandela conclude separately that compromise was unavoidable? An analysis of all the factors which brought them to the negotiation table is beyond the scope of this work.[6] But, even while war was being declared in the mid-1980s, both the ANC and the government were realising that conflict would not defeat the 'enemy', and were seeking an alternative.

The ANC's guerrilla war never held out a serious prospect of overthrowing the apartheid state – the movement had seen guerrilla attacks more as a supplement to other forms of pressure than as a route to power. By the last years of the 1980s it was not at all clear that it could wage even limited guerrilla war. The physical and economic cost of hosting ANC bases was becoming unsustainable for neighbouring states, and the movement faced the prospect of being driven further and further away from the borders it sought to penetrate. Its chief source of armaments, the Soviet Union, was undergoing profound changes and was dis-

tinctly unwilling to continue funding military activity; indeed, it began pressuring the ANC to settle the conflict by negotiation.[7] Domestic insurrection had seemed to offer a better prospect of success, but the state of emergency had underlined the state's ability to contain this threat.

And, while the campaign to isolate the state by encouraging economic and other sanctions was making ground, sanctions were an ineffective revolutionary instrument; they were far better suited to forcing an adversary to the bargaining table than to its knees. The changes in the Soviet Union also for the first time raised the prospect of a joint western/Soviet initiative to settle the South African conflict; if the ANC was seen to be unwilling to co-operate, sanctions might not last long. For a movement which had based so much of its strategy on winning the diplomatic war, this was probably more persuasive than its military set-

F W de Klerk and Nelson Mandela address the press after signing the Groote Schuur Minute, 4 May 1990.

F W de Klerk and Nelson Mandela at the National Peace Convention, 14 September 1991.

backs. In 1987, when it appeared to be preparing for a lengthy war, the ANC published a statement which proposed negotiation, not revolution, as the route to a post-apartheid order.[8] When the opportunity came to negotiate, it was taken.

The opportunity was created by similar pressures on the NP and the government over which it presided. The state was in no danger of collapse, but the costs of ruling by force were becoming unsustainable – in the longer term at least. As long as order could be maintained by force alone, and sanctions remained, the country faced an inevitable economic decline. The NP's strategists had known since the mid-1980s that it could not continue to rule indefinitely without black co-operation; the mix of reform and force was designed to achieve that on favourable terms, not avoid it. The emergency was not designed to prevent negotiation or black participation in central government, but to ensure that the NP would have to deal with black parties willing to accept it on government terms.

It failed: 'moderate' black leaders such as Mangosuthu Buthelezi of the Inkatha Freedom Party did not see security action against 'radicals' as an opportunity to negotiate; he refused to talk until the repression ended. And, in October 1988, the strategy's failure to strengthen black 'moderates' was illustrated when, despite the removal of 'radicals', only a small minority of township residents voted in the Black Local Authority polls in which they were supposed to express their enthusiasm for 'moderate' leadership.[9]

The international dimension was again crucial. The erosion of Soviet power, together with increased South African international respectability

THE RELUCTANT RECONCILERS

created by its role in negotiations which led to Namibian independence, sharply lowered the risk of negotiation – and created the expectation that concessions to international opinion might hold concrete gains. In sum, the costs of not negotiating were growing, but so too was the hope of rewards for doing so. As reports began to reach South Africa that some Soviet analysts were advocating a settlement which would offer the white minority safeguards which even western opinion had seemed unwilling to entertain, the prospect that a negotiated settlement with the ANC might not entail 'surrender' to majority rule seemed far more realistic than it had ever been.

These were among the forces and factors which prompted De Klerk, in February 1990, to deliver his celebrated address in which he lifted the ban on the ANC and the Pan-Africanist Congress and committed his government to a negotiated end to exclusive white rule.[10] They also explain why the ANC quickly accepted the offer, and returned to negotiate. In those euphoric early days of 1990 De Klerk became, among the disenfranchised, the most popular white minority leader in the country's history, fêted in black townships as 'Comrade F W'. Mandela, released from prison shortly after De Klerk's speech, was fêted by blacks but was also hailed by white decision-makers as the guarantor of a negotiated future.

The reluctant negotiators

But, while much was made of the 'chemistry' between Mandela and De Klerk, the excitement hid a continuing and seemingly unbridgeable gulf between their two organisations. Both camps had turned to negotiation as a reluctant 'second best' because there seemed to be no alternative, rather than from a desire for a historic reconciliation. Initially, both seemed more concerned to be *seen* to be negotiating – in the hope that the other would be manoeuvred into appearing unreasonable in the eyes of the foreign brokers who had mediated the attempt at reconciliation – than to bargain an agreed future.

The ANC's expected role was particularly difficult: it was expected to convert itself from a revolutionary 'liberation' movement into a party organised and coherent enough to negotiate a difficult compromise with a bargaining partner which still firmly held the reins of power, and whose negotiating skills had been honed in complex negotiations with the American, Soviet and Cuban governments over Angola and Namibia. Not only was a negotiated settlement not what the ANC's following was expecting; it was not a challenge for which years of exile had equipped it. The ANC's transition was difficult and, for much of the next two years, incomplete – some would argue that it still is.

Indeed, the ANC was arguably only ready to negotiate a new constitution after June 1991, when it held its first national conference inside the country in decades. It was here, for the first time since its return from exile, that it elected a leadership with a mandate to negotiate.

Mandela was, predictably, elected president. And, in a step which was to prove increasingly important as the negotiation process unfolded, it also elected Cyril Ramaphosa, general secretary of the National Union of Mineworkers, as secretary general. A seasoned negotiator and organiser, Ramaphosa seemed equipped to help steer the ANC into a new environment in which negotiating skill and strategy, as well as organisation, had replaced populist rhetoric and revolutionary activity as strategic priorities.

But the ANC's change of identity was a secondary obstacle. While negotiators on both sides soon realised that there was no alternative to a negotiated settlement, compromise remained a strategic necessity, not a preferred option, for both. Nor had those they represented reconciled themselves to compromise. Both sides therefore assured their camps that negotiation was a means of achieving the old goals by new means. De Klerk repeatedly insisted that the NP was not about to surrender to 'simple majority rule', leaving its fate in the hands of a nonracial electorate: it would demand a guaranteed share in power, whatever the outcome of a popular vote. ANC leaders insisted that negotiations would produce precisely the 'majority rule' – and hence the surrender – which 'people's war' and international isolation had failed to achieve.

These contending visions were so contradictory that the two could not agree on how a new constitution should be negotiated, let alone its contents. The ANC, consistent with its continued demand for majority rule, insisted that only a constituent assembly, elected by all adults, could devise the new order. To the NP, and Buthelezi's IFP, this was an attempt to decide the outcome of negotiation before it began: to say that the majority should draw the constitution was to say that it should rule – and, therefore, to insist that the key issue to be negotiated should be decided even before the bargaining started. The NP therefore proposed a multi-party conference, comprising all political parties 'with an identifiable constituency', as the constitution-making body. It was not difficult to see this as an attempt to revive, with ANC participation, the strategy of the 1980s: in 1986, then Constitutional Affairs minister Chris Heunis had proposed a 'council of leaders' which would include African representatives and would rule by 'consensus', ensuring that white representatives could not be outvoted. To the ANC, *this* was to decide the outcome in advance, since to insist that all parties, regardless of support (which would, of course, remain untested), enjoy an equal say in the constitution was to deny the majority's claims even before they had been stated.

This divide ensured that, although the ANC and NP kept talking – and, at meetings at Groote Schuur and Pretoria, reached agreements on steps which opened the way to constitutional talks, such as the suspension of hostilities by MK and the release of political prisoners – their discussions concerned only the obstacles which were to be removed before negotiations could begin.[11] It took almost two years before constitutional talks began. By then, the chief product of their mutual commitment to

negotiation had been levels of violence greater than those which had prompted the states of emergency.[12]

Nelson Mandela and Mangosuthu Buthelezi at the National Peace Convention, 14 September 1991.

Seeds of compromise

The 'breakthrough' which made even this belated start possible was a statement by Mandela – then still ANC deputy president – in January 1991. This called for an 'all-party congress' to negotiate the route to a constituent assembly. While the ANC retained its central demand for an elected constitution-making body, this was, in effect, an agreement to multi-party negotiations. While it would obviously put its demand for an elected assembly to the other parties, they would, equally obviously, reject it – allowing the bargaining, and the compromises, to begin.

Nor was a compromise impossible; the government and its allies were opposed to an elected assembly, not in principle, but because they did not want the representatives of the majority to write the constitution. But this was not an inevitable result of agreement on an elected assembly: decisions could be taken, as they had been in Namibia's constituent assembly, by a 'special majority' – two thirds in Namibia – which could give minorities a veto. The ANC had never demanded decision-making by a simple majority (50 per cent plus one), and its strategists were already beginning to concede the need for 'special' majorities.[13] Nor, despite the rhetoric it used in the early days of the process, did it seem committed to 'simple majority rule': in April 1990 Mandela had suggested that the first elected government would consist of all parties which gained significant support at the polls.[14] The 'unbridgeable' gulf seemed bridgeable after all.

Nevertheless, if strategists were shifting ground, they were still unwilling or unable to carry their constituencies with them. The next few months provided grim evidence that it would take more than finely crafted strategic shifts by leaders to end the polarisation of decades; conflict continued and the all- (or multi-party) conference remained an intention in the minds of its architects.

Indeed, in May, negotiations broke off altogether when the ANC withdrew, charging the government with complicity in the violence and demanding measures to restore its confidence in negotiation. If this indicated how deep the divide remained, the manner of its return to the table showed too how great the pressures for a settlement were. Some, but not all, the ANC's demands were met, but it returned to negotiation nevertheless. It said in effect that it was doing so because the violence would persist as long as the NP remained in power. Only an interim government, in which the ruling party would be forced to share power, could address the problem, and only negotiation could achieve that. This response revealed a pattern to be repeated countless times throughout the negotiation process: concessions and compromises would be made, but in terms which presented them as new ways of continuing the conflict.

It was not until September that the foundations of multi-party (or all-party) talks were laid. The vehicle was the National Peace Accord, a formal agreement in which political parties and interest groups committed themselves to a joint peace effort, agreed to submit to disciplines imposed by the accord, and to establish structures to monitor it. The NPA's contribution to peace-making was to remain limited. But it was the first formal multi-party accord, and it built sufficient confidence among the parties to persuade them to proceed to constitutional talks.

Indeed, it seemed for a time that these talks would be even more inclusive than most commentators and politicians had expected. In October the PAC, which saw both majority rule and constitution-making by an elected constituent assembly as non-negotiables, joined the ANC at a Patriotic Front conference held in Durban. Designed as a forum to weld a common front of 'liberation' movements, the gathering appeared to end in an agreement by the PAC to join the all-party talks.

In a paper presented to that meeting the ANC spelled out its rationale for, and expectations of, the all-party meeting. It was necessary, it said, because neither parliament nor the government could legitimately make decisions 'about such critical questions as the body to negotiate the new constitution, and how the country should be governed during the transitional period'. In other words, even an elected assembly would have to be arranged – and the government could not be allowed to arrange it alone. The all-party meeting was not an alternative to a constituent assembly, it was the only way to achieve one. The ANC saw the conference sitting for a short time to discuss measures which would be needed before an assembly could be elected: a free political climate; reincorporation of the TBVC 'states'; constitutional principles; interim government; the mechanism to draw up a constitution; the role of the international community; and a time frame.

Inevitably, the ANC said it would put to this meeting its view that the constitution be written by an elected constituent assembly, and added that the gathering might sit for several months: while the PAC insisted on referring to the meeting as a 'pre-constituent assembly conference', implying that it would meet briefly to endorse this demand and then adjourn to implement it, the ANC implied for the first time both that its demand would not automatically be endorsed, and that it would take some time to negotiate a compromise.

It (the ANC) added that it saw an 18-month period between the end of the conference and the first elections under a new constitution, during which the country would be ruled by an interim government of national unity. It would be 'composed of an effective mix of political forces', but would have a definite life span and 'would not persist indefinitely (as has happened in other situations)'. It would need a legal and constitutional form to prevent 'legal, political and possibly armed counter-revolutionary challenges by the extreme right wing'.

The statement was significant in two ways. It seemed to signal firstly that the ANC was aware that it was committing itself to substantial compromises; secondly, that it had found a way of presenting these as a necessary step on the route to 'liberation', so much so that it had convinced the PAC as well as its own doubters.

On 22 October, then, the ANC's national executive committee formally endorsed an all-party conference to which all political groupings, including the PAC and Azanian People's Organisation on the 'left' and the Conservative Party and Afrikaner Weerstandsbeweging on the right, would be invited. According to the ANC's *Negotiations Bulletin* (no 2), the NEC also confirmed the agenda spelled out at the Patriotic Front conference. It noted that the ANC and government had met three times in October to discuss details of the conference.

This decision was followed by a preparatory meeting, twice delayed but eventually convened at an hotel near Jan Smuts Airport. This gathering suffered a setback when the PAC withdrew. Having demanded that the conference convene outside the country under a 'neutral' chair – it rejected the appointment of two judges to chair it, on the grounds that they were functionaries of the state which was party to the talks[15] – it found not only that its position was rejected but that the ANC, despite the camaraderie of the Patriotic Front conference, joined the government in rejecting it. It retired to seek a mandate from its constituency to join the talks, which it was vociferously denied.[16]

Nevertheless, the other parties, primarily the ANC and NP, had clearly decided that the conference would proceed whatever the PAC thought, and progress was smooth and swift. At the end of the second day South Africa had finally come to the end of the 'pre-negotiation' phase. Further talks would now take place within a forum called the Convention for a Democratic South Africa (Codesa).

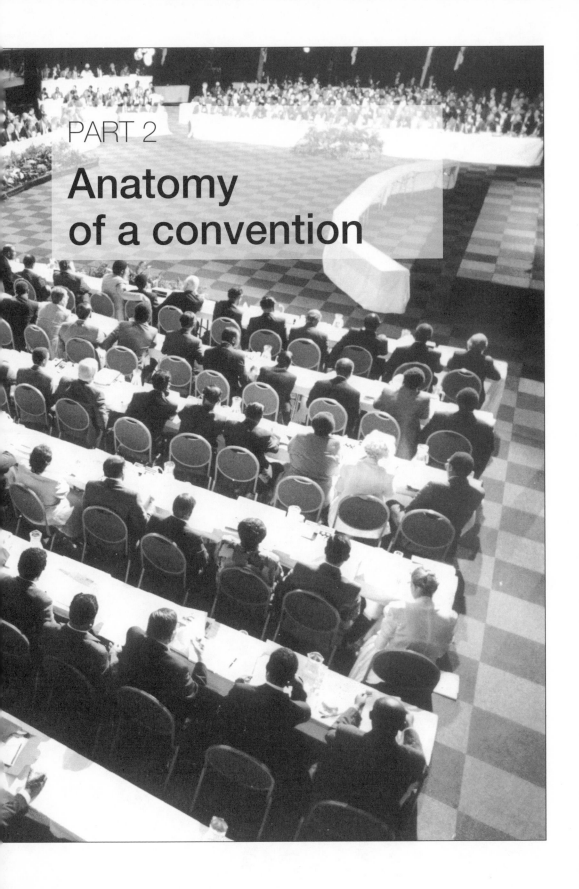

PART 2

Anatomy
of a convention

From breakthrough to breakdown

Codesa's first plenary assembled at an unlikely time in an unlikely place. The gathering had been convened in some haste; negotiators in both the ANC and NP camps had repeatedly promised that negotiations would begin before the end of 1991. Repeated delays had threatened to undermine public confidence; the two major parties were clearly determined that this was one promise which would be kept. The convention assembled, therefore, on 20 and 21 December, in the midst of the 'silly season', when politicians usually left on their annual holidays and the national preoccupation turned to preparations for the festive season. The venue, the World Trade Centre outside Johannesburg's Jan Smuts Airport, was neither imposing nor rich in history. At the time the choice seemed odd: in retrospect, perhaps its lack of political – or any other – symbolism made it the nearest the participants were to get to a neutral venue. Certainly, the first formal attempt to negotiate the future was sited in a venue with little association with the past.

More symbolic, perhaps, was the identity of the convention's chair. Two judges, Piet Schabort and Ismail Mohamed, had been chosen; the latter was the country's first black judge, who had previously gained his reputation in several exceptionally able appearances as advocate for the defence in political trials. Schabort had won respect for both fairness and competence, but was a pillar of the established judicial system; to some commentators, the chair seemed to represent a fusion of the best elements of the present and future.

But, if the plenary seemed to herald a fresh beginning, it did not convene without a reminder of the divided past. One key participant, the IFP's Mangosuthu Buthelezi, was absent – because he had chosen, very deliberately and loudly, to stay away. In the period before Codesa 1 (as the first plenary became known) Buthelezi and Inkatha had insisted that an IFP delegation was not enough. They had demanded that two additional delegations, one headed by the king of the Zulus, Goodwill Zwelethini, and the other representing the KwaZulu administration, be seated too.

Buthelezi was later to insist that he was demanding what others had already been granted. The Transkei, Venda and Ciskei administrations were represented (their leaders were military rulers who were not elected, nor did they lead parties; they were, therefore, representing the administration). So why not KwaZulu and the king of its 'citizens', who purportedly represented all Zulus, while the IFP spoke only for some? To IFP critics the demand seemed to be purely a power play, an attempt to set terms which would make it clear that its participation could not be taken for granted; that it would negotiate with the NP and ANC as an equal which could set its own conditions, or not at all. And the demand that the king be seated seemed to be an attempt to stress the importance of Zulu ethnicity, a theme which the IFP had begun to emphasise.

But, whatever the motive, the demand presented Codesa's organisers with a political and logistical nightmare. The ANC, too, had been wooing traditional leaders – a Congress of Traditional Leaders had been established with its encouragement – and the IFP condition prompted counter-claims that the King was not the country's only traditional leader, indeed not its only king ;[1] all the others would have to be seated as well. So too, presumably, would the administrations of other 'homelands', since only their ruling parties had been invited. No agreement could be reached, and Buthelezi stayed away in protest. The IFP did attend – the delegation was led by national chairman Frank Mdlalose. Many commentators saw the decision to send a delegation as a sign that the IFP too saw no alternative to negotiation and that Buthelezi's gesture need not be taken too seriously. But, as we shall see, these events did have a bearing on discussions at Codesa – and the IFP's purported fear of a NP/ANC pact at its expense was to pose important problems for the negotiation process.

Ritual and rhetoric

As the broadest ever cross-section of the country's political leaders gathered at the World Trade Centre, however, all that lay in the future. Nineteen parties were represented: the ANC was joined by its allies, the SACP and the Transvaal and Natal Indian Congresses (who shared a delegation); the NP was joined by a government delegation, a distinction presumably designed to demonstrate that the ruling party and the state

were different entities. It probably had the opposite effect, since the leading figures in the government team were usually NP cabinet ministers – as, of course, were the key members of the NP delegation. The IFP's – and, perhaps, the Democratic Party's – were the only other delegations which were expected to exert a significant influence on the convention. Five parties which controlled 'homeland' administrations,[2] the four TBVC administrations and three parties drawn from the tricameral parliament[3] completed the list.

Codesa 1 was in the main a ritualistic event, apparently designed more to impress a domestic public and foreign dignatories (who attended in some force) than to transact any business: a procession of speakers

Judge Ismail Mohamed, left, Chief Justice Michael Corbett and Judge P J Schabort at the opening of Codesa 1, 20 December 1991.

trooped to the podium to read prepared speeches, usually to polite applause. The real bargaining, it was assumed, would occur later.

However, even this bland gathering was not without drama. A speech by De Klerk questioning MK's continued existence prompted an impromptu and extremely angry response from Mandela; the two 'major' delegations then departed from the script for a while as old wounds

were opened. The incident was followed by a seemingly inevitable healing of the rift, and the planned schedule was resumed. Few experienced observers believed that the incident threatened negotiation: they saw it as a piece of (presumably unscripted) theatre which served mainly to show that the plenary was not entirely removed from the reality it sought to change. But in hindsight the incident was symbolic of two themes which were later to run through Codesa. The first was the multiparty forum's tendency to become, the moment serious issues were at stake, an arena for the NP and ANC alone. The second was the inability of the convention's single-minded search for surface consensus to breach the important divides between the two 'main' parties.

F W de Klerk arrives at Codesa 2, 15 May 1992.

The first point was illustrated by a 'technical' procedural rule agreed at Codesa 1 – 'sufficient consensus'. Where agreement from all parties – full consensus – on a particular point could not be secured, it would be enough for the parties to reach 'sufficient consensus'. According to one account, this magical principle was announced to a senior Codesa participant the night before the convention began by a key NP negotiator and his ANC counterpart. 'What does "sufficient consensus" mean?' the participant asked. 'Whatever we decide it means,' was the reply. Publicly this rule was never explained in understandable terms, but no one was in any doubt about its real meaning: 'sufficient consensus' was achieved whenever the ANC and NP agreed.

This did not mean that other parties were entirely passive: 'sufficient consensus' was applied rather earlier than Codesa's organisers had hoped when three parties opted out of the convention's first attempt at public unanimity. The centrepiece of Codesa 1 was the signing of a Declaration of Intent, consisting largely of vague statements of goodwill and designed primarily to avoid possibilities for disagreement: it committed participants to an undivided South Africa, peaceful constitutional change, a multi-party democracy with universal suffrage, a separation of powers, and a bill of rights. But the IFP initially refused to sign, insisting that the reference to an 'undivided'[4] South Africa ruled out the federal system which it demanded; it was joined by Ciskei and Bophuthatswana. The IFP and Ciskei did later sign (Bophuthatswana did not) – the former after securing an amendment which explained that the offending clause did not commit Codesa to a unitary state. But, as with Buthelezi's absence, the initial refusal was seen more as an irritant than a serious obstacle. And again, later events were to query the wisdom of that judgment.

The ceremonials having been duly completed, Codesa appointed five working groups whose task it was to prepare the way to a second plenary. It was in these groups that the real bargaining was expected to occur. It agreed also to convene the second plenary at an unspecified date in 1992 when, it was suggested, the first signs of concrete progress towards a negotiated settlement would be revealed. As delegates left to begin their Christmas holidays, there was little in their mood to suggest that they anticipated the travails ahead.

The gulf behind the glitter

If the parties really did expect plain sailing towards a settlement, they had no reason to do so. Despite the movement on both sides which had made Codesa possible, the difference between their visions of the transition to a new order remained unbridged. And a key difference concerned the purpose and lifespan of Codesa itself: what it was to achieve, and how long it would sit.

The rhetoric in which the ANC had clothed its decision to seek an 'all-party' conference may have been designed to 'sell' this compromise to the PAC and the ANC's own constituency. But it nevertheless described the goals with which the movement entered the convention. It still sought a swift transition from rule by a minority government to a new order shaped and ruled by the elected representatives of the majority. This meant the existing order had to give way as quickly as possible to an interim government and an elected constitution-making body. And it meant that as little as possible about the shape of the new constitution should be decided ahead of the election, since the more detail was agreed in the multi-party convention, the less leeway there would be for the elected body to frame the rules of the new order. Codesa's task was therefore to negotiate rapid progress to a constituent assembly, and to avoid agreements which would restrict that forum's freedom.

The NP – and its presumed allies – wanted as slow a transition as possible; the longer it lasted, the slower the change to a new order would be. It wanted, too, a process in which as much as possible was decided by all-party forums where it – and they – could expect to retain an influence they might be denied if the elected majority could decide. If there was to be a transition to majority rule at all, it would be a very long one: the fateful day would be preceded by at least a 10-year period of shared rule.[5] Codesa's role, therefore, was to agree as much as possible – and so to limit an elected assembly as much as possible. Nor would the NP relinquish sole power – to an interim government or elected assembly – until it had the guaranteed power sharing it wanted. Slow progress was not essential to the NP's strategy. But it clearly expected Codesa to be a more significant body than the ANC hoped – and this implied that it might have a longer life span.

Perhaps the only clear source of agreement was procedural – an acceptance that parliament would remain sovereign while Codesa talked, but would be bound by the convention's agreements. It was agreed that 'Codesa will establish a mechanism whose task it will be, in co-operation with administrations and the South African government, to draft the text of all legislation required to give effect to the agreements reached ...' The government added a declaration confirming that it considered itself 'bound by agreements we reach together with other participants in Codesa ... and hereby commit ourselves to the implementation thereof within our capacity, powers and authority'. This, of course, assumed that agreements would be reached at all. As events were to show, the fundamental gulf between the parties hardly made that inevitable.

Perhaps the only substance at Codesa 1 was provided by a De Klerk speech which seemed to narrow this divide and prepare the way for a compromise. He signalled his government's consent to an elected constitution-making body, but with an important rider: it would act as an interim government too, thus ostensibly agreeing to another ANC demand. But the ANC, as we have seen, demanded a multi-party interim authority whose life would be short and which would not be elected, since its prime task would be to prepare the way for elections without a single party (the government) gaining an unfair advantage from using the resources of the state. The government plan suggested both an elected authority and one which, its strategists suggested at the time, would rule for a long period – 10 to 15 years was mentioned – and would be governed by an interim constitution which entrenched the NP's proposals for enforced power.[6] The plan would be agreed at Codesa, put to a referendum of white, 'coloured' and Indian voters, and only if it was then approved would elections be organised to usher in interim rule.

NP strategists seem to have believed that this proposal would offer the ANC an opportunity to meet the government's demands without losing face. It would get its elected constitution-making body and its

IFP supporters demonstrate outside Codesa 2, 15 May 1992.

27

interim government; they would simply be fused. Indeed, government negotiator Tertius Delport said later he had persuaded the ANC to accept an elected interim government.

These expectations did not disappear when the ANC angrily denounced the proposal, accusing the government of 'skilfully trying to subvert the demand … for an interim government and an elected constituent assembly'. In January its *Negotiations Bulletin*, distributed within the movement, declared: 'The regime's approach makes the interim government an end in itself. We need to place emphasis where it belongs: the goal is the drafting and implementation of a new constitution. Unless agreement is reached on this matter, interim government can only serve as a trap.' The key purpose of interim government, it added, was 'to facilitate the bringing into being of a constituent assembly and the implementation of a new constitution'.[7] Only if it was agreed that an elected constitution-making body would be established, would it join an interim government.

Behind the rhetoric lay the objection that the government's plan had not really bridged the divide over Codesa's purpose at all. If the convention's task was to approve an interim government, ruling for a decade or more and governed by the NP's power-sharing model, then Codesa, rather than an elected body, would indeed be shaping the future for the next 10 years. If anything, the 'compromise' confirmed that the government did not intend Codesa to end until the NP's future was secure, regardless of anything an elected assembly might decide. As long as the ANC insisted that the convention was merely preparing the way for the elected constitution-makers, and the government was not prepared to leave Codesa until it had agreed the future, the parties remained deadlocked over the very nature of Codesa, let alone its outcome.

Despite the NP's optimism this divide was never bridged before the second plenary. Instead, the convention spent the next five months appearing to agree on everything except that which divided its parties.

Slow dance in a beleaguered ballroom

For the next five months Codesa was the dominant – in some ways the only – political event: even its opponents, such as the PAC, were compelled to spend much of their energy denouncing it. But its prominence owed more to the issues it was discussing than to the transparency or comprehensibility of its proceedings.

The negotiators disappeared into working groups operating behind closed doors – and, while Codesa's best-kept secrets were never that well kept, its proceedings became increasingly incomprehensible to even the most informed citizens. Unnamed sources from within the convention fed newspaper readers with a constant diet of cheerful assurances that 'major breakthroughs' had been achieved, followed almost as often

Great expectations: NP, DP and SACP delegates at Codesa 1, 20 December 1991.

by sombre warnings from equally anonymous insiders that agreement was far from near: usually the cheer seemed to emanate from government sources, the gloom from those in the ANC.

What precisely negotiators were agreeing (or disagreeing) was far from clear. The convention became impenetrably complex as ever more intricate proposals were made, to be countered by even more complicated responses. To activists anxious for 'liberation', business people eager for certainty or merely an end to sanctions, and citizens longing for peace, the manoeuvrings of the negotiators seemed ever more remote from their daily experience. A dance step called the Codesa was invented, in which the couple moved without changing their position on the dance floor. At township meetings, a person who talked at length without apparent purpose was dubbed a 'Codesa'.

The impatience was partly a symptom of exaggerated expectations:

although impatience was fuelled by the long wait before Codesa began, several months is not an excessive time in which to resolve a deep-rooted conflict which had lasted for decades, if not centuries. But the negotiators bore a sizeable share of the blame. If the citizenry expected Codesa to deliver either an instant constituent assembly or quick assent to power sharing, it was because political leaders often implied that it would. And if the public did not understand what was happening within the convention, it was because the negotiators never told them: indeed, even activists in both camps often appeared unaware of where their leaderships were taking them.

Perhaps most importantly, public disenchantment grew not only because the parties could not reach agreement on the country's future, but because they could not implement one they had already made about its present. While the politicians remained sequestered behind the doors of the World Trade Centre, the National Peace Accord seemed unable to prevent violence – or to stop the leaders who had committed themselves to a mutual effort to end it from blaming their adversaries for each failure. If the NPA was a guide, the citizenry had no great reason to feel confident about negotiations, particularly when the process seemed to grow more remote each day.

Growing public disillusionment had an important effect on Codesa: it created great pressure to 'show results', whether or not they had really been achieved. Constant assurances of 'breakthroughs' were one symptom, but they did not threaten the convention. What did was the perception within the World Trade Centre that Codesa would have to show visible public results soon. The second plenary had been promised in May (after some earlier promised dates had proved over-optimistic), and in May it would convene.

To close observers, who were beginning to make some sense of Codesa, a successful May plenary seemed implausible: DP negotiators, who had less of a stake in claiming instant success, warned that agreement on the issues which mattered was simply not achievable by the deadline. But this assumed that Codesa 2 was supposed to reach substantial agreements. For one major party, this was not necessarily so.

It was here that the divide we noted earlier became crucial. We have argued that the ANC needed the convention to produce quick concrete results, but that the NP was in no hurry. As disenchantment grew, therefore, it was government negotiators who sought to lower public expectations by insisting that decades-old problems could not be solved in a hurry: the diagnosis may have been accurate, but since it emanated from politicians whose sole hold on power would continue as long as the attempt to find solutions did, it lacked a certain plausibility. Government negotiators suggested, therefore, that Codesa 2 would hear 'progress reports' from the convention's working groups. The plenary's purpose would be to assure an anxious public that the parties were still talking and the process was still moving – even if it offered them little on where it was headed and when it would arrive.

The ANC remained in a greater hurry. Violence – which affected its constituents far more than the NP's white voters – continued, and the conditions of township life remained unchanged. The ANC had insisted repeatedly that conditions would not improve as long as the NP retained sole power. Its members clearly agreed – posters brandished at meetings upbraided Mandela for talking endlessly while 'the people' remained at the mercy of those who preyed on them. A series of choreographed

'progress reports' would do little to defuse impatience within the movement. The ANC needed more than a soothing spectacle at Codesa 2 – it had to have an agreement.

Chris April, Allan Hendrikse, Miley Richards and other LP delegates at Codesa 1.

The inevitable end

The outcome is well known. Pressed to resolve conflicts which it had at best only partly addressed, Codesa 2 collapsed – in a seemingly arcane dispute about percentages, which further diminished public understanding of the convention and respect for its participants. For months afterwards, negotiators insisted that agreement had been close and that someone – the other side – had sabotaged it. The reality was more sobering: agreement was not near, and the final dispute may merely have administered the final blow to a patient already doomed to die. To understand this, it is necessary to examine in detail the discussions within Codesa's working groups.

CODESA'S WORKING STRUCTURE

Before we begin a journey through the maze of Codesa's working groups, a word is needed about the convention's structures and workings: if the content of its discussions often seemed obscure to many, so did its mechanics.

Between Codesa 1 and 2 its work was delegated to five working groups in which each participant was represented by two delegates and two advisers. Their task was to reach agreement on key issues assigned to them and to compile a report, reflecting this consensus, to the next plenary. In theory, their reports were not binding since they needed ratification by the full convention; in practice, the presence of all delegations in each group made it unlikely that they would be rejected.

The working groups were responsible for discussing the creation of a free political climate; constitutional principles and a constitution-making body; a transitional or interim government; the reincorporation of the TBVC states; and time frames for the implementation of agreements. Each working group was to appoint a steering committee to streamline its work. In response to complaints that the 53 per cent of the population which happened to be female was barely represented at Codesa, the convention also established a Gender Advisory Committee, whose structure was similar to those of the working groups, to advise it on the 'gender implications' of its agreements.

In practice, Working Group 5 (time frames) had little to do since

Zach de Beer, centre, chaired Codesa's daily management committee. The ANC's Mac Maharaj, right, headed its secretariat.

there were no agreements to implement – an irony since the ANC, for example, placed one of its key advisors, lawyer George Bizos, in this working group, since it expected it to be of great importance: he and other delegates assigned to this group had a very quiet Codesa. The group did meet – it even began work on an electoral law, although this did not progress beyond the collection of information – but, through no fault of its own, spent most of its time waiting for a task which it was never called on to perform.[8] It will therefore not be analysed here.

While the working groups carried out their task, a body was needed to manage the convention as a whole. A daily management committee of eight individuals, each drawn from a different delegation, was appointed. Chaired by DP leader Zach de Beer, it was responsible for maintaining Codesa's momentum and for settling procedural disputes within the working groups. It was responsible to a bigger management committee, but played the major role in steering the convention. Finally, the DMC – and through it the working groups – were served by a secretariat, headed by former Constitutional Development director general Fanie van der Merwe and the ANC's Mac Maharaj, which was responsible for administration. Besides officials nominated by the parties, the Consultative Business Movement, a business alliance committed to aiding negotiation, offered administrative personnel and support.

Hard labour, scant reward

Working Group 1 was, in principle, a crucial one. First, it was part of its task to remove obstacles to open and fair competition between the parties – and so create that 'free political climate' which had been set by the ANC as a precondition for a settlement since the Harare Declaration.[1] For the ANC and many independent analysts, the parties could not negotiate – let alone compete in an election – on equal terms if one of them, the government, remained in sole control of the instruments of force, armed with a battery of security laws and control of the state media. For the government, 'intimidation' or the continued existence of armed ANC formations was an equally important barrier. Working Group 1 was therefore not only to clear the way to a settlement, but to begin preparing the rules for a South Africa in which free political competition would replace coercion.

Second, WG1 met at a time when the very absence of these rules made coercion an ever-present reality for many citizens: continued political violence, together with claims and counter-claims of 'intimidation', formed the backdrop to its work. It was this group, then, which was to address the issue – violence – which did most to damage Codesa's credibility, at least in the townships, as the convention wore on.

The sheer range of obstacles which lay in the path of free politics may explain why WG1 was presented with the lengthiest 'shopping list' of issues, many of which were to prove crucial obstacles in the path to a negotiated settlement. But it does not necessarily explain why, despite producing the longest report to the Codesa 2 plenary, it may well have achieved less than any other group.

Delegates gathering for WG1's first meeting contemplated an agenda comprising no less than 17 items (including a catch-all 'any other matters' clause) related to the 'creation of a climate for free political participation'. By Codesa 2 they had reached substantive agreement on very little. The group did achieve agreement on control of the public media, a key issue later in the process, but even this was only partial. Another firm agreement devised amendments to the Public Safety Act[2] in an attempt to liberalise emergency legislation – but this, as we shall see, hardly showered some negotiators with their supporters' gratitude. It also spent a great deal of energy suggesting improvements to the National Peace Accord; its proposals for more detailed NPA structures may in future play a part in reducing conflict, but, during 1992 they had no noticeable impact on levels of violence – or on the working of the NPA itself.

Several key issues, which were to prove central after Codesa, were hardly discussed at all. Some were left, implicitly or explicitly, to bilateral talks between the NP and the ANC, while one, the role of the international community, did not even come up for discussion until the final meeting of WG1 10 days before Codesa 2. Not surprisingly, that discussion was fruitless since the government was then hostile to any direct international involvement in the negotiation and peace process, and was not eager to discuss it. As with other key issues which remained unresolved, this question was only finally dealt with in the Record of Understanding of 26 September 1992 between the government and the ANC.[3]

Some participants deny that WG1 was a failure: NP delegate Boy Geldenhuys notes that the group 'addressed 60 per cent of the issues' scheduled for discussion, and refers to the length of its report. Others acknowledge that the ability to solve problems and reach binding agreements are more valid measures of success than the capacity to work through agendas – and that little was achieved on the first score. They advance many explanations – one on which they were, predictably, unanimous is that the size of the workload was an obstacle.

White right-wingers demonstrate outside Codesa, 20 December 1991.

Besides the number of issues to be canvased, WG1 received no fewer than 98 internal submissions (from Codesa delegations) and 102 external ones. Many were bulky, comprehensive documents. Participants say they took internal submissions seriously – almost all were allocated time for debate – and this was in itself a reason for the lack of productivity. As Law and Order deputy minister Gert Myburgh puts it: 'On each issue, each of the 19 parties would present their position. Discussion would go on for days.' And, having formally stated their position, parties would show a marked unwillingness to compromise on them.

The external submissions, meant as a means through which citizens' organisations not directly represented at the table could influence the future, were a perhaps inevitable victim: delegations would only raise points culled from them when these were seen to add to the debate. In practice, these submissions were effectively ignored – with a few exceptions, of which the main example was the work of the Campaign for Open Media, which the ANC alliance used almost exclusively in discussions on the South African Broadcasting Corporation and public broadcasting.

But WG1 faced obstacles other than its workload, some of which shed light on the broader problems which faced Codesa.

INSIDE WORKING GROUP 1
Skirting the centre

WG1 began its discussions on 6 February by allocating the matters for debate to three subgroups. Subgroup 1 (or SG1 as it came to be known) was to examine issues grouped under the general heading 'completing the reconciliation process'. These included finalising matters related to the release of political prisoners; the return of exiles; and the amendment and/or repeal of any remaining laws militating against free political activity, including the elimination of discriminatory laws.

SG2, charged with 'continuing the security and socio-economic process', was to focus on political intimidation; the termination of the use or threat of violence to promote political objectives; the successful implementation of the NPA; the prevention of violence-related crime; the role and composition of the security forces in South Africa and the TBVC 'states';[4] the need for improved socio-economic conditions; fostering tolerance among political parties; and the role of education and information campaigns on political tolerance, the working of democracy, and the Codesa process.

SG3 was mandated to examine the creation of 'a climate and opportunity for free political participation'. Specific topics for consideration were the political neutrality of and fair access to the state-controlled media, including those of the TBVC 'states'; the funding of political parties; fair access to public facilities and meeting venues; and the advisability of laws guaranteeing equal opportunity to all parties to establish and maintain their own means of mass communication. SG3 shared with

SG2 the responsibility to examine political tolerance between parties, and education and information campaigns on democracy.

'Motherhood and apple pie'

Each subgroup's debates deserve attention in their own right. But there were some common dynamics and trends among all the working groups. Perhaps the most obvious was that delegates spent much time discussing and agreeing on what IFP delegation leader Ed Benard terms the 'motherhood and apple pie' issues – the virtues of peace, democracy, tolerance and economic development and the baleful nature of violence and intimidation. Predictably,

The ANC's Kader Asmal ... formidable intellect, unhelpful style.

Benard notes, delegates had little difficulty in agreeing on these vague and self-evident truths: he rarely, he says, found himself in disagreement even with the ANC. In a society with a history of severe conflicts it could, of course, be argued that any agreement – even if only on general principles – represents progress. But, for an exercise which sought to hurry that society along the road to settling pressing and concrete conflicts (which were claiming lives even as the delegates debated), these agreements fell short of the minimum needed to show tangible progress to citizens eager for decisions which would make a visible difference to their lives.

Issues on which agreement might well have made that difference were those which participants were least willing to debate. The most important were the fate of political prisoners and exiles and the future of MK; the former remained a point of dispute until the Record of Understanding of September 1992, while the latter remained unresolved, at least for one of the key parties, until well into 1993.

The first issue concerned people who had committed common law crimes (such as murder) and who, in the ANC's view, were political prisoners since they were motivated by political goals; they had not been released by the government, who insisted that they were simply common law criminals.[5] The second turned on the ANC's insistence that MK, although it had suspended military activity, should continue to exist until it was merged with the South African Defence Force.[6] The NP and the South African government repeatedly urged the disbandment of MK, while in late 1992 the IFP was to demand its dissolution as a precondition for its return to negotiations, from which it had by then withdrawn. Both issues, then, were to be crucial points of tension.

But neither was debated in earnest by WG1. The first, political prisoners, was relegated to bilateral talks between the ANC and the government – on the grounds that it concerned these two parties only – despite the fact that, as we shall see, at least one key Codesa party had strong reservations about bilateral discussions between these two parties. The future of MK, which should have been discussed by SG2 under the heading 'The role and composition of the security forces', was touched on only cursorily, but seems not to have been directly referred to bilateral discussions. Bilateral talks on the subject were held, but the outcome was not disclosed to Codesa.

The importance of personality

The personal dynamics between the major players in the group were of some importance to the outcome of discussions in WG1. The ANC delegation was initially led by assistant secretary general Jacob Zuma, a senior official with a reputation as an able and conciliatory negotiator. But he played little part in its work and the mantle of leadership fell on law professor and constitutional specialist Kader Asmal. The first effect was to downgrade the seniority of the ANC delegation – Asmal is an elected member of the ANC's NEC, but, unlike Zuma, not of its national working committee, its most senior executive body.

Equally, or more importantly, Asmal's role brought a particular dynamic to WG1. He is arguably one of the most formidable intellects in the entire negotiating process, and even his opponents were forced to concede that his contributions brought clarity and insight to complicated issues; he did, as we shall see, play a particularly important role in the debate over emergency powers. But his critics, not all of them outside the ANC, insist that his style was less than helpful. Participants commented on his penchant for 'long-winded' contributions, delivered in the style of 'a lecture to a university undergraduate class'. The implication was that he 'talked down' to other delegates, perhaps unnecessarily stiffening their hostility – and that he believed that force of argument alone would be enough to win his point.

In the view of one third party observer, events within WG1 showed starkly that intellect and powerfully constructed argument often has a limited role in the sort of bargaining in which WG1 was engaged. This says something about the Codesa process itself, to which we will return. But the outcome was affected also by the reality that the only seasoned and senior negotiators in WG1 were the SAG delegation (IFP delegation leader Benard is, for example, the party's Sandton branch chairman). It was apparently common cause among Codesa insiders that many parties placed their most senior and experienced negotiators in WG2 and WG3 where what were seen as 'the most important issues' were to be dealt with – while, for obvious reasons, 'homeland' groups placed theirs in WG4.

The government negotiators were also Asmal's two main opponents – Justice minister Kobie Coetsee and Law and Order minister Hernus Kriel, aided by Coetsee's deputy, Danie Schutte, and Kriel's deputy, Gert Myburgh. Coetsee and Kriel are seasoned politicians – Coetsee had played a prominent role in negotiations which led to Nelson Mandela's release, and the talks which produced the Groote Schuur and Pretoria Minutes. Time and again they – Coetsee in particular – brushed aside Asmal's inputs. 'They [the two ministers] were powerful and often belligerent. Asmal was often simply outmanoeuvred,' says an observer. Simply brushing aside arguments is not necessarily a sophisticated negotiation tactic: but, for reasons which will become clear, it often proved effective, at least in the short term. Nor did Coetsee in particular merely restrict himself to ignoring opposing arguments: the debate over the state of emergency and other security legislation was, as we shall see, a prime example.

Coetsee's and Kriel's momentum was, say some participants, partly halted at times by two ANC allies, the SACP and the NIC/TIC delegation: SACP delegate Essop Pahad 'often stood up to Coetsee when Asmal was being pressured into giving ground,' says one. Mo Shaik of NIC/TIC did the same on occasion – delegates recollect a spirited speech by him outlining his experiences in detention without trial. On the whole, though, the government was forced into giving very little ground.

Asmal's own recollections reflect some of this: 'Codesa was little more than a debating society,' he says. 'Because of the "sufficient consensus" requirement, unless the government and NP agreed there was no forward movement. It was the intention, for example, not only to have identified laws which required repeal (because they were discriminatory or hampered free political activity) but also to have formulated agreements in the form of legislation by May. This did not happen.' (This presumably because the NP/SAG did not wish it to happen). Clearly, the delegates' position was strengthened by the reality that they were not quite a party like any other; they held power, were not under immediate pressure to settle, and so they retained an effective veto over change.

Nor were they the only delegations to adopt this stance. A further hindrance to progress, in the view of ANC delegates, was the position taken by Ciskei and more particularly Bophuthatswana, who tended to use *their* hold on power as a weapon in much the same way as the SAG. (Transkei and Venda were broadly part of the ANC's PF bloc at Codesa and were generally supportive of the ANC alliance.)

Points from a submission by the Bophuthatswana government illustrate this.[7] First, it insisted that it presided over a democracy in which parties were free to form and to contest for power. Their political freedoms would be guaranteed and they would enjoy access to public facilities – as long as they did not resort to violent or destabilising activities. But, to enjoy these rights, parties would have to register under the territory's law. The difficulty was that its opponents, such as the ANC, did not simply reject the territory's ruling party: they denied also that its government was sovereign or legitimate (see WG4). In effect, Bophuthatswana was saying that they could enjoy free political activity in order to campaign against its legitimacy only if they accepted the legitimacy against which they wished to campaign. Similarly, it insisted, its publicly owned media were the property of the people of Bophuthatswana, and its management structures could therefore not be interfered with by outsiders – which meant any South African groups. This, of course, meant that the future of its public media was not even open to negotiation by the – clearly South African – working group.[8] The Ciskei took a similar though slightly less uncompromising view.

Another important and unique feature of WG1's dynamics was the absence of a strong DP role as a mediator and 'facilitator'. In other groups this was a vital element; the DP often played an active role in maintaining some sort of momentum. Here it was hardly evident – except, perhaps, for DP participant Peter Soal's contribution to the debate on the future of broadcasting. David Dalling was the DP front runner, and by all accounts he adopted a particularly confrontational attitude towards the NP and its allies, so ruling out the possibility of acting as an 'honest broker'. Dalling has since resigned from the DP and joined the ANC.

The spirit of 17 March

The referendum of 17 March 1992,[9] held less than six weeks into WG1's operations, is seen by observers of both the ANC alliance and 'middle-of-the road' groups to have played a central role in triggering a more aggressive government stance at Codesa. In their view this manifested itself in WG1 specifically when Coetsee, at the first post-referendum meeting, stood up and announced: 'No one thought I would be able to deliver a "yes" vote in the Orange Free State, and I did.' In hindsight, that statement was read as a signal that the result had given him the power and right to set the tone in WG1.

'Coetsee's role changed noticeably after the referendum,' says one WG1 participant. 'It was as if he had decided that government could now either get the decisions it wanted in the group, or scupper it. It was probably the size of the "yes" vote that did it. Had the result been narrower, we would probably have made more progress.' Asmal agrees: 'The referendum sent inappropriate signals to government. A week before, they were trying to resolve issues at Codesa. Thereafter, there was a perceptible change in attitude.'

Inevitably the government disagrees, blaming the ANC alliance for failures to make progress. The NP/SAG delegates were firmly committed to resolving differences, according to Myburgh – even more so after the referendum, since the NP's constituency had voted for a negotiated settlement. It was the ANC which 'tried in every possible way to delay proceedings'.

NP/SAG representatives became particularly unhappy at the ANC's perceived use of its SACP and NIC/TIC allies, whose delegate would 'innocently' throw out an idea 'to test the water', prompting 'clearly orchestrated' interventions by other members of the alliance. This the NP/SAG participants saw as a deliberate attempt to cause delays: 'We were very frustrated by their delays,' avers Myburgh. The NP, he says, did not use such tactics simply because it did not have as well-developed an alliance with those groups that generally sided with it.

Why would the ANC alliance want to delay proceedings? Because, says Myburgh, it recognised the government's sense of urgency. 'Perhaps they delayed in the hope that our commitment to progress would induce us to give in to their often unreasonable demands. But we were not going to give the country away.'

Are these very different perceptions simply a sign of the cynicism which many outside the process claimed to detect at Codesa – in which each side allegedly hid its own tactical manoeuvrings by blaming the other? Perhaps. But neither side's perception of the other is easy to substantiate. WG1's minutes provide no real evidence of a hardening in the NP position on any issue after 17 March; Coetsee's statement, seen by some as a signal of a new hard-line position, could have been a reflection of the general jubilation among Codesa parties which greeted the referendum result. And the ANC alliance's 'delaying tactics' could have been no more than an unwillingness to accept without demur any position advanced by the NP/SAG negotiators.

Government negotiator Kobie Coetsee ... his role changed noticeably after the referendum.

If there was a 'villain', it may well have been precisely the post-referendum jubilation which Coetsee expressed. The overwhelming 2:1 white vote in favour of a negotiated solution naturally raised hopes – not only in Codesa – for an early resolution of differences. But elation at the electoral triumph over the white far right obscured the reality that the referendum did nothing to clarify the terms of a Codesa settlement. Voters were asked merely to endorse negotiation in general terms and, while the NP did inject into the campaign, at a late stage, its vision of constitutionally enforced power sharing, 'yes' voters spanned a spectrum from white ANC members on the left to right-wingers eager to avert economic and sports sanctions. (At one polling booth, the SACP's Jeremy Cronin enthusiastically cast his ballot – and then obligingly left, lest his party T-shirt alienate white fellow voters. Similarly, the white miner who voted 'yes' as an act of homage to the national cricket team then doing battle in Australia[10] was by no means alone). The ANC could conclude – as it probably did – that white voters had given unqualified endorsement to a settlement on any terms, while the NP could – and did[11] – conclude that it now had the unqualified backing of white South Africa for a transition on its terms alone, and that the ANC would have to heed this.

The ANC's failure to note precisely what the NP thought it was asking voters to endorse may explain its chagrin when and if the NP merely restated its position after 17 March. And, while the NP position in WG1 did not discernibly change after the poll, the message which it thought the white vote had impressed on the ANC may well have prompted it to hold to that position more firmly. The claim that Coetsee felt the NP could block progress unless it 'got what it wanted' was, as we argued earlier, consistent with its approach well before the referendum. The poll may simply have made it more confident that it could get 'what it wanted'.

The referendum may have had another, less noticed effect. It enhanced international and local expectations of speedy progress; certainly it increased perceptions by Codesa participants that this was what was expected of them. This increased pressure to regularly supply evidence of progress, even when progress was vague or illusory. The result was the already noted spate of announced 'breakthroughs'; in WG1 it may also explain the stress on 'motherhood and apple pie'.

Benard argues that post-referendum expectations were not the only factor impelling participants to demonstrate progress to an increasingly sceptical local public. It was, he suggests, a pressure sensed by delegates throughout the process. Since there were few examples of concrete progress to convey, WG1 was left with little choice but to reach agreement on matters of vague and uncontroversial principle and then to present them to the public as evidence of progress. In WG1 the pressure may have been heightened by the fact that it was supposed to tackle the issues on which the public most wanted and needed progress. The stress on 'motherhood and apple pie' may have concealed from public view the distinct lack of progress, and may have encouraged some outside the convention to believe that relief was at hand. But it may also, as we have suggested, have strengthened the scepticism of a public which noted the widening gap between the reported achievements of the negotiating forum and the travails they witnessed around them.

To see how these tendencies played themselves out in practice, let us examine the work of each of the subgroups in greater detail.

INSIDE SUBGROUP 1
Political prisoners

The first meeting of SG1 on 11 February focused on the question of political prisoners. But, besides agreeing that this issue was 'a priority in the completion of the reconciliation process',[12] it merely referred it to bilateral discussion between the ANC and the SAG. There was some debate over whether this was appropriate, but it was – ironically, bearing in mind the ANC and NP's later enthusiasm for 'bilaterals' and some other parties' hostility to them – the ANC alliance which argued that this issue, which had been the subject of bilateral discussion for nearly two years, should now be resolved by Codesa. The SACP's Essop Pahad explains that the alliance had concluded that previous bilaterals had deadlocked, leaving, by its calculations, 400 prisoners still in custody. A significant section of the ANC's constituency suggested that this showed the impotence of the negotiation process. There would, the alliance believed, be greater pressure on the government to concede this point if the issue was debated 'more in the public eye'.

But all other delegations did not appear to see this as a 'make or break issue'; they argued that, since this was a matter purely between the two parties, they should attempt to reach agreement between themselves. Nor, apparently, was this seen as a particularly difficult task: minutes of the 11 February meeting record the wildly optimistic statement that 'the question of political prisoners will be finalised ... at the next meeting', scheduled for a week later. That this was highly unlikely might have been apparent to any participant who had studied the government's early submissions to WG1[13] – which stated simply that the prisons held no more political prisoners, and that the issue was therefore resolved – and who were aware that the ANC believed the issue to be anything but settled.

We have noted that it took the breakdown of Codesa 2 and a period of severe conflict before the issue was settled by the Record of Understanding, which agreed to the release of the prisoners. Even then (see note 4) the government, relying on the Norgaard principles,[14] continued to regard these prisoners as ordinary criminals. Their eventual release was, according to Myburgh, a concession the government felt it needed to make if the ANC was to return to negotiations before the end of 1992. By then, of course, the issue which was to have been settled amicably by two parties within a week had contributed to a delay of several months in the negotiation process.

Despite all this, this was another issue on which an illusion of movement was maintained; this time the increasingly impatient and disbelieving audience was not the public but SG1 itself. Through the rest of WG1's life the government and the ANC delivered regular reports on this issue to SG1 and the working group as a whole, often reporting that 'good progress' was being made – a judgement belied by later events.

But while SG1 did not contribute to a solution to this issue, its early debates did throw light on the way in which bargaining positions have sometimes shifted during the negotiation process. At the first full WG1 meeting on 6 February the SACP, presumably with the consent of its alliance partners, called for the urgent implementation of a general amnesty – which would cover offences committed by right-wingers, including, presumably, those in the security forces – and agreement on a cut-off date beyond which the amnesty would not apply. Its motive was pragmatic – this would, it believed, secure the release of ANC cadres and, it argued, discourage right-wing terrorism: 'While this problem is unresolved,' the SACP argued, 'it encourages right-wingers to engage in killing sprees, because they feel that if arrested they will gain later from indemnities which must come for McBride[15] and others. A clean slate is required – there should be a general amnesty, and once a cut-off date has been established, individuals transgressing the law must suffer the consequences.'[16]

Later in the year, the government's decision to implement a similar approach – through the Further Indemnity Act – triggered strong opposition not only from its co-signatory to the Record of Understanding and other 'liberation' movements but from

opposition parties in parliament; it was ultimately compelled to force the bill into law by using a much-criticised feature of the tricameral system.[17] While it could be argued that the government had acted unilaterally and had, therefore, violated the spirit of the SACP proposal, the reaction did suggest that, for the ANC alliance, the strategic ground had by then shifted.

SACP delegate Essop Pahad ... argued that detentions would not work against the right.

'Discriminatory and repressive laws'

At first glance, the repeal of any discriminatory laws which might remain in force was an issue on which agreement could readily be reached, creating some much-needed credibility for the negotiators: after all, the government was by then firmly committed to the abolition of legalised discrimination. But, while at least one comprehensive submission on this issue was received by SG1, the topic was hardly discussed; it was referred to a task group which was rendered stillborn by the collapse of Codesa 2.

An obvious explanation might be that delegates, preoccupied with weightier matters and an awesome agenda, did not see this 'straightforward' topic as one which need delay them overmuch. But a closer look suggests that this issue is neither as straightforward nor as easy to resolve as it may seem.

The repeal of some of the statutes in this category – such as the Republic of South Africa Constitution Act[18] – depended on a settlement of the broader constitutional issues under discussion in other working groups. Many of the other 'discriminatory' laws contain no direct references to race, but are, in the view of their critics, effectively racist.

This is illustrated by the submission mentioned above which was compiled by the Law Reform Project, a division of the liberal organisation Lawyers for Human Rights.[19] It listed 34 'racially discriminatory' acts of parliament, covering issues such as local government franchises, referendums, defence, pensions, squatting, education, local government, training, community development, housing, welfare, probation programmes for prisoners, town planning, and various part appropriation acts.

The issues which did not depend on a constitutional settlement would require major financial and administrative adjustments by the SAG: equal pensions had obvious cost implications, while abolishing racial defence clauses might require a substantial reordering of the military. Some might need major changes in social policy – changes to the law prohibiting 'squatting' or housing might require totally different approaches to these problems. Agreement on these issues could well have triggered a substantial reordering of public service practices, and might have had important implications for key interest groups in the NP constituency, such as property owners. Whether SG1 delegates were aware of this at the time or not, a settlement on these issues would have touched on some of the core disputes in South African society and may well have proved beyond the capabilities of a forum unable to reach agreement on political prisoners.

Whatever its reasons may have been, SG1 chose instead to focus on laws affecting political activity, which themselves proved to be highly controversial. SG1 can claim credit for the repeal of that section of the Internal Security Act requiring newspapers to pay substantial registration fees; for the rest, security laws in general and emergency laws in particular became the subject of heated debate – and the latter the cause of serious embarrassment to the ANC alliance.

Its opening negotiating position suggested that its goals were clear – the repeal of the security legislation which had been used almost exclusively against it and its members. It demanded the repeal of the ISA, the Public Safety Act and all other legislation restricting individuals or organisations for security reasons. But here, perhaps more than on any other issue, it was the government and Kobie Coetsee in particular which effectively set the agenda.

The ANC's retreat on this issue appears to be a clear example of a case in which it was outmanoeuvred by the government. But this is not self-evident: the alliance, which brought to the table many long-held positions born in its life as a repressed 'liberation' movement, arguably entered this debate with an unsustainable position. It could be argued that, once it was intellectually – if not emotionally – persuaded to accept the need for some form of emergency legislation in the future, its representatives – Asmal in particular – and the DP played an important role in ensuring that the law would be hedged with safeguards comparable to those in 'enlightened' democracies. In this view, its most obvious 'defeat' was in reality one of the few examples in which WG1 produced a workable, defensible and effective compromise. But, if this is was happened, the ANC's constituency and at least some of its negotiators saw matters differently.

The Public Safety Act

The government argued strongly for retaining security legislation on two grounds; that the political situation remained unstable, and that security measures might be needed to maintain order. In any event, it added, democratic constitutions invariably provide for emergency powers in certain circumstances. The second argument is not unconvincing; as some ANC lawyers were to argue later, there are few, if any constitutions in which the controlled use of emergency powers is impossible. But, as events were to show later, the history of security laws in this society makes this a difficult argument for the ANC to accept.

Asmal suggests that the ANC's compromise on this issue was indeed a reluctant bow to the power balance, rather than a shift in thinking: 'Keeping the PSA on the books would allow an interim government to declare a state of emergency. The ANC wanted the act repealed, as it does not want such an act even for itself. But government would not agree to this,' he says.

That he is expressing a firmly held 'gut' position within the ANC is confirmed by the fate of this particular compromise. It became a political hot potato, at least partly because the alliance's handling of the issue was coy in the extreme. Instead of preparing its middle-level leadership and rank and file – many of whom had been detained under security laws in the 1980s – for an agreement, it concealed the debate from public view. When details of the agreement were 'leaked' to the media during the latter stages of Codesa, there was an angry reaction from ANC members, Codesa opponents such as Azapo, and human rights organisations such as LHR. For those outside the ANC the reaction was fuelled by the suspicion that it and the NP planned to form an authoritarian alliance which would use force to suppress its opposition. That possibility cannot be excluded: but the agreement on emergency rules was not the product of collaboration between conniving elites.

It should be evident by now that the ANC did not seek the emergency clause; it and the DP reacted to the government's determination to retain emergency powers by seeking to hedge them with safeguards. The final agreement provided that a state of emergency could be declared by the president only on the advice of the multi-party interim executive or cabinet; this was one of the earlier 'concessions' won from the government. It was also agreed that the proclamation of an emergency or 'unrest area' should be objectively justiciable; the courts would be able to rule on whether the situation justified the measures.

The ANC insists that it was further agreed that the PSA should be amended to provide for certain 'non-derogable' (inalienable) rights and procedural controls over detention without trial. Although the detail was not written into WG1's final report, Asmal had spelt these out at an SG1 meeting on 21 April.[20] They included specific bars on torture, discrimination on the basis of race, gender or religion, and any interference with the right to life. Further, security officials found guilty of contravening these laws would not be eligible for indemnity. Other safeguards were that detainees, as well as a friend or family member, be told the reasons for the detention, that there should be unrestricted access to legal representatives, and that the validity of each individual's detention should be reviewed by a judicial board with the power to order a detainee's release.

The retrospectivity of any emergency declaration was the subject of long and heated debate. The PSA presently allows for a state of emergency to be declared by up to four days retrospectively, and the government wanted to have this clause retained. This was opposed by the ANC alliance, supported by the DP. The SACP, seemingly already uncomfortable with the entire subject of emergency laws, went so far at a meeting on 27 April as to threaten to 'reserve its right to return to its original position, that of the total repeal of security legislation' if the government refused to remove retrospectivity.[21] The government insisted that the situation 'on the ground' sometimes demanded that emergency powers be proclaimed retrospectively, and that a bill of rights would be sufficient protection against abuse.

The debate raged on through the final WG1 meeting on 5 May, just 10 days before Codesa 2; even there the government delegation could agree only to refer the matter back to its principals. But at some point in those 10 days it decided that this limit on emergency powers was dispensable if the alternative was to push the alliance, led by the SACP, into rejecting the PSA. By the opening of Codesa 2 it had yielded, and agreement on the removal on the retrospectivity clause was written into WG1's final report.

A victory for the alliance? If so, many ANC supporters and analysts argue, it was only a Pyrrhic one, since even the greatly softened emergency rules which it won were too harsh for its constituency. Whatever the practical argument in favour of emergency powers, particularly powers of detention, alliance leaders now believe that they will probably be unable to sell the idea to their supporters. While stressing that the ANC considered itself still bound by Codesa agreements, Asmal adds as a rider that the emergency legislation section 'may be worthy of being looked at again'. Pahad puts it less diplomatically: 'No one in the movement accepts that we should have detention without trial under any conditions, even under a state of emergency.'

Here again, an issue 'resolved' in WG1 may be far from settled. But the issue may leave the ANC with a painful dilemma; since the negotiation process resumed in late 1992, it – like the NP – has insisted that all Codesa parties are bound by the convention's agreements: to reopen this issue would invite other parties to reopen others. And, if the issue is left to a power-sharing interim government, the NP would presumably be able to exercise a veto, leaving the Codesa agreement – or, indeed, the PSA in its present form – intact. Despite its strenuous efforts, the cost of negotiating an agreement on a sensitive issue without gaining support from its constituency could prove to be considerable.

The Internal Security Act

The ISA is the other key vehicle of security law, but on its future not even the fragile agreement reached on the PSA was achieved. Decisions were, as with discriminatory legislation, referred to a task group. Nevertheless, some of the arguments raised on this issue are of interest to the future of the negotiation process.

SG1 agreed early on that laws 'militating against free political activity' could be dealt with in one of three ways, one of which was to enact an interim bill of rights against which laws could be tested. This was the most popular option – but it was rejected by the ANC alliance. This had more to do with a general ANC reading of government strategy than a question of principle. As in WG2 and WG3, the ANC feared that any interim bill of rights (like an interim constitution) would become entrenched forever and would bind a constituent assembly. Says Asmal: 'A primary concern of the ANC [at Codesa] was the realisation that whatever is agreed to in the interim will influence and mould institutions in the longer term ... The intention of the ANC is to organise the transition such that inordinate power is not given to a future democratic government.' He adds: 'The government wanted to bring into Codesa issues that would shape the future constitution. Can one have an interim bill of rights? This type of question should be the prerogative of the constituent assembly, not of Codesa.'

The alliance, the DP and some smaller parties argued in favour of scrapping the ISA, although they accepted in principle that 'certain powers above normal [ones] are needed'. They argued against any provision for detention without trial of suspects or witnesses: 'I told Coetsee that we did not plan to deal with the right wing through detentions,' says Pahad. 'It didn't work on us, and it will not work against the right.' The alliance and DP also argued against the banning of organisations (although the DP was willing to countenance bannings of groups which sought to overthrow the democratic process – a provision in the German constitution used in November 1992 against a neo-Nazi group). They argued too that the definitions of terrorism and other offences in the act were inappropriate. But the government was unwilling to move much further than it had already done towards 'humanising' detention law; as with other issues this ensured a deadlock, and 'sufficient consensus' meant that government rejection barred further progress. As we have already argued, there was little apparent cost to the government in fili-bustering on matters such as the release of prisoners and the reform or repeal of security legislation – particularly as it basked in the glow of international approval following the referendum.

At the same time the alliance had concluded that these were not appropriate issues on which to deadlock the negotiating process. Says Pahad: 'We asked whether we should make the political prisoners issue the sticking point. We decided not and proceeded with other things, because when the transitional executive council (the first phase of inter-im government) was set up, it would take the issue out of the hands of the regime.' The result is that the issues remain unresolved. Nor will interim government take the matter 'out of the hands of the regime'; it will, as we shall see, remain an influential member of that government.

INSIDE SUBGROUP 2
Nothing of substance

Of the seven items allocated to SG2, the group focused its attention pri-marily on one – the National Peace Accord. It devoted some attention to the role and composition of the security forces, but steered clear of the most ticklish questions. On other issues, nothing of substance was dis-cussed. Its selection of a topic was not without irony, since a forum com-posed chiefly of NPA signatories chose to concentrate chiefly on 'im-proving' an earlier agreement which they had reached but failed to implement. It was unclear why the atmosphere at the World Trade Cen-tre would make it easier for them to conclude workable agreements than that at the venues where the NPA signatories met.

That substantive agreement on other issues was not achieved is illus-trated by the final WG1 report to Codesa 2. It declares, for example, that: 'There was agreement on the need for an improvement in socio-economic conditions as an essential part of the reconstruction of society. However, due to lack of time, the matter was not discussed further.' In truth, it was raised by government, the IFP and the SACP in initial written submissions and in an early discussion, but in terms which merely illustrated the lack of progress. The NP/SAG argued that economic development required a free market system. The SACP, not surprisingly, disagreed, suggesting that socialism was the only solution. And the IFP used this heading and that related to violent crime to raise one of its hobby horses – that socio-economic conditions would improve, and levels of violent crime decline, only if the ANC alliance agreed to call for the lifting of sanctions. The par-ties repeated time-worn positions rather than detailed remedies.

As the socio-economic 'agreement' suggests, 'motherhood and apple pie' was the chief product of SG2's work. On the crime question, it 'resolved' that the security forces should halt the flow of illegal arms into the country, that political parties should adhere to NPA guidelines on mass action, and that socio-economic conditions 'should be improved'. It even went as far as to agree that 'a spirit of tolerance needs to be fostered amongst political parties', only to add that 'there was no consensus on any further recommendations'. Political intimidation was discussed at some length, merely to end with a reasonably self-evident list of coercive acts which were defined as intimidatory. Time constraints prevented any discussion on education and information campaigns on democracy. On issues of substance – such as the death penalty or sanctions – no consensus was reached.

One agreement of note does seem to have been reached – on paper. But it clearly was not seen as binding. Thus one of the agreed definitions of intimidation was: 'The possession, carrying or displaying of dangerous weapons or firearms by members of the general public when attending any political gathering or meeting'. This was aimed at the IFP, whose members' inclination to bear 'cultural' weapons at political gatherings has been a constant point of dispute during the negotiation process. But while the IFP presumably agreed to this definition, its insistence on bearing these weapons has become more pronounced.

The future of the security forces

The role and composition of the security forces is one of the key issues in the negotiating process; at issue is not only who will maintain order, but also the balance of power between the parties. It is also, of course, a very sensitive issue, and that is perhaps why it was discussed in depth only once by SG2, on 24 March. Again, the ANC used one of its allies – the NIC/TIC – to float the issue; since this was only a week after the referendum, the alliance may have been expected significant movement. It did not get it, the government showing little interest in pursuing the debate.

The result, yet again, was that only the 'motherhood' aspects of the NIC/TIC's submission[22] found their way into the final WG1 report. These included a commitment to the peaceful settlement of political disputes; that the security forces be bound by the principle of constitutional supremacy; that they be politically non-partisan and committed to resolving conflict primarily through peaceful means; that they respect human rights, non-racialism and democracy; and that they should strive to be representative of society as a whole. Unspecified mechanisms to ensure public accountability were recommended, as was the drafting of a code of conduct and the implementation of a programme to improve relations between the security forces and the community.

Perhaps the most substantial point in the final report arose not out of discussion in WG1, but in WG3. This was an agreement that all security forces be placed under the control of interim government structures, an issue not directly addressed at the meeting of 24 March.

Probably the most crucial point in the NIC/TIC submission was not addressed. It argued for 'the reconstitution [of the forces] with a view to establishing new national, legitimate and representative security forces inclusive of the SADF, MK and the TBVC states and self-governing territories. All special forces and formations not included in this reconstitution shall be dismantled.' According to the minutes of that meeting, the NP/SAG's only contribution was to favour a largely professional defence force with a small conscript element. It said it opposed the politicisation of the force, and agreed that should the TBVC states accept reincorporation, their armies would become part of the national defence force. Also, private armies should not be permitted.

These last points begged the question of how the government saw MK, an issue it had apparently decided to avoid at that stage. As noted above, it – like the IFP – has often called for the disbanding of MK, labelling it a private army. Why, then, ignore the issue? Probably because for the government (rather than the IFP) its stand on this issue

The IFP's Frank Mdlalose, centre, with fellow delegates ... in WG1 the party played a surprisingly limited role.

was political theatre; it and the ANC had reached a secret protocol as part of the D F Malan Accord of February 1991, which became public knowledge only in August 1992. The accord was revealed because the ANC submitted it to the NPA in response to a formal IFP complaint alleging that MK's existence was a violation of the accord.

According to the secret protocol, the government accepted that MK did not fall under the provisions of the NPA dealing with private armies. The parties had agreed that: 'The ANC should begin a process of informing the government of the extent and nature of arms under its control. Such arms and ordnances will be placed under the joint control of any transitional authority and MK upon the formation of an interim government. MK will be disbanded upon the completion of the ... transition to a democratic constitution.' This may, of course, explain the depth of IFP hostility to NP/ANC bilateral agreements. As Ed Benard puts it: 'The IFP felt strongly this issue [MK] was not appropriate for bilateral solution. IFP people are being killed; it affects us too.'

What it does not explain is why the IFP hardly raised MK's status vigorously within WG1. Benard says the question rarely came up because of the perception that it was, like political prisoners, a matter for bilateral resolution. Pahad argues that the fact that the IFP delegation failed to raise it more than once – and then in a low-key fashion – suggests that it is just a political football for the IFP, an issue raised later when it seemed politically opportune to do so. More likely, given that the IFP continued in early 1993 to present the disbanding of MK as a precondition for multi-party negotiations, is that this represented a failure of its WG1 delegation, and of its co-ordinating structures, to ensure that the issue was pressed more strongly. This raises the broader issue of the IFP's usually limited role at Codesa, to which we will return.

The National Peace Accord

As noted above, this issue consumed the bulk of SG2's time. National peace committee chairman John Hall and national peace secretariat chairman Antonie Gildenhuys were two of a small number of outsiders invited not only to make extensive oral submissions to Codesa but to participate in lengthy discussions (in this case, with SG2).

There was initially some unease at Codesa that the convention seemed to want to take over NPA functions. Although most Codesa parties were also party to the NPA, some signatories were not political parties. These doubts were overcome when Hall expressly invited SG2 to contribute ideas aimed at strengthening the NPA. It did so, eventually providing a five-page section on the issue as part of WG1's report to Codesa 2.

Among SG2's recommendations were a number related to the operation of regional and local dispute resolution committees. It proposed the appointment of a full-time official to each RDRC; the establishment of permanent, equipped and staffed offices in the country's main areas;

and that representatives of local and tribal authorities be appointed to all RDRCs and LDRCs. The NPA and RDRCs should appoint subcommittees to deal with socio-economic reconstruction. RDRCS should be entitled to make recommendations to the South African Police and some 'homeland' police forces on the selection of senior officers and, where circumstances permit, security force action in conflict situations. It was suggested that the dispute resolution committees encourage the formation of non-partisan 'self-protection or neighbourhood watch groups', monitor their activities, and encourage co-operation between them and the police.

SG2 also devoted much attention to the establishment of commissions, constituted of representatives of NPA signatories, to monitor compliance with the NPA. It also noted the NPA's shortage of financial resources, and resolved to call for foreign aid and to suggest that the NPS prepare a budget for submission to the government.

Since SG2's ideas could potentially contribute to the strengthening of the NPA, they might be seen as an important part of Codesa's work. But it is unclear what impact Codesa had on NPA operations. The debate also leaves a sense that, unable to make any impact on the continuing high levels of violence, SG2 instead sought sanctuary in constructing ever more complex structures through which the NPA could theoretically work.

INSIDE SUBGROUP 3
Control over state media

Control over broadcasting and the SABC is another of the WG1 issues which was to become a key question after Codesa. Government critics see the state media as an instrument of the NP, and argue that fair elections are not possible if one party monopolises television and radio, the country's two most powerful media. This view has coalesced around a demand for an independent broadcasting authority, and non-partisan control of the SABC board. While this issue has not subsequently threatened to halt the negotiation process, it has been the source of heated public controversy. Again, therefore, WG1 was dealing with an issue which was anything but obscure.

This was also the one question debated by WG1 on which, non-government participants sensed, the NP was aware from the beginning that it would make substantial concessions, although the NP politicians did ensure that they were not conceded easily.

At an early SG3 meeting on 17 February, the NP/SAG stance suggested that they would not be made at all; they presented a spirited argument that the status quo was already fair. They were satisfied 'that the SABC's code of conduct, values and present editorial policy meet the requirements for political neutrality'; the corporation was also 'free from government intervention', and the status quo should therefore be maintained as an interim measure.[23] But Kobie Coetsee and his colleagues kept their options open during the second half of February by saying they were still studying the report of the Viljoen Task Group on Broadcasting,[24] and that they wished to study the submissions of other parties.

This was followed by an apparently substantial NP/SAG concession. At an SG3 meeting on 30 March, agreement was reached in principle on the establishment of an independent broadcasting authority, tentatively named the South African Independent Telecommunications Authority. The rationale was that an independent body should allocate broadcast licenses and so break the government's monopoly on access to broadcasting; participants argued that diversity was an important guarantee of the free flow of opinion.

The political direction behind this agreement was provided largely by the COM through the ANC alliance. But the technical expertise on broadcasting, electromagnetic waves and similar issues was provided by government and, notably, Peter Soal of the DP. The government brought to a meeting an expert who delivered a comprehensive lecture on broadcasting technology. An early DP submission went into important detail on such matters as the use of the electromagnetic spectrum, the allocation of licenses to independent broadcasters, the obligations of the SABC to provide technical services to the independents, and advertising regulations and the like. All these technical issues were aimed at addressing the practicalities of ensuring broadcasting diversity.

But this agreement was not the final word on the subject. Agreement on Saita did not necessarily imply agreement on the future of the SABC board. The former would be responsible for governing and administering the airwaves as a whole – a function now exercised by the postmaster general. The latter would directly control the state broadcasting corporation.

While consensus was reached on all details of Saita, there was no agreement on when the SABC board was to be changed; the ANC alliance wanted immediate action, the NP/SAG insisted that this was impractical. Nor was there much clarity during SG3's debates on the difference between the SABC board and Saita: ANC alliance representatives, in particular, often appeared to speak of the two as one and, presumably, to assume that agreement on Saita also implied consensus on a non-partisan SABC board. The final WG1 documentation is also imprecise: while it does record the detail of the agreement reached on Saita, it is far vaguer on the SABC. It implies, but does not baldly state, that agreement was reached on the 'reconstitution' of the SABC board. It notes the disagreement on timing, and agrees that the current chairman of the board will be approached for a discussion on when the 'reconstitution' of the board would be possible. And it talks also of a proposed body to monitor the SABC's impartiality.[25]

The phrasing of the final report is vague enough, then, to leave unresolved precisely what final agreement was reached on the SABC board. Nevertheless, the text does imply that agreement on 'reconstitution' was reached – and this was certainly the understanding of SG3 participants. The final text may therefore simply have been the product of clumsy and hasty drafting. But the following comment by Essop Pahad implies that the government did not necessarily concede an independent SABC board: 'We got the impression, although it was not stated in so many words, that both [SABC board chairman] Viljoen and Coetsee were not averse to a number of more widely acceptable people being brought onto the board, provided the present incumbents' terms were also extended; the size of the board would be increased.' He adds: 'We could never accept this.' It may be significant here that the agreement stipulated that the board would be 'reconstituted' – not that it would be entirely independent – and that this issue was still contested in early 1993 when a Campaign for Independent Broadcasting, which had mobilised against government control of the SABC, was negotiating the composition of a new SABC board with the authorities.

Even the agreement on Saita was not achieved without another dispute which hinged on the ANC alliance's already mentioned fear that agreements reached at Codesa would become permanent, thus pre-empting an elected constitution-making body. Consistent with this – and despite the fact that it had advanced independent control of the airwaves as a principle and, therefore, presumably, as a permanent state of affairs – it insisted that Saita be an interim body only; debate on this continued for several meetings. It is here that the DP played a key role in breaking the deadlock. It raised the practical point that broadcasting was a capital-intensive endeavour, and that no new broadcaster would be willing to make the investment needed unless it was assured that it would be allowed to exploit it for a long time. If a broadcasting license was to apply for a brief interim period only, the diversity of broadcasting which the ANC sought would not materialise. This appears to have persuaded the alliance to drop its objections.

Despite Pahad's reservations, he suggests that SG3 did produce a binding agreement on an important issue. 'I still think it is a bloody good agreement. And not enough is made of the fact that the ANC is being very magnanimous; control [of broadcasting],' he adds, 'will not pass to us.' When compared to WG1's discussions on other key issues, the broadcasting debate did seem to produce concrete results. Even here, however, the agreement (not yet implemented by the beginning of 1993) may not have been watertight enough to prevent later disputes.

BIG ISSUES, SMALL RESULTS

WG1 dealt with issues which crucially affected both the process of negotiations and the lives of South African citizens. Many were less technical than those dealt with in other working groups. Had substantive agreements been reached here, they could have played a major role in moving negotiations forward and in boosting sagging public confidence in Codesa.

But, despite the broadcasting agreement – which, important though it might prove to be, was of less immediate concern to many citizens than issues such as violence – and that on emergency powers, which, as we have seen, may have created as many problems as it solved, participants in WG1 recognise that very limited progress was made.

Part of the problem may have been specific to WG1. Despite the importance of the issues it discussed, the parties do not seem to have given the same priority to them as constitutional principles and transitional arrangements: hence their decision to assign their most senior

negotiators elsewhere. WG1 also had a far more diffuse task than the others; its discussions were focused on a wide range of issues, rather than a single task or a number of clearly related ones. WG1 might have achieved more had the Codesa parties focused on the key issues which needed to be resolved, and limited WG1 to these.

Nevertheless, some of the problems which beset WG1 also revealed obstacles which seemed to apply to Codesa as a whole. One of these was the pressure to 'show results', almost as a substitute for actually achieving them: hence the spate of 'motherhood and apple pie' agreements. Another was a confusion about what precisely Codesa was. On one level

F W de Klerk waves to supporters after winning the referendum on reform, 18 March 1992.

WG1 showed all the trappings of an earnest, problem-solving convention. Submissions were invited and debated, practicalities examined, helpful suggestions made. On another, it showed all the hallmarks of a tough political bargaining session between the parties. This is an uneasy mix, and it was ironically the NP, which preferred a multi-party forum to an elected assembly, which was less inclined to see WG1 as a problem-solving body than the ANC. Thus Asmal assumed that the power of debate would carry the day while, Pahad suggests, the alliance believed that an issue not resolved in 'bilaterals' with the NP – political prisoners – would somehow be more winnable in Codesa.

The oddity is perhaps explained in another way: at times the ANC acted as if it were already at a constituent assembly, while the NP, which had sought a multi-party forum, had no illusions about the difference. But negotiators on both sides – only some of whom were at WG1 – did seem to be more certain of where the real action was being played out; they not only reached a crucial agreement on MK outside Codesa, but felt no need to tell the convention that they had done so.

Was WG1 convened simply to add a gloss to deals struck between the big power players, or an all-party forum to discuss common problems besetting the society? While it purported to be the latter, WG1 *was*, as we shall see, intended as a bargaining forum, and the protagonists were the NP and ANC alliance. Their bargaining strategies are thus worth a closer look.

On one level the NP pursued a strategy we commented on earlier: despite Myburgh's complaints about ANC delays, there is no reason why the NP needed to hurry the process; it had far less to lose by simply saying 'no'. But the NP also had goals which WG1 was meant to achieve. The chief one was to win consent for continued security measures – before, it had imposed them against its bargaining partner; now, it hoped to do so with it. Where the NP was pursuing its objectives, it had an interest in firm agreements; on the principle of continued emergency laws, for example. Where its opponents were pursuing theirs, on limitations to those laws or an independent SABC board, it preferred vague agreements or no agreements at all.

The ANC's chief goal appeared to be to sweep aside the restrictions – security laws, control of broadcasting – which in its view gave the NP an unfair advantage, and raised the spectre that the transition was really just a way of perpetuating NP control in a new guise. Had WG1 simply focused on this rather than on a host of issues, many of whom were better suited to a problem-solving task force, greater progress may have been made.

But the ANC negotiators seem to have had no effective counter to the

NP's strategy. Asmal's complaint that 'sufficient consensus' allowed the NP simply to say 'no' was technically correct, but reflects a failure to understand the nature of negotiation. A bargained agreement cannot be reached until all parties agree – and it is hardly uncommon for one to begin by refusing. The task for its opponent is to force or persuade it to change position, and the ANC found no way to do this. Certainly, Asmal's powers of argument, considerable though they were, were insufficient. The unequal balance of bargaining power may also explain ANC negotiators' relative lack of concern about achieving binding written agreements.

Some of Asmal's limitations on emergency rule were not written into the final WG1 report, yet the ANC seems convinced that it won them. Pahad's understanding of the SABC agreement reflects a perception of what parties thought they were agreeing, rather than the contents of the written accord. Was this a result of inexperience – or a mistaken assumption that the details of agreements did not really matter, since the 'people' were on the road to victory regardless of the fine print of working group reports (witness Pahad's remarks on political prisoners)? Whatever the reason, the few agreements which were reached seem to favour the NP.

Some participants suggest that Codesa failed to recognise that there were, in reality, three chief blocs – led by the NP, ANC and IFP – and that the supposed representation of 19 parties was a time-wasting illusion (witness the need to hear lengthy submissions by each party in a particular bloc). They note that negotiation after Codesa has recognised this; much time could have been saved had Codesa done so too. (The possible entry into later negotiations of left- and right-wing parties may complicate this judgement, but not even that is certain: the PAC could find itself gravitating to the ANC bloc, right-wing parties to, say, the IFP's). More generally, they add, later events may have shown that a gathering of this sort was doomed to achieve little unless it was *preceded* by tough, direct, negotiation between the parties – which is the way in which negotiation has developed since.

Indeed, according to a senior NP source, the 'big three' approach was the way in which Codesa itself was supposed to work; in pre-Codesa negotiations, he says, the NP had agreed that only it, the ANC and IFP would be represented on all working groups; other parties would have at most token representation. However, having been invited to the convention, 'smaller' parties inconveniently insisted on participating in it. So Codesa was planned as a 'big party' bargaining forum, and, despite the irritations caused by 'small' party participation, that is what it was.

At WG1, as with the rest of Codesa, the multi-party nature of the forum was less of a hindrance than participants suggest. When key issues were debated there were really only two players, the NP and ANC (and their allies). What was time-consuming was the elaborate attempt to create an impression of multi-party debate. Codesa was a bargaining forum rather than a problem-solving exercise – for good reason. There is little point in joint problem solving until there is agreement on what the problems are. WG1's discussion on several issues shows clearly that there was no consensus on this – without agreement on the nature of problems (beyond vague commitments to peace and prosperity) there clearly can be no search for solutions.

What is harder to explain is why the third 'big' participant, the IFP, played such a limited role. It, of course, also had an important stake in the outcome: it was later to raise objections on many issues which it hardly addressed at WG1. Had it attempted to raise its strategic concerns, progress may have been more concrete – or the lack of it more apparent. To be sure, while it was apparently seen as a key party, no attempt was made to ensure that it played a major role; the ANC was not going to encourage it to do so, while the NP, according to one of its strategists, would not do so either since it wanted to avoid forming alliances with other parties – a point to which we will return.

But why did the IFP not force its way into the bargaining – by raising its concerns about MK or bilaterals, for example? One explanation, noted earlier, is that it simply failed to send a senior delegation. Another, suggested by a seasoned IFP watcher, is that Buthelezi's absence made it impossible for IFP delegates to operate effectively, since the only man who could really bind it to agreements was not there. In this view, Buthelezi did not expect the IFP to present a strenuous defence of its interests, since he expected the real bargaining to begin only when his terms were met and he joined the negotiations. But, whatever the reason, the IFP's comparative silence in WG1 limited even further the group's ability to solve problems which were to emerge later.

On a more immediate level, the IFP's Benard suggests that WG1 would have been more productive had technical matters been fully researched by specialist groups and then considered by negotiators. One example was the question of emergency powers; a small group of lawyers should have been commissioned to research emergency laws and regulations in democratic countries. This, he believes, could have saved a great deal of time. Certainly, other negotiation forums have recognised that there is a difference between negotiators and specialists, and that the use of the latter may speed the work of the former.

Ultimately, however, even had all of these problems been addressed, there is no guarantee that WG1 would have made substantially more progress; still less that it would produce firm agreements. WG1 showed that the government and ANC in particular approached Codesa with very different assumptions. For the government, WG1 was an exercise in consultation: it would listen carefully to participants' views and then decide, as the sovereign authority, whether to implement them – hence its perceived unwillingness to discuss proposals which it did not plan to implement. For the ANC alliance the government was a party, among many others, which had gathered to clear the way for an election in which it would surrender power and retire either into the opposition benches or obscurity. This ensured that both parties underestimated what they would have to give, and overestimated what they would receive in return.

WG1 was meant to clear part of the way to a settlement. But since the parties did not agree on what it was they were clearing the way towards, it is perhaps no surprise that they failed to do so.

End of innocence

'The long and short of the situation is that there is no time now to debate the proposal and to see whether one could reach a further compromise.' – Deputy Constitutional Development minister Tertius Delport to the last meeting of Working Group 2.

'We never thought that we would be on the verge of packing our bags and departing from this room. We have now reached that point.' – ANC secretary general Cyril Ramaphosa to the same meeting.

Thus did Codesa's Working Group 2 draw to a weary close towards midday on 15 May. As delegates rose from their chairs and moved to the exit, IFP delegate Ben Ngubane announced: 'My principal has considered the whole proposal. He has said that he agrees and that we go to 70 per cent on clauses in the national assembly.'[1] Few, if any, participants heard him. The time for trading was over, and Codesa with it. Only the death rites remained.

In the days before Codesa 2, WG2 had become virtually the sole focus of the convention's – and the media's – attention. Here alone, the citizenry was told in ever more dramatic press reports, agreement was elusive, and here alone a compromise was desperately sought. While other working groups waited to deliver their completed reports, this one bargained on. The appointed day of the plenary arrived and WG2 met again, delaying the session as it sought the elusive agreement a final time.

It failed, and the aura of imminent agreement which had surrounded Codesa collapsed as the main parties traded insults at separate media conferences and then took their animosities into a ritualised public debate redolent of the country's polarised past, not its presumed reconciled future. The delay of several hours became one of months as the

negotiation process entered a period of apparent deadlock. Months later, the issues which had divided WG2 remained seemingly unresolved.

Chief government negotiator Gerrit Viljoen ... his withdrawal from WG2 was a setback to negotiations.

A predictable surprise

That Codesa'a fate should hinge on WG2 was not surprising. Its task was to examine the central issues on which a settlement depended and it was here, therefore, that the parties were assumed to have sent their most senior negotiators. The nature of the issues and the composition of the delegations ensured that, if Codesa was indeed tackling the divisions in the way of a settlement, agreement in WG2 would be most important and hardest to achieve.

But when WG2 deadlocked, both delegates and observers professed to be surprised. Conventional wisdom had insisted that its task – to agree on a set of constitutional principles and on a mechanism which would produce a constitution – would be relatively simple, since it would merely formalise an agreement already largely in place.

Before Codesa, progress towards a settlement seemed barred by the gulf between the NP's insistence on a multi-party conference and the ANC's on a constituent assembly – a divide which expressed competing visions not only of how to reach a new order, but of that order itself. The ANC wanted a constitution framed by the representatives of the majority, because it wanted a new order ruled by that majority. The NP wanted one shaped by several parties – including itself – because it wanted a future in which power was shared by these parties.[2] These positions went to the heart of the gulf which negotiation was meant to bridge.

But conventional wisdom was that the broad outline of an agreement on how the constitution was to be framed had taken shape in late 1991 and had been given substance by De Klerk's speech at Codesa 1. We have argued already that this did not then resolve the gulf between them: for the ANC, the interim was a brief prelude until the old gave way to the new; for the NP, the old would recede as gradually as possible. This too went to the heart of the divide.

But it did not seem to do so then. De Klerk's offer seemed to bring the government as close to a constituent assembly as it was likely to get. Although the ANC did not endorse his plan, its objection seemed to centre purely around the life span of the elected interim government/constitution-making assembly. To be sure, it was at pains to stress that this was to it a vital issue: the movement's confidential[3] newsletter, *Negotiations Bulletin*, noted on 16 January: 'We need to place emphasis where it belongs: the goal is the drafting and implementation of a new constitution. Unless agreement is reached on this matter, interim government can only serve as a trap …'[4] How long the interim period would be would, of course, decide how long the new order the ANC wanted would be delayed – hence its warning. But a dispute over time frames seemed one which could be resolved by horse-trading; hence the expectation that a deal was in sight. ANC negotiators seemed to share that view: they seemed convinced that a workable compromise was possible, until hours before Codesa 2.

On constitutional principles, the other aspect of WG2's brief, consensus seemed equally secure. Because the NP feared a constitution drafted by an elected majority, it insisted that a constitutional assembly be bound by principles negotiated between the parties. But the ANC seemed to have accepted this already: the Harare Declaration had proposed the use of certain principles 'as the basis for the adoption of a new constitution'. It added that, 'having agreed on these principles, the parties should then negotiate the necessary mechanism for drawing up the new constitution'.[5]

The mere fact that the ANC was participating in Codesa, a multi-party gathering, was seen to confirm a consensus born of more than two years of strategic rethinking on both sides; it was assumed that WG2 would simply add the finishing touches to the 'deal'. Why then did 14 working group meetings, and the combined efforts of some of the country's most senior politicians, fail to consummate the compromise? Why did they only achieve, as analyst and DP WG2 participant David Welsh wrote later, 'an agreement on the balance between central, regional and local government that is so general as to be of little value to constitution drafters', and one on the 'meaningful participation of political minorities', which he described as a 'non-principle'?[6]

Part of the answer lies in understanding how close to – or far from – agreement the parties really were. Expressing a widely held view, TIC delegate Firoz Cachalia insists that WG2 delegates were 'tantalisingly close to agreement'. Did WG2 fail simply because its participants were unable to grasp a moment which history had prepared for them – or was this a symptom of a more fundamental problem?

To attempt a clear-cut explanation of the deadlock is a task to be approached with the utmost humility. The stakes were high – to examine WG2 is to a undertake a journey into the very heart of the South African political divide, and the issues are far from resolved. No doubt unopened files and unspoken agendas remain. But precisely because they are unresolved, and are crucial to the search for a workable settlement, the bewildering tapestry of developments – in and outside the meeting room – which shaped the deadlock must be confronted, for only an understanding of past failures will prevent future ones. The task must begin with a careful account of events within WG2.

INSIDE WORKING GROUP 2
A toughness of will

WG2 held its first meeting on 20 January; it was a routine discussion of procedures. But a glance around the table showed that this was where the parties had concentrated much of their top personnel. Delegates included Ramaphosa and Albie Sachs of the ANC; the SACP's Joe Slovo; Constitutional Development minister Gerrit Viljoen; Ben Ngubane of the IFP; Rowan Cronjé of the Bophuthatswana government; and Colin Eglin and Denis Worrall of the DP. These well-known figures were complemented by able lawyers and analysts.

That first, easy-going, meeting helped to set the tone. Eglin recalls the atmosphere: 'On a personal level, it was very good. No one raised their voices; everybody was polite and amenable. But towards the end, as we came closer to a moment of decision, there was a toughness of will, if not of manner.'

Ironically, given the importance of the task, the negotiators spent relatively little time debating the ground rules of a new order. Where the other working groups broke into subcommittees charged with detailed assignments, WG2 met only in plenary and then only 14 times; meetings usually continued for two days. As in WG1 progress was not made easier by the need to discuss formal submissions from all 19 delegations; each was read out to the meeting, followed by questions. Perhaps inevitably, Welsh recorded that 'progress on the constitutional principles was painfully slow and inconclusive'; there was 'not much debate on principles per se'.[7] The problem was partly addressed by appointing an eight-member steering committee which met before each meeting, but the fact that not all parties were represented was a nagging source of resentment among excluded delegations.

As early as the second meeting it emerged that the 'consensus' on constitutional principles was an illusion; while both the ANC and government agreed that Codesa ought to agree on principles to guide a constitution-making body, they disagreed fundamentally on their nature. This was to be a constant theme within WG2; the failure to bridge the gap contributed greatly to the final deadlock.

The essential divide was over the difference between a principle and a detail. This was anything but technical. The NP/SAG wanted as much as possible agreed, for it wanted to leave as little as it could to an elected assembly; the ANC wanted as little as possible agreed, and as much as possible left to the assembly. Thus the government proposed the 'principle' that power be shared in the executive, a central NP goal. The ANC countered that this was a detail; an assembly elected by 'the people' should decide if the NP's chief condition for a settlement would be met. In WG1 it was the NP's strategy which often prompted it to avoid detailed agreement; in WG2 it was the ANC's.

Vijoen's successor, Roelf Meyer ... for him, when Codesa collapsed, the bargaining began.

We have already noted that this was a debate, in effect, over Codesa's purpose. The ANC therefore argued, in a document[8] which foreshadowed WG2's later disagreements, that Codesa was 'a self-appointed body'. It therefore had 'no legitimacy to draft a constitution'; its function was 'not to draft a constitution by stealth'. The ANC added that Codesa's consensus mechanism was 'functional rather than democratic', again illustrating the clash between its and the NP's vision: consensus implied that the new order was to be negotiated between the parties, and for the ANC this was to frustrate the will of the majority. But what of the minority, which also had to accept the legitimacy of the process if it was to live with the constitution? Its confidence, the ANC said, would be promoted by the use of proportional representation to elect the assembly (which enhances minority representation); agreement that clauses in the constitution could be adopted only by a two-thirds majority;[9] and by adopting constitutional principles before the assembly met. But principles were meant to govern the basic character of the constitution, not its detail.

For Viljoen, this stance ensured that 'WG2 was not successful in producing formulations for basic constitutional principles'. The government, he says, feared increasingly through WG2's discussions that the ANC had 'lost their concern about formulating principles beforehand'. It was concerned that the ANC's 'sensitivity that we should not be too specific' meant that it believed the principles 'were not that important and should remain vague'. To the government, the ANC stance amounted to an unwillingness to agree on anything that might allay its fears of an elected constitutional assembly.

Since this went to the heart of the division WG2 was meant to overcome, it seems logical to expect that it would debate and resolve this issue before it did anything else. It did not.

Regionalism: agreement on what?

Instead, between 6 February and 9 March, it debated two specific principles: the balance between central, regional and local government, and the 'meaningful participation of political minorities'. These demanded so much attention that, at its seventh meeting on 9 March, WG2 left it to the steering committee to produce draft principles on outstanding issues. This it did, producing proposals on a bill of rights, the role of traditional leaders, economic freedom and the diversity of cultures, all of which were to glide through WG2 with little dispute. The first two issues, however, since they raised the core concerns of the parties, had been far more fiercely contested.

At WG2's fourth meeting on 17 February the government proposed agreement on four aspects of a principle on the balance between the three levels of government. These were: recognition of the three tiers; democratic representation at each tier; legislative, executive and fiscal autonomy at each level, enshrined in the constitution; and the delegation of powers from central to lower levels of government.

The last two aspects in particular indicated, as Welsh later noted, the government's 'vigorously federal stance' which was, he added, shared by the IFP, DP and some homeland delegations. On this issue the NP and the 'homelands' had a clear community of interest; the former, which had reasonable hopes of winning power in at least one and perhaps two regions,[10] saw strong regional powers as a further key protection against 'simple' majority government, while 'homelands', with somewhat less convincing reasoning,[11] saw them as a means of retaining influence after apartheid went. The government proposals reflected this, since the insistence on delegating powers to lower levels meant, for example, that the central government would surrender these permanently to lower tiers. By contrast, Welsh noted, the ANC wanted 'a unitary system with some federal characteristics'. The government noticed this divide in a submission on 2 March. It listed those parties which had 'expressed themselves unequivocally in favour of regional autonomy' as those given by Welsh as well as the LP; the 'homeland' groups it listed as allies were Ciskei, Dikwankwetla, Venda, and the Ximoko Progressive Party.

At first, however, this issue seemed to be resolved surprisingly swiftly. The ANC reacted to the government's submission merely by suggesting that a bill of rights be enforceable at each level. The steering committee was mandated to draw up a draft principle on what had ostensibly been agreed and, at the fifth meeting on 24 February, WG2 endorsed the wording of a principle on the balance between the levels of government.[12]

The agreement was seen as a victory for the government, since the ANC had apparently accepted that the powers delegated to lower levels should be enshrined in the constitution, not left to the discretion of central government; a major step towards strong regional powers. But differing interpretations of what had apparently been agreed surfaced at WG2's sixth meeting on 2 March.

The government argued that functions assigned to the different levels by the constitution could only be performed with 'the necessary financial capability'. It followed, therefore, that 'fiscal competency must accompany the allocation of powers to the highest practicable degree'.[13] In other words, if lower levels were to have more powers, they needed the financial muscle to exercise them, a further argument for federalism. The ANC replied that fiscal powers were the same as legislative ones, since budgets were the product of legislation. But this was a symptom of a wider disagreement: it also now noted that, in its view, the principle agreed to did not reject the concepts of concurrent or overriding powers and the creation of metropolitan governments with a special status.[14] Since concurrent powers, for example, meant that, where lower levels were granted powers on a particular function, the central government would also retain powers over it – to perhaps set the policy guidelines in which lower levels would have to operate[15] – the ANC was saying in effect that the agreement had not committed it to strong powers for the lower levels. And that meant that it had done little or nothing to guarantee what the government wanted. The agreement had therefore not moved the parties much closer to a settlement: Welsh notes that, while there was 'agreement of a kind' on entrenching the powers of lower levels in the constitution, the sharp differences over federalism were not resolved conclusively.

So the government and ANC now put vastly different interpretations on what they had 'agreed'. This pattern of finding 'agreement', and then to continue negotiating as if none had been reached, was to haunt all of WG2's discussions on constitutional principles.

Differences of interpretation on one or two issues – even where the 'agreement' seemed clear – could be dismissed as misunderstandings, or as one or other party's attempt to wriggle out of a concession made earlier. (Indeed, Codesa insiders suggested at the time that the ANC delegation had made an error in committing themselves to too binding an agreement and had then quickly sought to extricate itself – a claim denied by an ANC negotiator.)

But in WG2 these disagreements were routine. According to one insider, once a principle had been phrased, participants could rarely agree on what it was they had 'agreed': the fact that a principle was read out and apparently adopted did not seem to bind parties to it or prevent them from raising later qualifications which watered down the principle. Indeed, says the insider, there was not always agreement even on the recorded wording of the principle. One suggestion was that the principles be adopted as recorded in the minutes. This was accepted, but parties then insisted on the right to add to these principles to 'spell out their implications'. It was decided that delegations could add a 'formulation' of their own to an agreed principle; if this was adopted it would appear alongside the principle in WG2's final report. The effect was to ensure that any issue apparently settled could be reopened; as we shall see below, one 'formulation' so altered a principle that the outcome of a key debate was turned from an NP into an ANC 'victory'. If the object of defining principles was to inspire confidence in a future constitution-making process, it was tending to have the opposite effect.

At the heart of many of these 'differences of interpretation' ran the divide over principle and detail, raised again by the ANC at the meeting of 24 February; according to insiders, Ramaphosa argued in all three of WG2's initial meetings for broad rather than detailed principles. But the issue was not tackled head-on and was left to gnaw away at WG2's work.

Minority participation: principle, not detail

Having failed to reach binding agreement on the three levels of government, WG2 turned to negotiating a principle on the 'meaningful participation of political minorities'. The draft principle prepared by the steering committee read: 'A new constitution should provide for effective participation of minority political parties'; at the ANC's insistence the words 'consistent with democracy' were tacked on, a condition clearly designed to prepare a challenge in the constitution-making body to the enforced power-sharing model unveiled by the NP the previous September.[16] This again gave early warning that the parties were further apart than conventional wisdom had believed: the principle was to undergo more radical revisions in the meetings that lay ahead.

This issue was of course crucial to both sides. For the government, minority participation meant not merely the right of minorities to organise parties and express themselves, but the guaranteed right to participate in government: its September principles had confirmed this. And it was this that the ANC, committed to majority rule, wished to reject. The government's aim was to see its model entrenched in a principle which would bind the constitution-making body – the ANC's, to allow that body the freedom to reject the NP model.

The government's outlook was expressed in an NP submission[17] which argued that 'sustainable democratic structures' should not be equated with 'simple or unqualified majoritarian rule'. It went on: 'We could have a long debate on whether the fear of domination of some of South Africa's ethnic, religious or linguistic minorities is realistic or not, but if we are to deal with our constitutional future in a responsible manner, the mere existence of such perceptions should be accepted as a reality which must be accounted for in a new constitution.' In other words, whether the NP constituency's fear of majority rule was well-founded

was less relevant than the depth of that fear, since this would prompt it to reject any constitution which did not allow for it.

The ANC's Cyril Ramaphosa ... determined to extract tangible concessions from government.

The NP said it wanted the principle of meaningful participation of minorities formally included in the constitution 'instead of relying on the development of appropriate conventions'; the collegiate presidency (see note 16) would go some way towards satisfying its demands. It was not enough to promise participation in broad principle: the details of how this was to be achieved should be stipulated.

The ANC's reply[18] implied that the NP's brand of 'minority participation' was a code for guaranteed power for racial groups. While minorities had 'legitimate interest(s)', these could be recognised under majority rule; a minority could play a role as the opposition in the legislature, while freedom of association, proportional representation and the development of civil society[19] would 'lend vitality to the legitimacy and status of political minorities/opposition'. It reiterated its rejection of 'enforced coalitions/power sharing/minority vetoes'. So the parties were no closer to each other on this central question, and the ANC was clearly unwilling to endorse a 'principle' binding itself to the NP vision.

Unless this agreement was resolved, Codesa could bring the parties no nearer a settlement. But it was not. Instead, a compromise was reached in which a 'formulation' was added to the agreed principle. It read: 'The principle does not imply or reject constitutional prescription for the participation of minority political parties in any executive structure of government, simple majoritarianism, or veto powers by minority political parties on any issue.' In other words, it did not prevent the constitution-making body from selecting any form of government at all.

The effect, of course, was to deny the government's demand that a detailed commitment to its brand of power sharing should bind the assembly. Inevitably, the impression that the ANC had 'won' this issue, and so the first round of WG2, was widely held among participants. ANC negotiator Mohammed Valli Moosa – the leading ANC participant for much of WG2, since Ramaphosa was largely absent after the first few meetings – expresses this: 'I think we were quite happy with the way the discussions had gone, and the tentative decisions on constitutional principles. They were very much in line with ANC thinking ... they were broad and general sorts of principles.'

Towards the precipice: a constitution-making assembly

The ANC's 'victory' was to prove more apparent than real. The steering committee was mandated to draw up draft principles on remaining issues for the eighth meeting on 24 March; that meeting turned its attention from principles to the constitution-making process.

This was, of course, the other issue on which consensus was supposed to have emerged even before Codesa; again the optimism proved unfounded. The government's willingness to concede an elected constitution-making forum had been based largely on the expectation that agreement on principles would prevent that body from ignoring NP concerns. Since the 'agreements' on the powers of central government and power sharing had failed to do that, the government now sought to secure its interests by winning the next round: it proposed a detailed interim constitution which would spell out what the principles had failed to specify. The ground for WG2's deadlock was now prepared. Viljoen explains the direct link between the vagueness of the principles agreed by WG2 and an interim constitution. 'If there was no interim constitution which binds the interim government and the constitution-making body, then that body will be its own judge as to how far it could proceed in interpreting principles.' Valli Moosa offers his own interpretation: 'Because the government could not get its way on constitutional principles, it then insisted that we would need a transitional constitution. Obviously everybody agrees that you need some sort of a transitional constitution – but their plan was that it should be of such a nature that the elected constitution-making body would not be in a position to change it.'

In different words, and from different perspectives, the two are saying much the same thing: that the government would not leave its and the society's future solely to a constituent assembly and that, having failed to secure the controls on this body which it demanded, it now sought to secure its future by other means. But initially the ANC does not seem to have realised this: it believed, perhaps on the strength of its early 'victories', that the government had conceded a sovereign constituent assembly which would shape the new constitution.[20]

Government proposals for transitional government were presented to WG2 on 23 March. They envisaged negotiations on a transitional constitution to replace the present one; the government said it would propose draft legislation at the end of April for 'meaningful discussion, consideration and negotiation in Codesa'. The detailed proposals envisaged a two-chamber interim parliament in which a senate would comprise regional representatives or members of existing legislative bodies, depending on progress in negotiations on regional issues. A collegiate presidency operating by consensus, its chair rotating every six months, would also be established. This would be preceded by a 'preparatory phase' to 'maintain good government and to provide for the responsible management of the transition process'. Transitional multi-party councils would be established to deal with election preparations, regional government, local government and state finances; they would meet together in a joint transitional council.

The effect of this proposal can hardly be overstated. While the ANC criticised the proposed transitional councils as 'toy telephones' (since they would, in its view, have advisory powers only), its objection was far more fundamental. If the government were to win this issue, its power-sharing model would become entrenched during the (lengthy) interim phase. The ANC feared the final constitution would be tacked, almost as an afterthought, onto a long and complicated process. There might be little scope for parties sharing responsibility for government in a difficult period to thrash out a constitution; the interim might become permanent – or at least last a very long time.

Battle was joined at the ninth meeting of WG2 on 31 March, where the government spelled out its model of the transition to a new order.[22] The convention was to agree on a transitional government, to be established in terms of a transitional constitution drafted at Codesa and made law by the current parliament. This would provide for a new legislature, including a senate which would ensure minority participation. It was this body which would write and adopt a new constitution. Its model, it said, provided for participation by all parties, in contrast to 'a simple majoritarian system which is actually the goal or desired outcome that some parties seek to achieve by the negotiations'. In a reference to the recent referendum, the government insisted that it 'has no mandate to enter into a constitution-making process by imposing simple majoritarian decision-making'. An elected constitution-making body that did not function by consensus 'reduces negotiation to a level of insignificance' and amounted to a 'transfer of power to the masses'. In an apparent reply to ANC criticism of Codesa's legitimacy, the submission concluded: 'Codesa does not have the required political legitimacy to institute a government superimposed on the present constitutional government. It does, however, have sufficient legitimacy to institute structures charged with the responsibility to prepare the way for an elected transitional government, and to draft a transitional constitution by consensus.'

The government's proposal sought, in effect, to turn the elected assembly into the multi-party negotiating body it had first sought. The senate, with its weighting in favour of minorities – it could well comprise the 'homeland' and tricameral parties – would be able to block any decision taken by the elected lower house and so force the majority and minority to bargain the shape of the new order.

It also rejected another ANC expectation – that the existing parliament, since it was elected by the minority, would give way before elections to an interim government comprising all parties. The ANC believed such a government would have greater legitimacy, since it and other parties speaking for the excluded majority would at last be included, thus ending minority rule. The government replied by giving the ANC's criticism of Codesa's legitimacy a new twist. Since the convention was indeed a self-appointed body, it argued, it – and an interim government composed of its parties – was less legitimate than the existing parliament, which derived its authority from a constitution. Until elections were held to bestow legitimacy on a new constitutional authority, it was preferable to leave power in the hands of the old one, thus ensuring continuous constitutional government. For the ANC the existing order was less legitimate even than Codesa, for it excluded the majority; for the NP it was more legitimate, since it was constitutional.

For philosophers, this might represent two very different sets of political values. As far as the negotiating process was concerned, it represented two different practical outcomes: the ANC's required the speedy replacement of the existing parliament before an election; the NP's, that parliament remain the final authority – albeit advised by transitional executives – until a ballot.

The ANC's reply[23] further crystallised the division on this central issue: 'Codesa has a vital but limited function, namely to create the conditions for the adoption of a new constitution, not to draft [it] itself.' It reiterated that an elected assembly should write the constitution; elections would 'take away the sense of distance and incomprehension which unfortunately at present separates the public from Codesa.' The ANC also seems to have detected an emerging alliance on this issue between the NP and other parties (see below); part of the document was a reply to IFP positions on an elected assembly.

The IFP was opposed to any elected constitution-making body. It insisted that the constitution be drafted in a multi-party forum and then put to the electorate in a referendum since, in framing a set of political rules which would apply to all, minority views were as important as majority ones (an elected body would sharply reduce the influence of minority views); it had also argued that a fair election was impossible while violence continued.[24]

In reply, the ANC said that a referendum to adopt a new constitution was 'a grotesque device for ensuring that a long and complicated document corresponds to what the populace thinks is correct' (despite this, it later proposed just such a referendum in an attempt to break the talks deadlock). Those who argued that there could not be elections before violence abated were encouraging conflict since, by implication, it was perpetrated by those who sought to prevent elections. The ANC argued that its opponents had no principled objection to 'simple majoritarianism' but were dissatisfied 'with whom the majority will be'. Majoritarianism, it repeated, was qualified by the safeguards it had earlier offered (proportional representation and the two-thirds majority; now, perhaps as a result of the direction of earlier debate, the constitutional principles were no longer cited).

The ANC's justification for the two-thirds stipulation was particularly important, since it touched on the issue which was ostensibly to deadlock WG2: the size of the majority needed to pass the constitution. It argued that no single party would gain a two-thirds majority in an election, so all would have to seek support from rivals to gain the clauses they wanted. This acknowledged that debate over the size of the majority might have little to do with principles, and far more to do with calculations of eventual support. Later events may have shown that the NP trusted the ANC's electoral arithmetic as little as it did the movement's other assurances. In any event, the ANC insisted that the two-thirds provision was superior to the second chamber which the government favoured; the latter was a 'built-in deadlock' and equivalent to 'assuming inevitable conflict between the majority and minorities, and then setting them against each other on a collision course'.

Motives and intentions

These exchanges showed that the divide remained as wide as it had been when the negotiation process began. Behind the technical proposals and counterproposals lay the stark reality that the ANC still insisted that the 'people's representatives' write the new constitution – albeit with a guaranteed veto for any party which could muster more than one-third support for its view – and that the NP still wanted one bargained between the parties. The ANC still wanted quick movement to majority rule; the NP still wanted a slower transition and a guaranteed future role, regardless of the outcome of elections.

As in WG1 some participants explained the NP's 'tough new stance' by its referendum victory – which it explicitly mentioned in its submission. The ANC clearly felt this: in its *Negotiations Bulletin* of 9 April, it implied that the poll was the chief reason why the government had begun to insist that MK disband as a 'precondition' for interim government; a further implication was that this was also why the NP had 'backtracked' on its commitment to a 'sovereign' constituent assembly.

Again as in WG1, there is little evidence to support this. On the MK issue, the referendum may have emboldened the government. But on the constituent assembly issue, the claim that it had 'backtracked' ignored the point that it had never been willing to agree to a 'sovereign' assembly in the first place. As we implied above, it originally sought to reduce the assembly's power by negotiating detailed constitutional principles which would bind it. When that was rejected, it turned to bicameralism and the rotating presidency to achieve the same end. While the

The DP's Colin Eglin, right, with the NP's Dawie de Villiers. Eglin tried unsuccessfully to engineer a last-minute compromise between the NP and the ANC.

referendum might have made it more assertive, it did not substantially change its position.

To other participants, pressure on the ANC was also a factor in the apparent hardening of positions. One such pressure was political violence. It undermined the credibility of the Codesa process and all its parties; hence their attempts to blame each other for it. The government's demand that MK be disbanded was, according to the *Negotiations Bulletin*, an attempt to shift the blame onto the guerrilla army. The ANC insisted that violence was meant to undermine negotiations – and so progress towards an interim government.

As evidence, the ANC-aligned Human Rights Commission cited figures to show that violence seemed to increase as Codesa progressed: it found that the number of politically related deaths was higher in March (437), April (356), May (296) and June (373) than in any month in the preceding year; March to June was the only period in the 12 months since June 1991 in which more than 200 people had died in the PWV area each month.[25] And, as we have seen, while violence undermined

the process itself, it particularly weakened the credibility of ANC negotiators.

Nor was violence the only factor persuading key sections of the ANC
constituency that Codesa was going nowhere; some who had been sceptical of multi-party negotiation from the start were bolstered by a growing grass roots perception that Codesa was a 'talk shop' which was delivering
none of the breakthroughs the negotiators had promised. Eglin explains:
'Things were going badly outside as far as the ANC's support was concerned. The ANC had no victory inside [Codesa], and it was a shambles
outside.' A sense among ANC negotiators that they were losing touch
with their constituency must have been strengthened by the paucity of
response by ANC structures to the negotiators' efforts. The *Negotiations
Bulletin* of 9 April noted: 'With reference to the issues raised for discussion in *Negotiations Bulletin* no 7, it is rather disturbing that we have
as yet not heard the views from any of the regions. It is important that
these bulletins be used as discussion documents. The views of branches
and regions are of great importance.'

These factors, combined with the realisation – prompted by the
debate over a constitution-making body – that the parties were further
apart than they had thought, combined to heighten mistrust between
them. The divide was widened by a 'new' factor – greater agreement
between the NP and IFP, which strengthened ANC suspicions that the
two were co-operating to prevent a 'democratic transition'. This had not
always been so. While the IFP and some other parties were assumed to
be government allies when Codesa began, they were often – particularly
during the earlier stages of Codesa – suspicious of its intentions, since it
engaged frequently in bilateral discussions with the ANC; they feared
that they were being 'sidelined' as the two 'big parties' sought common
cause. The dynamics of WG2 did little to allay their fears: chief government negotiator Viljoen and his ANC counterparts had frequently left the
room together to thrash out disagreements. But this pattern was to end
at the end of the April, when Viljoen withdrew from WG2 to be replaced
by his deputy, Tertius Delport. ANC negotiators came to believe that
Delport was more determined than Viljoen to have his outlook prevail –
and that he brought the government far closer to the IFP.

'Natural' alliances

Nevertheless, Viljoen's departure and Delport's arrival may have been at
most a symptom, not a cause. A senior NP negotiator suggests that, for
much of Codesa, the party was eager not to form alliances with other
delegations, including the IFP. Later it was approached by 'smaller parties' which feared that minority concerns, particularly on regionalism,
were being ignored – only then did it and they begin taking common
positions. Delport's explanation does not entirely exclude this: in a later
interview, he insisted that the government and IFP drew closer to each
other because of their 'common thinking' on federalism.

But another explanation is that the government's change of strategy, prompted by its failure to secure its constitutional principles, had given it a common cause with the IFP. When the government had seemed willing to countenance a 'sovereign' constituent assembly, there could be no alliance. Its new proposal might not meet all the IFP's requirements, but it was close enough to ensure Inkatha's support. The government/IFP 'convergence' owed far more to the change in the NP's position – towards an attempt to dilute the role of the constitution-making body more overtly – than to changes in negotiating personnel. We hinted earlier that positions on the constitution-making body were based more on demographic calculations than on political philosophy, related to expectations of the likely results of a non-racial election. Since the IFP's calculations of the likely outcome of a ballot were not that different to the NP's, a proposal aimed at diluting that outcome created a 'natural' alliance between them.

Why had that alliance taken so long to emerge? Before it did, WG2 had seemed to be the arena for bargaining between the ANC alliance and the NP: other parties, including the IFP, had seemed peripheral. SACP delegate Jeremy Cronin was later to argue that, while the presence at Codesa of 'homeland' parties and those in the tricameral system could have favoured the government, it proved 'relatively inept' at using this potential alliance: its allies were seldom quite sure just where the government stood on issues, he claimed. He argued that the open nature of Codesa was not conducive to the government's style: it preferred closed diplomatic negotiations at which it showed 'tactical cunning'.[26] That an ANC alliance negotiator should seize on the government's inability or unwillingness to cement alliances as a sign of 'ineptitude' is to illustrate the extent to which Codesa's chief parties still saw each other as adversaries whose weaknesses were to be exploited; but it also confirms that the government's 'allies' were being sidelined.

One possible explanation is the suggestion by several insiders that, for much of the time Codesa sat, the government had concluded that the IFP was an unreliable ally,[27] and that it was also influenced by polls suggesting that it could win more black votes than the Natal-based party. Certainly, the NP seems to have believed during this period that it did not need allies to negotiate a favourable agreement with the ANC.

What is not explained is the willingness of the IFP in particular to accept a marginal role on all issues except perhaps federalism. One explanation saw Codesa as a very inappropriate forum for a party such as the IFP: in this view, the convention's emphasis on parties and modern political structures created an ambience in which the ethnic concerns which were at the heart of the IFP position could not be easily raised; this was illustrated by the exclusion of the Zulu king.

Another explanation (see WG1) suggests that Buthelezi never intended his party to make an impact on Codesa, once he had failed to secure participation on his terms. The IFP delegates, notes an observer with a close knowledge of the party, would never agree to anything substantial without the approval of their leader – and as long as Buthelezi was not at Codesa, he had little interest in helping the convention to make progress by giving his approval to particular positions. Until he felt willing to join the convention, therefore, the IFP would make only a token attempt to put its position, keep its powder dry – and wait for its opportunity to intervene in negotiations on its, rather than other parties', terms.

Be that as it may, even when the IFP and other 'homeland' parties did find themselves on the government's side, they were clearly junior partners: throughout WG2 the IFP never received more than a polite hearing. Notwithstanding rhetoric to the contrary, the NP was well aware that the ANC held the key to international acceptance of a settlement, and that agreement with it was a necessary condition for a 'deal'. To name but one example, a government willingness to side with the IFP in its opposition to an elected constitution-making body would have weakened world support for the agreement, since it had an undemocratic ring in a world in which liberal democracy had become a new orthodoxy. It was not that other parties were 'unimportant'; simply that they could not give the government what it needed. As long as it believed that agreement with the ANC could secure its conditions, it concentrated on achieving that. Only when it concluded that the ANC was unwilling to meet it, did an alliance with other parties (whether at its or their behest) seem necessary.

In sum, the 'convergence' – and the increased polarisation between two blocs within WG2 – was a symptom of the two 'major' parties' failure to find common ground. It was in the nature of the Codesa process that even a rift as fundamental as this should be cast as a procedural disagreement – a technical difference over details such as time frames – rather than a dispute of substance, and that it should be attributed to negotiating styles rather than the convention's lack of progress in finding that common ground. Certainly, the WG2 steering committee seemed to assume that the disagreement was one of detail, not substance. It proceeded briskly to lay the ground for a settlement in a manner which implied that the issue at hand was another item on a busy agenda, not an attempt to bridge the basic gulf in South African politics.

Arriving at the abyss

WG2's 10th meeting, held on 7 April, was handed a steering committee document entitled 'Suggested Discussion on Constitution-Making Body'. The issues facing the negotiators were, it suggested, whether the CMB should be elected; whether it should have a second chamber and provision for special majorities; how far Codesa should proceed in drafting principles to bind the CMB; the status of TBVC voters (their eligibility to vote if the CMB was elected); the functions of the CMB as an interim legislature; whether a referendum should be held, and when; and the desirability of regional constitutions and a constitutional panel.

By the 12th meeting, on 28 April, the committee was able to present a specific proposal on a CMB and how it might be achieved. And at the 13th meeting, on 24 April, it distributed a proposal which appeared to be an agreement to take the country forward to non-racial elections and an agreed constitution-drafting assembly. It suggested that Codesa agree to a law establishing a CMB operating within the framework of an interim constitution; that the non-independent 'homelands' be consulted on the law and the interim constitution; and that Codesa agree on a set of constitutional principles. An interim constitution would provide for an elected interim parliament which would also draw up a new constitution; a multi-party interim executive; justiciable civil and political rights during the transition; the balance between the three tiers of government; regional boundaries; elections; special majorities for clauses of the constitution (especially on regional structures and the balance between tiers of government); legal provisions to prevent a constitutional hiatus; and an independent body to determine whether general constitutional principles had been enshrined in the constitution (the constitutional panel mentioned earlier). This proposal was to be submitted to the delegates' principals and discussed further at the next meeting.

The committee – on which both the ANC and NP were represented – seemed to have achieved a startling breakthrough: the fundamental divisions which had emerged over a CMB had been settled in a few weeks. By 12 May, at the start of its final scheduled meeting before it was due to submit its report to Codesa 2, WG2 had ostensibly arrived at the brink of an agreement on the writing of a new constitution. If the ANC had 'won' the first few rounds at WG2, the proposed agreement suggested that the NP had more than regained ground. Its basics – a transitional constitution drawn up at Codesa in accordance with agreed principles, clauses of which could only be amended only by special majorities – met the NP's requirements for a settlement.

A closer look at the steering committee proposals might have sounded a warning that its suggested agreement was hardly watertight. True, the NP had won its interim constitution. But the proposal said little about the details of that constitution; the NP's concern to entrench power sharing and to ensure a senate representing minorities which could block any proposal had not been agreed. There was more than enough room for deep disagreement later, even if the proposal was adopted.

In the event the disagreement emerged even before it was adopted – on the details of a principle which both the ANC and NP had accepted, the need for special majorities. Over the next four days there was an intense struggle to determine the precise percentages needed to adopt particular constitutional clauses.

A steering committee proposal drawn up on 13 May read: '... every clause in the final constitution shall be adopted by a majority of 66,7 per cent, 70 per cent or 75 per cent in the national assembly' (the name now proposed for the CMB). It added: 'Provisions in the final constitution affecting regional government and the distribution of power between central, regional and local levels of government shall also require a special majority of regional representatives in the NA, such special majority to be agreed upon by Codesa'. Between the three proposed percentages lay enough division to prompt the WG2 deadlock.

The government outlined its position in a proposal on 14 May.[28] Ordinary constitutional clauses should require a 66,7 per cent majority, it said. Clauses dealing with a bill of rights, the principles of three-tier government, multi-party democracy and effective participation of political minorities would require a majority of 75 per cent. Those dealing with the regions were to be decided by an unspecified special majority. It now also proposed that a senate approve the entire constitution by a 66,7 per cent majority, but offered to drop this proposal in exchange for a 75 per cent majority on clauses dealing with the regions. At first glance its agreement to a two-thirds majority on 'ordinary' clauses seemed like a concession. But the senate proposal, together with the insistence that on all issues the government considered central a three-quarters majority would be needed, reduced the 'concession' to a symbolic one: unless the majority party won more than 75 per cent of the vote, minorities – of which the most important was the NP itself[29] – could veto the constitution.

This proposal was significant in two ways. For many analysts it expressed NP expectations of its likely electoral support – more than 25 per cent, but less than 34 per cent.[30] But it also raised again an issue which had never been far from the surface but had been partly obscured by divisions on power sharing: regional government. Until two days before Codesa 2, the government seemed content to pursue its goal through three devices: agreement at Codesa on regional powers and boundaries; a system of national and regional lists for elections to a CMB; and the senate. The first had proved a broken reed, while the second was not a serious source of dispute but was also likely to do little to further the government's cause, since the fact that delegates were elected on regional lists did not mean that they would necessarily vote for strong regions in the assembly. It was, therefore, the third, the senate – disagreement over its composition and functions had been papered over previously – which it now stressed.

The last wrangle

This proposal began the wrangling which was to end in deadlock. Welsh describes how it happened: 'In the flurry of last-minute negotiations on the eve of and indeed on the very day of the opening of Codesa 2, relations between government and the ANC deteriorated dramatically. With the utmost reluctance, the ANC had agreed to push its 66,6 per cent figure up to 70 per cent and to require that amendment of the bill of rights needed a 75 per cent majority. The government now insisted (reportedly at the behest of some of the homeland governments) that a 75 per cent majority be required to amend relations between the central and regional governments.'[31] According to Welsh, the government withdrew its insistence on a senate in the CMB on condition that the ANC accepted a senate with co-equal power to the lower house in the final constitution. The ANC, in exchange for its 70 per cent concession, demanded a deadlock-breaking mechanism in the form of a referendum which would be held if a national assembly could not agree on a constitution within six months; a simple referendum majority of 50 per cent plus one would be needed to adopt the constitution.

The ANC's explanation of its position appeared in the *Negotiations Bulletin* of 18 May. It had been presented, it said, with government demands which sought to ensure that the interim constitution, with its 'undemocratic' senate, became permanent: 'The regime, having agreed to an elected constitution-making body, set such stringent conditions that the national assembly would take many years to draft a new constitution.' This would mean 'that the interim constitution would remain in force, and may even become the final constitution. This was the trap set by the NP.' In an attempt to avoid deadlock, the ANC had agreed to a 75 per cent majority on a bill of rights and 70 per cent on all other issues 'if all other conditions were agreed to by the regime'. One of these was the referendum, demanded because 'the national assembly may never be able to take decisions with such high percentages'. When this was rejected, 'we were forced to deadlock rather than make such an unacceptable compromise'.

Government's Tertius Delport ... little authority to take decisions.

The NP insists that this apparent reasonableness masked an unwillingness to compromise. Delport summed up this view shortly after the deadlock when he insisted that the referendum demand rendered all other ANC compromises meaningless. This was so because it could effectively deadlock the national assembly and wait for a referendum, in which a bare majority would assure it of the constitution of its choice: the 'simple majoritarianism' which the NP feared had reappeared with a vengeance.

In the wake of the deadlock, many of these niceties were lost on independent observers and, perhaps, most South Africans. Two perceptions sum up their response. The one was that the politicians, faced with the prospect of an historic compromise, had fallen to haggling about trivia – a handful of percentage points in a constitution-making body. The other, popular among non-NP analysts not necessarily sympathetic to the ANC, was that the government had missed an opportunity to win an agreement largely on its terms. It noted that the ANC alliance, in conceding

70 per cent majorities to gain a settlement, had exceeded its mandate and might have faced a hostile reaction from its constituency. In so doing it had walked into a government 'trap', which would have locked it into precisely the permanent compromise on NP terms of which the *Negotiations Bulletin* warned. But the government, determined to win a settlement entirely on its own terms, 'blundered' and let the opportunity slip.

This view is put by Eglin. He suggests that the details of the proposals which flew back and forth were less important than the reality that the ANC wanted to settle, but needed a 'victory' to take back to its constituency – one which need not have anything directly to do with the issues under debate. He says a senior member of the ANC alliance delegation told him that the mere release of a substantial number of political prisoners would have given the ANC enough to take back to its constituency the compromises called for in WG2. The government, he suggests, was deeply suspicious of the ANC's real intentions; it 'went all out for victory' and so lost sight of 'the bigger picture'. His view is summed up by a remark he is said to have made to De Klerk some time after the collapse of Codesa 2: 'In politics,' he said, 'it is not clever to win everything.'

More importantly, it soon became a part of political lore that WG2 had been 'agonisingly close' to agreement. Had the negotiators kept their heads, the vital breakthrough would have been achieved. But, in reality, the stalemate may have been more inevitable than it seemed.

ANATOMY OF A DEADLOCK

Despite the public optimism exuded by the parties before the final deadlock, there were clear signs in the two weeks leading up to Codesa 2 that prospects of a deal were wilting by the hour. Viljoen insists that the ANC had, 10 days before Codesa 2, changed its approach. 'There was a marked change in the personnel who represented them in WG2 and in other groups and steering committees.' In WG2 the most important change was the reappearance of Ramaphosa, who had missed most meetings. He immediately adopted a far tougher stance than his colleagues, prompting Delport to exclaim angrily that the ANC general secretary was negotiating 'like a trade unionist' – a not entirely surprising allegation since, until his election to the ANC post, this was precisely what Ramaphosa was. Viljoen's perception was that the change of personnel toughened the ANC stance, a point to which we will return.

Evidence that the ANC did not necessarily believe itself to be on the verge of an historic reconciliation with the NP was provided by a statement issued by its Department of Information and Publicity on 13 May.[32] It reported on a 'summit meeting' of the ANC-led tripartite alliance: 'On the eve of Codesa 2, the ANC, SACP and Cosatu held a leadership summit ... which reviewed the current negotiations process. General progress made at Codesa was welcomed, while a number of unresolved areas were noted. The alliance reaffirmed that the central issue in the whole negotiation process is agreement on a democratically elected constituent assembly. The CA should be a single chamber structure. It should be sovereign, with no veto powers over its decisions. The summit called for implementation of first phase multi-party interim structures by the end of June and the holding of elections for a CA by the end of the year.'

It continued: 'If Codesa 2 deadlocks, only mass action will ensure that the democratisation process remains on course. If Codesa 2 produces a breakthrough, mass mobilisation will be critical to ensuring the effective and urgent implementation of the agreements.' Finally, the statement noted 'the present government's deep complicity in murder and wide-scale corruption'. Regardless of the outcome of the meeting, the alliance had agreed on the mass mobilisation which, later in the year, was to highlight the still enormous gulf between the parties. Whatever was happening inside Codesa, polarisation was clearly growing outside it.

On the other side of the table the mood was no more conciliatory. The next day, then Defence minister Roelf Meyer, a key NP negotiator, issued a statement which reasserted the government's insistence on formal power sharing, and its rejection of a 'monopoly of power' and the 'misuse of power by any majority, however constituted'. Meyer said the government wanted 'an entrenched constitution which can only be amended by a special majority in parliament'. It would insist on 'constitutional continuity, the maintenance of order, and negotiations in good faith'. This entailed compliance with agreements, 'rejection of hidden agendas', and 'reasonableness, with solutions in which there are no losers'. While none of these statements broke new ground, they underlined a deep mistrust of the NP's presumed partners in reconciliation.

Nor was the ANC the only party to change its personnel in the period just before the deadlock. Viljoen had attended his last meeting of WG2 on 28 April – with Finance minister Barend du Plessis, he was the second major government figure to leave Codesa within as many months. He was replaced by Delport.

Viljoen, a former Broederbond chairman, a man of enormous influence within the ruling establishment and until then perhaps the key intellectual force behind the constitutional strategy of the De Klerk presidency, had guided negotiations from their inception. Delport, seen by critics as more of an academic than a politician or negotiator, was later singled out as the cause of the deadlock. Stricken by flu and slightly hoarse during the last days of WG2, he gained a reputation for inflexibility which persisted long after Codesa 2's collapse. Valli Moosa insists: 'There is no doubt that Delport made a specific contribution to making it impossible for agreement to be reached.'

But these criticisms ignore the most important point about Delport's role: that his relatively junior status ensured that he had little authority to take decisions on behalf of the NP/SAG and that, whatever the merits or otherwise of his manner, it is therefore implausible to identify him as the deadlock's cause. Delport was a junior minister, left in full charge until WG2's final meeting, when Meyer, later to become Viljoen's successor at the ministry of Constitutional Development and as chief NP negotiator, sat in. Even then, Meyer said little or nothing, leaving Delport to mind the store. Eglin recalls the effect on WG2 in its last week: 'It was unfortunate that Viljoen had been withdrawn the week before. While there were defects in his makeup, he was a well-respected member and no one would have walked over him.' By not appointing Delport to Viljoen's post, the government 'was saying that Delport was not good enough to be number one – on top of this they did not bring in a number one'. He adds: 'While Viljoen's seniority and status would have allowed him to make adjustments, we had to adjourn every so often because Delport had to get on the telephone. And then he had to talk to a man he could not talk to as an equal. In the most crucial phase, the government left a junior team to strike a deal with a senior one.' This is partly confirmed by an often repeated story which insists that it was not Delport who turned down the ANC's 70 per cent compromise; it was the NP leader he phoned to ask for a mandate, which he was denied.

The key question, of course, is why the government should have left WG2 to the deputy minister. Eglin insists that it underestimated the importance of Ramaphosa's intervention and his resolve to extract a visible concession from the government. Certainly, in his last address to WG2 on the morning of 15 May, Ramaphosa leaves an impression of 'steely will'. His remarks to Delport are tinged with condescension and a hint of menace. In his irritation, Ramaphosa appears to disagree even with Valli Moosa, who had led the ANC in WG2 in his absence; when the latter seemed to suggest that WG2 could report to Codesa 2 and leave the unresolved matter of a senate until later, Ramaphosa insisted that all issues be resolved at the meeting. And it was Ramaphosa who, in effect, announced the deadlock by stating: 'We have never considered that a situation would come about where our delegation would feel so frustrated in participating in the deliberations of WG2. We have now reached that stage. This is a grave situation, because Dr Delport is once again trying to take us backwards. He is demonstrating a total unwillingness to drive this working group ... towards reaching an agreement ... In the light of the response we are getting from Dr Delport, I just wonder whether we are spending our time fruitfully. Let us adjourn, reconvene and this group reports that there is no agreement.' To Delport and perhaps other delegates, this was indeed the first time that the flavour of shop-floor bargaining had intruded on WG2 – and it was clearly more than the group's fragile apparent consensus could bear.

A gulf too far

Yet to reduce the deadlock to Ramaphosa's style is to ignore why he may have used this particular approach – indeed, why he may have reappeared at WG2 in the first place. For several months, despite the atmosphere of progress recalled by WG2 negotiators, the government and ANC had been waging a propaganda war on the timing and purpose of Codesa 2. That this

plenary was being held at all seemed, as we have suggested, more a function of the fact that Codesa had promised a second public meeting and
wished to preserve an illusion of momentum than with the likelihood that
there would be any concrete agreements to report. There were, of course,
few if any detailed agreements which could be unveiled by mid-May.

Government spokesmen reacted to this reality by insisting that Codesa 2 was merely an opportunity for working groups to present progress
reports. They added that it was not Codesa alone which would set the
pace of constitutional reform; the process might take more time than
most South Africans hoped, but that was inevitable if a durable settlement was to be achieved. Unresolved issues such as violence, the status
of MK and the government's insistence that the ANC transform itself from
a 'liberation movement' into a political party were important factors in
the timing of transitional arrangements. In sum, the NP suggested a
piecemeal approach in which agreement would be reached on those
issues on which it was possible, and more difficult issues would be left
until later.

The ANC, for reasons we explained earlier, was in a hurry. It argued
the need for a package of agreements; it could not accept a first stage of
an arrangement if the phases to which it would lead had not been
defined. It was 'all or nothing'; either a comprehensive settlement would
emerge from Codesa 2, or the gathering would be a failure.

These stances may have indeed been influenced by the post-referendum environment. The NP, secure in its white support and international
approval, had little reason to hurry; it was, as we have pointed out, the
party in power which had little reason to hasten the day on which it had
to share it. Insider gossip was to insist, in the days after the deadlock,
that the government had looked over the brink at the prospect of abandoning sole power, decided it was not ready, and resolved to bide its
time. The ANC, encouraged by the large 'yes' vote, and finally convinced
that the prospect of the NP losing power to the white right if it compromised was now past, may have decided that the time to press home a
settlement had arrived.

There is little doubt that the pressure on the ANC to secure a decisive
victory was greater than that on the NP. As we suggested earlier, important parts of the ANC alliance had concluded for some time that Codesa
was not worth the price they believed they had paid by joining it – it was
not, after all, yielding the 'sovereign' constituent assembly which they
were promised as the reward for resigning themselves to it. They wanted a transfer of power, not a compromise with the NP; and if Codesa
could not achieve it they suggested that mass mobilisation would. Equally important, there was a strain within the alliance, represented largely
by Cosatu, which did not reject negotiation and the compromise which
went with it, but insisted that the ANC negotiating strategy compared
unfavourably with that of the unions: in particular, it did not realise the
need to back talks with pressure, a strategy which is central to industrial
bargaining. During the referendum campaign, Cosatu's leadership had
skilfully deflected a demand from union shop stewards for 'mass action'

in protest at the whites-only poll (which they and the ANC feared, might have swelled the 'no' vote) by agreeing to a mass campaign in support of an interim government a couple of months after the white ballot. That averted the demand for mass action during the referendum – but it also meant that the bill would have to be paid, and the mass campaign launched, if an agreement was not swiftly reached. In sum, mounting frustration with Codesa placed ANC negotiators under severe pressure to reach a settlement which could clearly be portrayed as a victory. If they could not produce one, mass action was inevitable.

But the problem was more intractable even than this. One clue is provided by the ANC's statement of 13 May promising action even if a settlement was reached. A second is offered by the NP's clear message, ignored in the emotional days after the collapse, signalling clearly that it neither expected nor wanted a final agreement at Codesa 2. And the third is provided by this account of WG2 itself, which indicates that, despite an impression of progress, the working group failed to resolve any one of the divides between the NP and ANC.

The two parties were simply too far apart to settle, and WG2 had brought them only inches nearer. A deal was not 'tantalisingly close'; it was almost as far away as when Codesa first convened. The final disagreement was not a haggle over percentages – the NP still wanted a slow transition to power sharing; the ANC, through its referendum proposal, still wanted quick majority rule. This, together with the ANC's need for a quick agreement, was, far more than the personalities of the negotiators or the immediate tactical calculations of the parties, the cause of WG2's failure. It has been suggested that mediation could have brought the two major parties to agreement in those last days; Eglin had, in that final week, tried to engineer a compromise between the ANC and government/IFP positions. However, it was said that he had 'burnt his boats' with the NP by leaning towards the unitary rather than the federal camp in WG2. But it is unlikely that even skilful mediation could have bridged, in a few days, a gap which months had failed to mend.

Nevertheless, in a way not yet suggested by accounts of the Codesa breakdown, the intervention of one key individual on each side in those last days may have given a clue to the cause of the deadlock, and the likely road ahead.

POSTSCRIPT: HORSES FOR COURSES?

On 19 May, Valli Moosa and ANC spokesmen met a few journalists at the ANC's head office in Shell House for a briefing on Codesa 2. The WG2 deadlock had ensured a plenary in which the convention, now clearly polarised into two camps – with the DP in the middle – had dissolved into a rhetorical contest as the two sides found ever more eloquent terms in which to blame the other for the deadlock. The press briefing confirmed what the 13 May statement had promised: the ANC alliance would turn to 'mass action' to break the stalemate.

While a desultory attempt was made to retain Codesa, for much of the rest of the year the negotiating process would remain in apparent limbo as the two chief parties at WG2, joined now by an ever more assertive IFP, jockeyed for power on the streets and in angry statements rather than in the cloistered atmosphere of the World Trade Centre. By November the ANC and NP were talking again – but this time to each other only (and, in separate meetings, to the IFP). The illusion, maintained at Codesa, that the new constitution would emerge out of the earnest and (almost) public deliberations of a wide range of parties was dead forever.

But the groundwork for the November talks had been laid well before then – indeed, the process had started almost as soon as Codesa 2 ended. The vehicle was continuing contact, even in periods when NP/ANC relations seemed most venomous, between Ramaphosa and Meyer.

It is worth recalling, then, the role which the two played in the dying days of WG2. Ramaphosa was the skilled union negotiator whose experience had taught him that agreements struck in hard bargaining and worded carefully were far more durable than those which were vague but reached in a miasma of goodwill. One mine employer claims Ramaphosa never broke an agreement with him;[33] those who know they must stick to agreements tend to take their wording very seriously. But when the toughest of the ANC negotiators entered the WG2 fray, he did so, in effect, to put an end to it.

Meyer, on the other hand, was the rising star of the government negotiating team whose close links with the senior ranks of the National Intelligence Service, two of whose top men were to serve under him when he took over Viljoen's old department,[34] offered him access to strategic information and analysis which Delport may have been denied. The 'heavyweight' on the NP side did not kill WG2 – but he was content to issue an uncompromising statement at a crucial moment and then to watch it die, sitting through its death throes without a murmur.

A theory suggests itself, unsubstantiated by hard evidence but perhaps the only one that fits the known facts of the breakdown. It suggests that Ramaphosa and Meyer, independently perhaps, the one basing his assessment on strategic insights gathered in labour bargaining, the other on the advice of NIS, concluded that no amount of last-minute manoeuvring could produce an agreement at Codesa 2 which had any realistic hope of surviving. As their colleagues battled to reach an agreement which they had decided could not endure, they – independently or in concert – determined that Codesa should die, to be replaced by the hard bargaining which might bridge the divide.

Fanciful? Perhaps. But a vignette from the bruising Codesa 2 plenary may offer a clue. As the emotion-charged delegates vented their frustration at the lost agreement they had believed to be so near, an observer noticed, at the far end of the hall, Meyer and Ramaphosa locked in earnest and businesslike conversation. They did not seem like negotiators whose hopes had just been shattered, but like men in the midst of a task undisturbed – even, perhaps, strengthened – by the events of the day. For them the convention was over; the bargaining had begun.

Phoney peace in a phoney war

As Working Group 2 descended into the maelstrom, Working Group 3 sailed fairly smoothly and calmly to an agreement. Participants agree that there was a greater 'meeting of minds' in WG3 than in other groups; this they explain partly by insisting that the negotiation process was better managed here. But the contrast with other groups may have had far more to with the parties' belief that much less was at stake.

WG3's brief was to suggest the transitional arrangements, interim government or transitional authority which should manage the country before the drafting of a new constitution. As events in WG2 had shown, these were not merely technical questions: at issue was how much power the existing state would enjoy during the transition. This, as WG2's work briefly showed, was a key issue between the parties – it would decide the extent to which, and the speed at which, the old would give way to the new. But the stakes were lowered because WG3 agreements depended on consensus in other working groups – they would be implemented once constitutional principles were decided in WG2, and the future of the TBVC 'states' in WG4. Its task seemed more clear-cut and technical, less a matter of political life or death.

And yet, WG3 produced an 'agreement' which failed to bridge an important divide between the parties. Nine months later the issue on which it had 'agreed' was still unresolved.

Gliding through: a brief chronology

The 'major' parties may have sent their most senior delegates to WG2, but WG3 also included some key political figures. Delegates included Dawie de Villiers and Roelf Meyer for the NP, Barend du Plessis and Johan Scheepers for the SAG, Thabo Mbeki and Joe Nhlanhla for the ANC, Ken Andrew and Robin Carlisle for the DP, Musa Myeni and Alistair Macaulay for the IFP, and Jeremy Cronin and Nozizwe Madlala for the SACP. The chair was divided between Pravin Gordhan of NIC/TIC, Andrew, Luwellyn Landers of the Labour Party and Patrick Maduna of Inyandza, each of whom chaired one or more meeting.

WG3 first met on 20 January; initial discussions were largely procedural. By its fourth meeting, rapporteurs had drawn up a list of items which had emerged from the parties' submissions; by its sixth meeting on 2 and 3 March, an agenda had been drafted. It included: the method of implementing interim arrangements; their purposes, goals and time frames; the structure and functions of an interim executive and legislature; and the position and role of the existing constitution, the TBVC 'states' and self-governing territories, and the world community in the period leading up to an election.

During the next month the issues raised in the submissions were discussed. There was an exploratory meeting with the steering committee of WG4 on 24 March to discover whether it had reached agreements which would allow the TBVC 'states' to be incorporated into transitional arrangements; it had not, and this issue was not discussed in detail by WG3. There was a similar meeting with the steering committee of WG2 in April, where it was agreed that the chairs of the two steering committees would 'consult on a regular basis'.[1]

During the first week of April, discussions began moving towards the relationship between present and interim government structures. Mindful that Codesa 2 was set to meet on 15 and 16 May, at which time WG3 would have to submit its recommendations, Andrew, seconded by Cronin, proposed that a technical committee be established to concentrate on framing details of this report. The committee met for the first time on 10 April, after which there was a dramatic increase in the rate and depth of work: three reports were tabled in this committee, and by 11 May the final report was complete. This brisk progress was of course a novelty at Codesa.

A matter of technique?

According to some participants the use of a technical committee helped WG3 along significantly. As in WG1 they argue that the group was too large for effective negotiation. 'There were too many parties and representatives,' says Ken Andrew, 'and the formal meeting procedure made it difficult to negotiate any issue.'[2] The TC, appointed by the WG3 steering committee, was leaner and more efficient: it comprised key WG3 figures but also co-opted experts who were not members of the group. Walter Felgate of the IFP, Mac Maharaj of the ANC, De Villiers and Scheepers, although not members of the committee, attended some of its meetings.[3] Maduna chaired it and a drafting subcommittee consisting of Fanie van der Merwe, Arthur Chaskalson and Dawid van Wyk was also appointed.[4] Most participants agree that the TC achieved its purpose and that it was here that the issues were 'really hammered out'. But this method had its price: the list of those chosen to serve on the committee caused great acrimony. This highlighted one of the key themes of WG3 – 'progress' was achieved primarily by excluding some parties from an effective role.

As in the working group itself, discussion in the TC tended to start with statements of the party positions on an issue. But it would soon develop into an examination of technicalities and practicalities, and it was at this level that common ground was sought. Once it was found it would be taken back to the parties for ratification. Confidentiality was also easier to maintain in a smaller committee, and this too made for speedier progress. A further help was the experience within the drafting subcommittee: Van der Merwe was a pivotal government negotiator, Chaskalson had been deeply involved in drafting the Namibian constitution, and Van Wyk had been an advisor to the KwaZulu/Natal Indaba.

But WG3 was not without problems. Perhaps most importantly, principals were often not present when decisions were needed; because participants were not senior enough to take decisions, there were many delays for consultation. Many delegates also had other duties between meetings, and this was often disruptive. Weak chairing also hampered progress: participants were reluctant to accept a strong chair for fear

that it would allow an incumbent to direct proceedings in the interests of a particular party. Although WG3 seem satisfied with the role played by its chairmen, this made meeting procedure even more cumbersome and the role of the chair more difficult.

A more avoidable problem was the absence of secret ballots to nominate and select committee members. Besides placing a damper on discussion this made personal resentments almost inevitable; these would needlessly affect the negotiations. Nevertheless, participants recall that they developed a chemistry and camaraderie during the long hours they spent together which promoted co-operation and a desire to achieve results.

But camaraderie between negotiators does not always filter down to their constituencies; warmth between negotiators could produce agreements unpalatable to their supporters, alienating the negotiations from those who are expected to abide by their outcome. Since the constituencies of key Codesa parties were not convinced of the need for compromise, this was an ever-present threat. It also shows the danger of too great a reliance on technique: efficient management of negotiations can produce speedy agreements, but there is no guarantee that they will narrow the real differences between the parties. In some ways this was as much a factor here as in WG1.

INSIDE WORKING GROUP 3
Tackling the transition

In a published interview,[5] Colin Eglin describes the main difference between the government and ANC views of the transition: 'The government envisaged a transitional power-sharing government of extended, undefined duration. The prime task of the interim government would be to govern a society undergoing a lengthy transition, not the speedy formulation of a new constitution. The ANC saw things exactly the other way round. It envisaged a short transitional power-sharing period during which the interim government's major task would be to draw up a new

WG3 in session ... sailed smoothly and calmly to agreement.

constitution for the transfer of power.' Put in another way, the government's goal was to retain as much power for as long as possible, and the ANC's to wrest as much power from it as soon as possible. In WG2 this was one of several issues: in WG3 it was the central theme.

The chief debates centred around three questions: the form of the interim structures; the relationship between them and the existing state; and their relationship to a constitution-making body.

Debate began as in WG1 with presentations by the parties. But for some time there were two notable omissions: neither the government nor the ANC tabled formal proposals until late March, restricting themselves to verbal presentations during the early meetings. Several participants suggest that both were 'playing a waiting game' – watching each others' responses to proposals tabled by other parties in an attempt to sense the room for flexibility – before committing themselves. This may have put the formal presentations to better use than in other working groups.

But it also implied that WG3 was another forum for bargaining between the two 'major' parties: other presentations were not treated on their merits, merely as a means for the NP and ANC to size each other up. For the IFP, which had put more effort into WG3 than it seemed to have devoted to other working groups, this was frustrating. It had tabled a detailed proposal early in February, but did not feel that it was taken very seriously. One participant confirms this: 'People took note of the IFP proposals but then wanted to get on with "the real negotiations" – the positions of the government and the ANC.'[6] This increased the IFP's sense that Codesa was a thinly disguised two-sided table – which was to have important consequences after the collapse of Codesa 2.

But that lay in the future. During WG3's life it was the NP and ANC which set the tone for the discussion and final agreement.

Reigning in the interregnum: the form of interim structures

The two 'major' parties staked out opening positions in early verbal presentations. De Klerk's acceptance of the principle of an elected transitional government was, as we have noted, seen as a basis for compromise; it laid the foundation for discussion in WG3. But the government's first proposals revealed that this was not quite the concession to the ANC which it seemed at first to be. As our discussion of WG2 implied, the government's insistence on an *elected* interim government meant that it would not agree to transfer powers granted by the existing constitution ahead of elections. And that meant that all-party transitional structures established before a ballot would not take over powers from the tricameral parliament, but would be largely advisory.

The government rejected not only the details of the ANC's position but also the assumptions and language which lay behind it. For the ANC, the existing regime, based as it was on the exclusion of the majority, had the same task as those of Zimbabwe and Namibia – to make way as soon as possible for a new order. Even before an election, it should cede power to an 'interim' regime composed of all parties. The government insisted that it was sovereign – it was not a defeated 'regime' negotiating its departure – and legitimate, since it was elected (albeit by a minority) and subject to a constitution; it could be replaced only by a government which met the same criteria.

If this divide seems clear now it did not appear so then. There was so much confusion around this issue in WG3 that, at a TC meeting, Meyer chose to use a flip chart to explain how the government viewed the transition: there would be advisory bodies only before elections; only after a poll held under an interim constitution would a power-sharing government rule.[7] And the existing constitution could not be changed until the government held a referendum to consult its electorate. 'Colonial' regimes might have to disappear hurriedly; as a sovereign government, this one was not going anywhere until it knew by what it was to be replaced – and had supervised the transition from the old to the new.

Consistent with this vision the government first proposed an 'extended cabinet' which would include members of other parties in the relatively brief period before an interim government was elected. This arrangement would require only minor changes, since the enlarged cabinet would still be formally responsible to parliament. The government might thus largely retain power during the lead-up to elections, negotiate a favourable transitional constitution relatively quickly at Codesa, and then move into a prolonged period of power-sharing transitional government while the final constitution was being negotiated.

The ANC inevitably rejected this. It did not see the government as sovereign, merely as another party among many. A key purpose of the period leading to elections was to deprive it of the advantage it held over the others – control of the state, which allowed it to act as 'player and referee'. The 'extended cabinet' would simply co-opt members of other parties into the existing government, leaving its and the NP's hands firmly on the rudder, ensuring an unfair contest. The ANC therefore proposed more radical changes to allow for multi-party control before an election. It wanted a more powerful interim government, serving only for a limited period and clearly focused on preparations for elections. It would have final authority over those aspects of government where joint control was needed to 'level the political playing fields' – the state media, security forces, budget, and election preparations.

By the time the government submitted its formal proposals, less than a week after the 17 March referendum, it had modified details of its approach; the changes seemed partly prompted by events in WG2, but the fact that it retained the essentials in the face of ANC opposition suggests that it was also emboldened by the strength of the mandate it received from white voters. In addition to a transitional constitution before an election it proposed a first phase in which 'transitional councils',[8] called 'preparatory councils' in its later submission – their members chosen by Codesa's management committee and appointed by the state president – would be established to deal with elections; local and regional government; government finances; and housing and urbanisation. It left open the possibility of establishing other councils. The councils would 'pass resolutions' by consensus and would sit together as the joint preparatory council, also limited to taking resolutions – not decisions: the final authority would remain the president and the parliament to which he was responsible.

The ANC saw this as an important concession, arguing that it acknowledged the need for other parties to play a more significant role in government before elections; presumably because they would no longer be absorbed into the cabinet, and would be represented in separate structures. But it still fell far short of its demands, since the president and cabinet retained the power to ignore the councils' resolutions. The proposal was rejected because, an SACP participant[9] says, 'it did not give the ANC enough real power in the period of electoral preparations'. Debate therefore shifted to the powers which 'preparatory structures' should enjoy over the existing state.

In its formal submission the ANC proposed the appointment by Codesa of an 'interim government council' which would oversee cabinet committees composed of several parties; co-ordinate and supervise existing administrations; and carry out executive and legislative functions determined by Codesa.[10] The tricameral parliament would be phased out and the TBVC 'states' reincorporated into South Africa. All draft laws would need approval by the IGC, and in matters related to 'creating the conditions for free and fair elections', it would have the power to make laws by proclamation. While multi-party cabinet committees would be responsible for security, the budget, local government and foreign relations, the IGC would have the power to 'reverse or amend' any decision taken by a committee. This interim government would have a fairly short life and would concentrate on preparing for elections to a constituent assembly, which would agree a constitution and make laws. It also proposed an electoral commission and a media commission, independent of both the IGC and parliament, with clear powers and functions. This, of course, reflected the ANC's very different vision of the transition.[11] The tricameral parliament, a symbol of apartheid, would be replaced by an all-party council, so beginning the post-apartheid order.

The government later accepted the need for an overarching transitional executive council with subcouncils, but major differences on the powers, functions and composition of the TEC remained.[12] This, according to one WG3 participant, was the chief source of controversy between the parties – this was no surprise, since it raised some of the divisions on which WG2's discussions were to deadlock. But in WG3 agreement was reached – of a sort.

Symbols and substance: the powers of interim structures

WG3 was able to find consensus for two reasons. Firstly, all its agreements deal only with the first, 'preparatory', stage of the transition. The key issues of an interim constitution and constitutional principles were left to WG2 – and WG3's agreement would be implemented only if WG2 reached agreement on them (which of course it did not). And, on the issue which they did address the parties did appear to find the 'first prize' for any negotiation process, a formula which allowed both to claim 'victory'.

In its report which was to have been submitted to Codesa 2, WG3 agreed that during the first stage there would be a 'need for a multi-party transitional executive structure to function in conjunction with existing legislative and executive structures, subject to the possible consolidation of the tricameral parliament and the general/own affairs departments'.[13] This would comprise:

- A *transitional executive council,* appointed by the president on Codesa's recommendation. It would consist of at least one full-time member from each Codesa party but could be enlarged to include parties not at Codesa. Its functions would be to 'level the political playing field' and to create and maintain 'a climate of free political participation'.

TEC subcouncils with specific responsibilities in particular areas (see below) would be appointed, and it could delegate powers to them. But the TEC could negotiate issues for which subcouncils were not responsible.

The TEC would have access to all information relevant to its functions, including records of all participating organisations, proposed legislation, executive actions and proposed actions. It could 'require that any participating body not proceed with a proposed bill or action should it consider that such a step would adversely affect a free and equal political climate'.

- Disputes within the TEC would be referred to an *independent election commission* which would consist of 'respected and suitably qualified persons drawn from a broad cross-section of the population', appointed by the president on Codesa's recommendations.

- *Subcouncils* would be multi-party bodies, comprising up to six full-time members appointed by the president on the recommendation of the TEC. They would deal with regional and local government (including provincial administrations, 'self-governing states' and TBVC administrations which chose to participate in the TEC); finance, law and order, stability and security; defence; foreign affairs (if further discussion found this to be necessary); and elections (to provide information and services to the IEC).

Subcouncils would report to the TEC, which could overrule or change their decisions. Cabinet ministers would act in consultation with the TEC or relevant subcouncil where their powers related to levelling the playing fields and free political participation. In cases of disagreement, disputes could be referred to the IEC by any participant in the TEC or subcouncils. Ministers of a participating government or administration whose departments would be affected by the functions of the TEC could attend, on invitation, meetings of subcouncils or the TEC.

TEC and subcouncil decisions would be made where possible by consensus; if it could not be reached, by an 80 per cent majority. Any dissatisfied participant could however refer any disputed matter to the IEC for adjudication.

- An *independent media commission* would be established on the basis on WG1's recommendations.

While this seemed to be a more comprehensive and detailed agreement than those reached in other working groups, important details remained to be agreed. WG3 noted that the composition of the TEC and subcouncils, the composition, powers and functions of the IEC, and the suggested subcouncil for foreign affairs remained to be settled. The position of the TBVC 'states' and their relationship to the first-stage structures were also unresolved, since this was the province of WG4. By the beginning of 1993 they remained unresolved.

WG3 also acknowledged that this agreement, providing as it did for shared decisions between parties who were still fierce rivals at best, enemies at worst, would not on its own ensure a smooth transition. It noted that '… the lack of trust between parties will have to be resolved, so that it does not become an obstacle in the functioning of the above bodies'.[14]

What did this agreement mean, and how had the parties arrived at it? The ANC clearly saw it as a victory. An ANC WG3 participant[15] argues that 'the NP had to make concessions all along the way because they were not able to sustain their arguments – in public, in a multi-party context, and in the eyes of the international community'.

The DP's Ken Andrew … proposed a technical committee, which increased the rate and depth of work.

Certainly, the final agreement does seem to show that the government had moved significantly from its opening position. Two points stand out. The first is the TEC's power to 'require' the government not to proceed with any planned law 'or action' which related to free political participation and 'levelling the playing field'. This gave it a veto over government action in these areas, far more than the advisory role the government first offered. The second is the IEC – proposed by the ANC – which was given substantial powers to intervene in disputes between TEC subcouncils and cabinet ministers. This body would play a pivotal role in the transition period. And, since the IEC would be made up of independent 'respected and suitably qualified persons' recommended by Codesa, final decisions on issues involving political disputes would be taken by a non-political, independent body rather than the existing authority. So the government did significantly soften its position that the constitutional structures over which it presided should be the final authority.

Nevertheless, a government participant insists that it did not concede its insistence that the first phase structures should operate within the existing constitution. A look at the agreement supports this. Existing structures would not be phased out, and they would continue to govern. Their powers were limited only where it could be shown – to the election commission – that a decision or action related to 'levelling the playing field' or free political activity. And the 80 per cent majority (a compromise proposal by the IFP's Felgate, accepted by both the government and the ANC), he adds, would allow the state to function during the transition. While the ANC had insisted only that the TEC be able to prevent the passage of laws which might give the government and its allies an unfair advantage in elections, the government feared that any purely administrative decision could be interpreted as 'unfair'; the TEC would be able to block *any* decision, causing continual delays in routine administration. The 80 per cent stipulation ensured that the TEC could intervene only if the government and its allies agreed.

More generally, the agreement seemed to compromise between the ANC and government positions by stipulating that the TEC and existing structures exist side by side, rather than that one should have authority over the other. This followed a debate which centred on whether the interim structures would have power over existing ones, or whether the two would share power. This was in itself a government shift: it was no longer insisting that the existing structures be the *sole* formal power. The agreement, with its formulation that the TEC would function '*in conjunction with* existing legislative and executive structures', indicates that the ANC compromised by accepting joint power. Similarly, the agreement's reference to 'the *possible* consolidation of the tricameral parliament and the general/own affairs departments'[16] suggests that the government sought a compromise by suggesting that the three racial chambers in parliament could be collapsed into a single white, 'coloured' and Asian legislature and that racial 'own affairs' departments would be scrapped, thus abandoning the internal racial features of the system (the 'external' one, of course, is the exclusion of Africans). But it was not bound to do this; by early 1993 it had implemented the latter but not the former.

Nevertheless, the agreement does not seem to settle the balance of power between existing and interim structures. 'In conjunction with' is a very vague term. And the government's belief that it had avoided the possibility that just about anything could be labelled a ploy to prevent a level playing field seems overly optimistic, despite the 80 per cent rule, because any issue could be referred to the elections commission.

By giving this commission the central role, both sides had agreed to allow it to become the real source of power in the first phase – even though it was to be composed not of party representatives but independent people, whom they would presumably not control. And, having signed over to this body the power to settle all their differences, the parties did not decide its composition, powers and functions in detail. It was not entirely clear even who would decide on its members: was the president forced to act on Codesa's instructions, or merely to listen to it and then take his own decision? At the very least, the agreement opened the way for disputes if he decided to ignore the convention. In sum, the vagueness of key clauses suggests that the key issue which separated the parties – who was to have the final say during the first phase – was avoided.

The multi-party nature of the TEC and its subgroups, together with the 80 per cent requirement, reflects a key dilemma of the pre-election period. Since no non-racial test of representativeness would have been held, there are no 'objective' grounds for excluding any party or for stipulating that decisions be taken by a simple majority; 10 parties whose combined support may later prove minimal could impose decisions on two or three that represent the vast majority of voters. But allowing virtually all parties an equal say makes decision-making very cumbersome: not only could a collection of very small parties (if opinion polls are taken as a guide) block agreement, but a single one could appeal to the IEC, making it the final judge.

This is no legalistic quibble. While the key WG3 agreement clearly took the parties further by cementing significant compromises, it resolved very little. In early 1993, while the parties had made substantial progress on other issues, the one on which WG3 had agreed was ironically a key point of dispute between the ANC and NP. At issue was precisely the divide which WG3 was meant to bridge: the relative powers of the TEC and existing structures. Even Codesa's most detailed agreement proved to be less of a breakthrough than it seemed.

THE TWO-SIDED TABLE?
Blocs and alliances in WG3

The ANC and NP were not, as we have noted, the only parties to present proposals to WG3; indeed, they waited until most other parties had done so. While the NP and ANC views were decisive, other positions should be noted not only to offer a full record of WG3 but to reflect on one of Codesa's key issues – the extent to which it was an all-party forum or a disguised NP/ANC bargaining session, with the other parties falling neatly into the two camps.

The submissions of most other parties did tend to fall broadly into either the government or ANC camp, despite the fact that specifics varied quite widely. Proposals for the transitional presidency included the retention of the current president, the election of an acting president, and a rotating presidency.

Those for the transitional executive included a multi-party council of leaders, co-opting more ministers into the present cabinet, the appointment of an executive council by Codesa, the election of an all-party cabinet by a multi-party national assembly, and a cabinet with half its members appointed by a constituent assembly and half by the parties in parliament. Proposals for the transitional legislature included retaining the existing parliament, either with its racial divisions or sitting as one body with both the divisions between the three racial houses and the distinction between own and general affairs abolished; a multi-party national assembly constituted by all signatories to Codesa's declaration of intent; and that Codesa become that authority.[17] But, within this welter of detail, parties more closely aligned to the government tended to emphasise the retention of existing structures, while those closer to the ANC argued for the dilution of the power of the government and the system it ruled.

On the ANC side, the SACP argued that the election for a constituent assembly could not be supervised by the government but that transitional structures with control over broadcasting, violence, the conduct of the election and the role of the international community were needed. It made no specific proposals on interim structures. The NIC and TIC proposed the appointment of a sovereign interim government by Codesa; it would prepare for elections, and exercise control over particular areas of government. They also argued for the dissolution of the tricameral and 'homeland' parliaments.

The Transkei administration proposed the establishment of an interim government which would rule by decree and enjoy full government authority, including control over the security forces and the administration of the TBVC 'states'; Codesa would appoint an administrator and an executive council made up of one person from all delegations which would head the various departments of the interim government. This was perhaps the most radical proposal from the ANC camp. Venda's proposals were strikingly similar – an interim administrator and council of interim administrators would rule by decree, but only in certain areas, and the international community would play a role in both peace-keeping and the electoral process.

Intando Yesizwe of KwaNdebele proposed that parliament legislate Codesa into an interim government to control law and order, security, the budget, foreign affairs and the media and to take over TBVC administrations. In similar vein, the United Peoples' Front of Lebowa proposed that Codesa appoint multi-party cabinet committees to govern the country, including 'independent' and 'self-governing' homelands. The Inyandza National Movement of KaNgwane proposed that an interim constitution, involving multi-party structures at all levels of government, be negotiated by Codesa and passed by the tricameral parliament. The structures would be responsible for governing the country, passing laws, and preparing the way for constituent assembly elections; it also proposed an electoral and public service commission.

The LP's proposals also fitted quite neatly into the ANC-allied position. It proposed a transitional executive set up by Codesa and responsible for the security forces, the election process, the state-controlled media, budget, regional and local government, and foreign affairs. Parliament would merge into one house whose only purpose would be to legalise decisions made by the transitional executive. All other administrations and the cabinet would fall under the control of this executive.

Of the parties presumed to be closer to the government, Solidarity proposed an interim government made up of nominated party representatives and headed by the president. Multi-party cabinet committees and three independent commissions – an electoral, civil service and media commission – would also be established. The tricameral parliament would become a unicameral legislature, and a bill of rights would be enacted. The NPP proposed a short-term interim government which would obviate 'the drastic changes at all levels which will take a considerable time to implement'.[18] The NPP suggested converting Codesa into a constituent assembly to avoid 'problematic and time-consuming' elections; the TBVC and 'self-governing states' would remain unchanged until the future of regional structures was finalised by the assembly. Dikwankwetla of QwaQwa similarly proposed that Codesa form the nucleus of a constituent assembly. The executive of the interim government would be an enlarged cabinet elected by Codesa and serving as a supervisory body. It would be up to each TBVC 'state' to decide whether to participate. Parliament would enact any transition measures decided by Codesa. The Ximoko Progressive Party of Gazankulu distinguished between two transitional phases. In the first, Codesa would become a statutory body and would negotiate the principles and composition of a multi-party transitional legislature and cabinet (the second phase).

Ciskei's submission favoured a federal form of government and noted its opposition to interim elections or the reincorporation of TBVC 'states' before a new constitution was in place – both issues which were the province of other working groups. On the issues before WG3, it proposed that Codesa draft a new constitution and that a transitional government made up of all Codesa participants govern during the transition. Ciskei saw constitution-making and governing as separate, and argued that they should not be controlled by the same body.

To be sure, most of these proposals envisaged a primary role for existing government structures. But, in contrast with the ANC camp, there was a surprising exception: Ciskei's transitional government proposal did seem to suggest the replacement of existing structures – bringing it ironically closer to the ANC than the government. And several of the parties in this camp seem to have had different concerns to the government; they were for example eager to avoid an elected constitution-making assembly. This stemmed almost certainly from an expectation that they would receive very little electoral support and that their only hope of influencing the constitution was to retain Codesa, where they enjoyed, at least formally, equal status. The NP, confident of emerging as one of the 'big three' parties, was content to limit majority decision-making in the assembly in other ways.

The IFP's proposal struck similar themes, although, in keeping with its concern to project itself as a major party, its submission was far more detailed. More importantly, it departed enough from those of the two major camps to be seen as a distinct position. It proposed a 'transitional government of reconciliation' which would be more broadly based than Codesa and would be 'constituted under the state president and responsible to parliament under the existing constitution, amended as to certain unentrenched clauses to make this legally possible'.[19] This TGOR would be essentially a multi-party cabinet. The IFP, as we saw in WG2, was strongly opposed to the idea that a new constitution should be written by an elected assembly. Some of its reasons were mentioned then. But it also argued that the constitution determining the electoral process should be negotiated *before* an election could be held; only once a permanent constitution was agreed would it be appropriate to elect a new government. In a harbinger of later disputes, the IFP was also adamant that the future of regions needed to be resolved before any constitutional changes could be made.

Although the IFP did partly endorse the NP position by suggesting that its TGOR act as a cabinet, responsible to the tricameral parliament, it did want to subject it to controls imposed from outside the existing constitutional system. Thus it would have to govern the country in terms of agreements reached at Codesa on regional devolution of powers and a socio-economic charter; this would give Codesa some power over it. The TGOR would be served by advisory boards responsible for police, the SADF, the media, and privatisation.

A constitution-making body would also be appointed, which would be bound by principles agreed by Codesa. The constitution which it drafted would need approval from a national referendum before the first elections could be held. Before then, 'own affairs' departments would be abolished and the three houses of parliament would sit and vote together on all legislation, including passing the new constitution into law. (An electoral board would be established by the TGOR to prepare for the referendum.)

But the starkest divide between the IFP and most other Codesa parties was not its specific WG3 proposals – it was rather its insistence that its participation in a transitional government could not be taken for granted. Its conditions for joining included: agreement on seating the Zulu king and his delegation at Codesa; amendments to Codesa's Declaration of Intent, which, the IFP continued to insist, committed Codesa to a unitary state; proper consideration by Codesa of 'claims to the right to self-determination'; agreement that no 'self-governing' territory could be deprived of its status without its consent; agreement on the composition of the TGOR; the disbanding and outlawing of all private and liberation armies; and agreement on the principles and framework of the new constitution.

It should have been clear from this list that the IFP did not consider itself a junior member of the government camp. Indeed, apart from a common concern to prevent the ANC alliance 'monopolising' power through 'simple majoritarianism', it is doubtful whether the conditions placed the IFP in the NP camp at all. It was demanding a veto over the process – and some of its conditions might conflict with NP aims. Its insistence that the king be seated, which attracted most attention, was by no means the most important. As later events were to show, and our discussion of WG1 suggested, the demand for the end of 'liberation armies' – primarily MK – challenged bilateral agreements which the NP had made with the ANC. The IFP insistence that 'self-governing home-lands' enjoy a veto could create problems for the NP as well as the ANC – if one of these territories delayed a settlement by digging in its heels. And its rejection of an elected assembly undercut the fragile NP/ANC consensus on this issue. Its conditions were also likely to be so unpalat-able to the ANC that they raised the spectre of a deadlock which would be far harder to resolve than any caused by the divide between the ANC and NP. We might therefore have expected WG3 to take the submission very seriously. It did not.

Finally, the DP maintained its position between the major blocs – and its attempt to mediate between them – by offering a submission seem-ingly designed as a compromise between conflicting positions. It pro-posed that Codesa negotiate an interim bill of rights and establish a tran-sitional government of national reconciliation, which would appoint a 'council of leaders' composed of all main political groupings and the state president. Its functions would be to implement decisions made by Codesa and to resolve deadlocks referred to it by multi-party cabinet committees. The council of leaders would also be empowered to make changes to the cabinet, create interim provincial and local governments, and broaden the representativeness of the judiciary, public service and armed forces. The DP also proposed that the 'own' and 'general' affairs distinctions in the constitution be abolished and that single departments be established under a unicameral legislature. This 'package' left the existing constitutional system intact (with some internal changes), but transferred important powers to Codesa and the multi-party council which it would appoint.

Like the IFP proposals the DP's were largely ignored, reinforcing the impression that Codesa was not an all-party convention but an attempt to strike a deal between NP- and ANC-led camps.

How many blocs?

The IFP in particular believed that the government and ANC were cau-cusing behind the scenes at Codesa and that 'processes were rigged by this – finally leading to the breakdown of Codesa'. It felt it was being 'steamrollered'. Says the IFP's Felgate: 'Already in 1991 the IFP indicated that it would object to the constituent assembly becoming an interim government. Gerrit Viljoen assured the IFP this would not happen. Now the government is agreeing to exactly that. Important principles are being compromised. The government is weakening against the threat of mass action. F W could have agreed to a multi-party conference with or without the ANC. Negotiations are necessarily a three-way process and should continue until resolution is reached.'[20]

Although the IFP felt brushed aside at Codesa it did not, as in the oth-er working groups, choose to contest this vigorously in WG3. Felgate was a far more assertive figure in WG3 (despite the fact that he was not formally a member of the group) than its representatives in the other groups. But one WG3 participant insists that, in both WG3 and TC discussions, the IFP was 'rational' and 'non-problematical' – in other words that it not only accepted but contributed to the agreements reached. 'The IFP's bark was worse than its bite. It could appear intransigent, aggressive, belligerent, but at the level of specifics it was easier to reach agreement than one might have expected'.[21] We have already speculated (see WG2) on why this may have been so. WG3's failure to confront the IFP conditions which were later to pose a severe threat to negotiations may therefore have been at least partly of Inkatha's making.

The ANC's Thabo Mbeki ... among key political figures delegated to WG3.

Another reason for the IFP's amenability may have been that the 'specifics' at Codesa were not very specific. If the NP and ANC could accept agreements which did not bind them to much, so could the IFP. In WG3 it could accept the final report because implementation depended on agreement in WG2, where talks were running into major problems. Thus, while it accepted the WG3 agreement, it stressed that this should be 'dependent upon agreement being reached by Codesa in respect of the second stage of transition, including an interim constitution, and general constitutional principles'.[22] The IFP's easy manner in WG3 may have been a result of the group's ability to avoid issues. Certainly the IFP does not believe that WG3 committed it to taking part in the structures which were agreed.

But both the ANC and NP did largely behave as if Codesa was a 'two-sided table'. An ANC source insists that the NP and the ANC are indeed the two major forces in negotiation, if only because no agreement is possible if they deadlock. The ANC therefore believes that prior agreement between it and the NP on as many issues as possible is necessary before multilateral negotiations.[23]

And this is precisely how the NP and ANC approached negotiation after post-Codesa 2 talks were resumed in late 1992. It begs the key question of whether a final settlement is possible without at least the IFP's consent, an issue we will examine later.

The NP's position is more complicated. At first it insisted on a multi-party forum; when Codesa was launched, some analysts suggested that it hoped to strengthen its position by 'packing' the forum with homeland and tricameral parties which had a vested interest in siding with it. It was presumably in the NP's interests to stress the independence of these parties, since it could then insist that some compromises were not its alone to make. But by intent or accident dynamics at Codesa proved to be very different. There were greater, albeit at times subtle, differences within the presumed NP camp than within the ANC alliance. And the NP concentrated on striking a deal with the alliance; it made no concerted effort to force the concerns of its 'allies' onto the agenda, and often joined the ANC in ignoring them.

The ironic result, say some participants, is that the ANC put the multi-party format to better use than the NP. Its alliance (with the SACP, NIC/TIC, Lebowa, KwaNdebele, Venda, Transkei, Inyandza, and, increasingly, the Labour Party) was relatively solid, so much so that the allies formed a 'Patriotic Front caucus' which met regularly during Codesa. In the caucus they could agree that one party would introduce a point to gauge the government's response without the ANC having to openly commit itself. As one participant put it, 'the ANC especially used surrogates to run a position, and then came in as the conciliator'.[24]

The presumed alliance around the government position (the NP, NPP, Solidarity, IFP, Ciskei and QwaQwa) was far looser – as we have seen, one 'ally', the IFP, may have been no such thing. It was also more delicate and less reliable, as the parties had a long history not only of co-operation but also of conflict with the government. They were, in a sense, vassal parties to the NP. Labour could conceivably have been an NP ally, but was ambivalent since it had experienced what it saw as a history of NP 'manipulation' in the tricameral parliament; the parties had clashed over the Group Areas Act, to name but one example, and the NP later sought to gain control of the House of Representatives by recruiting Labour MPs[25] – a tactic prompted by the LP's occasional unwillingness to pass NP-initiated laws. One LP interviewee remarked: 'While the NP were having talks at Tuynhuys [the president's residence] with the LP, they were at the same time conniving to take over the House. They are ruthless in their quest for the maintenance of power.'[26] Whatever the merits of this assessment, NP critics insist that its ' history of political domination', its unwillingness to share decisions with its partners in constitutional structures, prevented it from building alliances with them. It was seen by some to 'use' them when convenient, discard them when it was not.

Similarly, some participants see the NP's indifference to its allies not as an attempt to placate the ANC at any price, but as a sign of an inability to adapt to a situation in which it could no longer impose its will. An SACP WG3 participant insists that the NP was ill at ease in Codesa: 'The government was used to a rubber-stamp, tight-caucus, style of operating, whereas Codesa leaked like a sieve. They were not used to operating in a multi-party environment while the ANC was, having always been an umbrella body to several organisations. Although the government pushed for the multi-party format of Codesa, they were much happier in bilateral situations.'[27] While the ANC was clearly the dominant party in its alliance – it is hard to see parties such as the SACP, TIC and NIC as 'independent' since their members and delegates are invariably ANC members as well – it certainly is far more used to operating in a 'front' or alliance of organisations.

The uneasy mix between a 'two-sided table' and a multi-party format did seem to hamper Codesa. Besides negotiating with each other the 'big' parties were also trying to build electoral alliances and were thus reluctant to alienate potential allies;[28] an LP interviewee believes that 'negotiations drove the two blocks even further apart'.

In many cases the 'two-sided' approach did seem to reflect reality, both in Codesa and the country. While there are no 'objective' tests of party support, opinion polls, party membership figures and influence can be measured; it is generally accepted that opposition parties in the House of Delegates are far less crucial to a settlement than the NP, ANC or IFP. Parties whose claim to influence rested largely on their participation in structures which Codesa was assembling to abolish and which were largely seeking to defend vested interests which rested on very tenuous claims to support, may not have enjoyed much influence, but they played an important part in delaying proceedings.[29] And, unlike the IFP, they did not appear to represent independent interests which needed to be accommodated; unlike the DP, they did not present independent perspectives which needed to be heard. They were content to attach themselves to major parties, and their presence served more to make Codesa cumbersome than to add to the settlement process.

But the cost was not only to ignore parties whose claims to independence were implausible; it was also to ignore some whose claims were real. If the multi-party format was meant to bind all parties to Codesa agreements, the fact that a two-party approach was used at an all-party forum ensured that it failed. Add to this the fact that some other parties such as the CP and PAC were not represented because they chose not to be, and the agreement reached at WG3, perhaps Codesa's most substantial, effectively bound only the NP and ANC – and then to an 'agreement' inconclusive enough to ensure that they were still divided on the issues months later.

Ruling the present, writing the future

If one effect of this approach was to ignore an interest which had the power to destabilise the process, another was to ignore one which might conceivably have made a contribution.

Thus, while the 'two-party' trend was the norm in WG3, on one issue a smaller party did launch a vigorous, albeit losing, attempt to influence the debate. This was the DP, which had far more influence over the process in WG3 than its outcome. (Andrew, through the introduction of the TC, ensured a brisker, more business-like approach which may have ensured that even a vague agreement was reached. But its proposals made little impact on WG3's final agreement.)

The issue on which the DP fought its battle was its rejection of the NP-ANC agreement that a single body act as both interim government and constitution-maker. The ANC was initially open on this issue. In its submission of 30 March it proposed two possibilities: the interim government council, appointed by Codesa, could continue to function until an elected assembly had drawn up a new constitution; or the assembly could function both as a constitution-making body and legislature until the new constitution had been adopted.

But after accepting the idea of an elected constitution-making body the government persuaded the ANC to agree that it should also make laws, despite the fact that, as we have seen (WG2), the ANC feared that the government's aim was to draw out the finalising of a new constitution – since constitution-making might have to be crammed into the regular law-making schedule – and so prolong the 'interim' power-sharing period. But the fusion of the two functions in an elected body had clear attractions for the ANC, which believed that it would emerge from an election as the strongest party and would be powerfully placed to control the passage of legislation. Both parties approached the issue as a strategic one – a way of outmanoeuvring the other; the workability of the arrangement was secondary.

The DP, which had no great strategic stake in the outcome, insisted that two very different functions were being fused and that both would suffer. The constitution-making process in particular would be a victim, it believed; not only would it enjoy less priority, since the drafters would have other preoccupations, but it might also be far more a product of day-to-day 'horse trading' than of a debate on the country's longer-term needs. It preferred interim government to be a mainly ad hoc adjustment which would take into account the results of an election for a constituent assembly: the government would not itself be elected, but its composition would change to reflect the balance of party support. It accepted that, once an election had been held, no one would want to see the old government structures still in place – if the NP had lost the election but F W de Klerk remained president he would not enjoy much credibility. A solution was needed which addressed this problem while not fusing the two functions.

The DP knew however that since the government and the ANC were agreed on this point, there was little other parties could do to dissuade them. So it introduced a new issue: '[It] then insisted that if there was going to be a newly elected interim government with full legislative, executive and constitution-making powers, this could not happen in a constitutional vacuum.'[30]

Its concerns echoed the NP's, but stemmed from a very different motive – it was concerned not only to limit the ANC but the NP too: an interim constitution drawn up by Codesa would be necessary, it argued, to prevent an elected interim government from governing indefinitely. As Eglin later argued: 'Although the major parties might believe it is merely an interim arrangement, they might also find it convenient to continue governing indefinitely, untrammelled by constitutional checks. All parties accepted this, which meant there would have to be an interim constitution.' The DP wanted at least these checks and balances: a comprehensive bill of rights; the separation of powers; an independent judiciary; and the devolution of financial powers to at least seven regions.[31]

The DP's view was largely ignored, although it did win minor victories where its position was relatively close to that of the 'big' parties. And, while ignoring the IFP could have damaging consequences, the DP did not wield the muscle to disrupt the process. But its concern that the deals reached by the powerful could be won at the expense of the (relatively) powerless was shared by many outside the World Trade Centre, including some who had little in common with the DP. Since Codesa was about power rather than debate, the DP made little impact. But its intervention did serve as a reminder that, while a settlement between the powerful may be the only route away from our past, it could be won at the expense of the rights and liberties of those excluded from the pact.

THE MAGIC OF THE SMOKE-FILLED ROOM

Behind the seeming simplicity of WG3's task lay important conflicts which it did not fully resolve. Perhaps because it focused so precisely on the issue of state power, it was here that the bilateral nature of the negotiations was perhaps most clearly revealed. No party other than the NP and the ANC had any real aspirations to win an election and to rule. Other parties may have had little option but to ally themselves with the NP or ANC – or be ignored. But in one case (that of the IFP) WG3's failure to address a third party's demands was to have serious consequences.

Equally importantly, WG3 deferred almost as much as it decided – by delegating to an independent commission, the IEC, issues which the parties could not resolve themselves. It is hardly guaranteed that a group of 'eminent persons', no matter how respected, will resolve differences which the parties themselves were unable to confront.

WG3 was by all accounts not only an island of relative tranquillity at Codesa, but also in a society which was then divided and beset by conflicts – its citizens united, perhaps, only by a growing scepticism on both sides of the divide of the negotiation process itself. The calm was partly induced by effective techniques and perceptions that the real battle was being fought elsewhere. But it owed something to the inevitable tendency of negotiators, removed for a time from their constituencies, to bridge their differences more easily than their warring supporters. The key question is whether agreement can be maintained once they leave the room and return to the society outside. In this case, for many bitter months at least, it could not.

Rescrambling the egg

On the face of it, the task addressed by Working Group 4 seemed the simplest. Its agenda seemed to raise none of the key issues which divided the major parties; it was discussing a measure on which the NP, ANC and IFP might be expected to agree with no risk to their strategies or principles.

But, like most other issues discussed at Codesa, divisions on this question proved to be more intractable – and agreement far more elusive – than they had seemed when the convention began. Reincorporation directly affected the most vital interests of some of the smaller parties which had played a minor role in other working groups, and so they played a more independent role here than elsewhere; parties which were willing simply to align themselves with the 'big two' in other debates were not necessarily prepared to do so here. WG4 had therefore to reconcile the interests of not just two parties or positions. And, as debate unfolded, it became clear that the issue did affect some of the 'major' parties' key strategic interests. Behind the bargaining on 'technicalities' lay some of the divisions which had proved so difficult to heal in other working groups. And this ensured that WG4 too failed to settle divisions which could obstruct progress later.

At issue was the future of four 'independent states' – Transkei, Bophuthatswana, Ciskei and Venda. They had acquired that status through the logic of grand apartheid which saw Africans not as citizens of a common South Africa, but as a collection of separate nations which were to be led to full statehood. The motive for this was not altruism: as a senior cabinet minister confirmed in the 1970s, the goal was to force all Africans to exchange their South African citizenship for that of an 'independent state', ensuring that 'there would be no black South Africans'.

The mere existence of these 'states' was seen by the ANC and many others as the most visible expression of the apartheid order. Their abolition and reincorporation into a 'united South Africa' was seen to be an obvious consequence of the end of apartheid; as long as they existed, so would apartheid.

Nor was there much reason, before WG4 began its work, to assume that the NP would oppose reincorporation. Since it accepted in the mid-1980s that there would always be a great many black South Africans, 'homeland independence' had lost its rationale: once P W Botha, in 1985, committed the NP to a single South Africa with a common citizenship,[1] its strategy was no longer apparently threatened by the reintegration of TBVC territories and the restoration of their subjects' South African citizenship. The IFP (then Inkatha) had justified its participation in the KwaZulu administration partly on the grounds that this prevented the territory being wrenched from a common South Africa. It had resolutely opposed 'independence' despite alleged government blandishments and threats; there seemed no reason to assume that it would oppose the end of an arrangement it had always rejected. Codesa's Declaration of Intent, with its commitment to an 'undivided' South Africa, seemed, despite the initial refusal of KwaZulu and Ciskei and the continued refusal of Bophuthatswana to sign it, to reinforce the view that reincorporation was a *fait accompli*. WG4's brief was also limited: it could not discuss the future of the non-independent 'homelands'. The wider debate about the constitutional relationship between central government and regions in a new order was outside it scope: this was, as we have seen, discussed by WG2. This too seemed to make agreement easier.

But the issues to be dealt with here proved to be far more complicated than they initially seemed. Despite the modesty of its goals, sharp differences within WG4 ensured that its final report stepped cautiously through the bland phrases of tenuous consensus. Even then, Bophuthatswana declared itself not bound by the agreement.

Within apartheid's logic

It soon became clear within WG4 that reincorporation was far from decided. Because Bophuthatswana had refused to sign the Declaration of Intent, insisting that it would not unconditionally consent to reincorporation, WG4's terms of reference were carefully worded to avoid prejudging whether reincorporation would be agreed at all. The SAG's first submission then made it clear that not only was it in no hurry to end TBVC 'independence', but that it was not necessarily inevitable that it would end at all. It claimed the decision was not its to make: it would support whatever each 'independent' territory decided. This 'neutral' stance effectively bolstered Bophuthatswana's position, prompted considerable tension within WG4 over the meaning of the declaration, and ensured that there would be no easy road to agreement.

Equally importantly, this submission set the tone for debates in which it was repeatedly assumed that the products of apartheid whose demise WG4 had purportedly gathered to discuss were legitimate and sovereign. Nor was it only the government 'camp' which used apartheid-derived logic; so did parties who were determined to see the end of TBVC 'independence'.

Bophuthatswana repeatedly stressed its desire to preserve its apartheid-derived status. The SAG, NP and even the DP, by arguing that each administration had a 'right to choose', assumed that they were both sovereign and representative of their 'citizens'. On the other side, Transkei, despite being the first TBVC territory to advocate reincorporation, insisted on its right to retain its status as long as the NP ruled alone. And the ANC came to support Transkei's desire to retain temporary 'independence'.

INSIDE WORKING GROUP 4
Strategies and symbols

WG4 addressed three main questions:
- Should the territories be reincorporated? How should this be decided, and who should decide? If they had not been reincorporated when transitional structures were launched, what would be done to enable their 'citizens' to participate in the transition?
- When should they be reincorporated? And
- What kind of South Africa would they 'rejoin' – one with strong regional powers, or with a powerful central government?

These questions raised vital strategic issues for the 'major' parties. Perhaps the most important was the effect of the timing of reincorporation on the first inclusive elections.

While the NP/SAG were not opposed in principle to reincorporation, an election in which millions of TBVC 'citizens' or residents[2] were not permitted to vote would sharply reduce the African electorate and dramatically improve NP prospects. This would be so even if only people resident in the territories were excluded – if all their 'citizens' were, no Xhosa-speaking people would be able to vote. The ANC, mindful that millions of voters in its heartland, the eastern Cape, were TBVC 'citizens', needed reincorporation before an election.

Bophuthatswana's Lucas Mangope ... declined to be bound by the final agreement.

Secondly, the NP and a number of 'homelands' wanted to ensure that the 'homelands' governments were replaced by powerful regional governments: one way of achieving this was to insist on it as a concession in exchange for reincorporation.

Not all these questions could be answered solely within WG4; they partly depended on progress in other groups, particularly WG2 and WG3. But this did not prevent complicated strategic battles in WG4.

Early sparring: WG4's structure

Like other working groups, WG4 elected a steering committee which oversaw protocol and, where necessary, referred issues of procedure to Codesa's daily management committee. It comprised the NP/SAG, ANC, IFP and TBVC representatives. In addition, four subcommittees were established to deal with testing the will of TBVC 'citizens' on reincorporation;

citizenship; the administrative, financial and practical implications of reincorporation; and the political, legal and constitutional implications. Each delegation was represented in each subcommittee, and representatives of 'smaller' parties were chosen to chair them. DP delegates chaired two – Errol Moorcroft chaired SC1, and Charles Simkins co-chaired SC3 with James Mahlangu of Intando YeSizwe. C D Marivate of Ximoko Progressive Party chaired SC2, and Devagie Govender of the National People's Party, SC4. The subgroups generally met every Monday – the day before WG4 plenary meetings.

Codesa protocol called for a rotating chair for plenary sessions. Stella Sigcau, prime minister of Transkei until she was deposed by Bantu Holomisa, and a Contralesa[3] office bearer since then, chaired an early meeting. Not all parties were impressed with her performance and there was some surprise when Pik Botha, leader of the SAG delegation, proposed that she retain the chair until Codesa 2. This was agreed.

More contentious was the question of rapporteurs, whose task was to extract common thinking from the debate and to try to construct a consensus. The NP/SAG proposed that Secosaf[4] officials be appointed;[5] the ANC camp replied that Secosaf was part of the machinery of the apartheid system. Transkei leader Bantu Holomisa effectively vetoed the proposal, pointing out that Secosaf could not intervene without the approval of all its members, including his administration. Much to the surprise of the ANC, the SAG then did not propose fresh nominees, and all ANC candidates were accepted: Geoff Budlender for SC2, Bulani Ngcuka for SC3, and G M Memela for SC4. (Moorcroft served as rapporteur and chair of SC1).

The ANC was delighted with this coup, while other delegations seemed reconciled to it – until the rapporteurs, called on much later to propose a way out of a threatened deadlock, presented a proposal clearly more acceptable to the ANC than its opponents. By then, the atmosphere of easy compromise which marked the opening sessions had evaporated.

Reincorporation into what? Regional government

For some parties, the question of whether reincorporation was desirable begged another: what were they to be reintegrated into? The key issue here was regional government. If the purpose of WG4 was to gain the TBVC territories' consent to abandon the current regional dispensation, they presumably needed to know what the new one was to be; many participants tried to draw just such a link.

WG4's terms of reference provided for this: it was to examine 'the relationships between South Africa, the TBVC states and the people of those states under a new constitution'. But since regionalism was the province of WG2 this was presumably seen as a logistical question, not a discussion of a core constitutional issue. WG4's agreements therefore had little to say on regional government. But the debate showed that this, not logistics, was the key issue; it was a vital undercurrent within WG4.

Early submissions to SC3 all reflected attitudes to regional policy. But this was not always explicit – some expressed their position by insisting that WG4 had to be guided by agreements in other working groups.

The NP/SAG, Bophuthatswana and Ciskei all suggested that WG4's work depended on agreements in WG2 and WG3. Important details of a new system of regional government – powers, functions and boundaries – would, they said, have to be agreed in advance of a transitional government or constitution. For them, reincorporation depended on whether strong regional government was agreed. The DP, from a slightly different perspective, suggested that, since reincorporation implied a new regional system which would affect the 'self-governing' territories (SGTs), their future too would have to be discussed. Again, this implied that the regional question needed to be settled before WG4 could move forward.

For the ANC alliance, reincorporation had first to achieve a reunited South Africa; a new regional system was secondary. It insisted too that an elected constituent assembly, not Codesa, should decide on regional powers and functions.

The issue was raised almost as soon as WG4 began its work. At the first meeting of SC3, on 17 February, the ANC and DP tabled submissions suggesting how the group should proceed; a week later the NP submitted its view. Although the three documents were short, dealing mainly with information needed for SC3's work, they gave an early indication of the differing approaches to the way the regional question would impinge on WG4 discussions.

The NP's first submission opened with a bland statement reiterating support for the controversial clause in the declaration of intent committing the parties to an undivided South Africa.[6] But it went on to argue that two factors made discussing the logistics of reincorporation more difficult: the need to first consult TBVC voters, and the relationship between WG4 and other working groups.

'Firstly and obviously, any ... recommendations which SC3 may come to can only be implemented once the people of each independent TBVC state have democratically decided in favour of reincorporation,' it said. 'Secondly, the results of negotiation in WG2 and WG3 will have a profound effect on [WG4's] final recommendations ...' This second point appeared to support the Bophuthatswana position: that reincorporation would depend on whether TBVC territories were satisfied with constitutional agreements, particularly on regionalism, reached at Codesa. To discuss detail was, therefore, premature.

Its second submission, a month later, did deal with the more technical details of reincorporation[7] – but in a way which stressed the regional issue. It noted that that the principle of strong regional government 'apparently' enjoyed general acceptance at Codesa. The most important of its recommendations on the effects of reincorporation into an 'undivided but regionalised new South Africa' were that new regional boundaries would have to be drawn to 'accommodate' the reincorporated 'states'; available infrastructure in TBVC capitals would be a vital factor in determining the capital of the new regions. Second-ly, TBVC government structures would have to be dismantled and assimilated into new regional government structures, or phased out. But TBVC police and defence forces would 'of necessity' have to be assimilated into the SAP and SADF; clearly the NP had no intention of seeing the dissolution of the latter agencies.

The ANC's first document, submitted on 18 February, drew no clear connection between reincorporation and the need for a new regional system.[8] It argued that the goal was the 'elimination of ... duplicate administrations, departments and services and the incorporation, so far as possible, of existing structures and personnel, into united South African ones'. The emphasis was clearly on a unitary state.

This document was given greater detail by a later SACP submission.[9] 'Since our party favours reincorporation of all TBVC states into a single, united, democratic South Africa,' it said, 'we would see the need for the TBVC states to eventually dissolve, for their administrations to be rein-corporated into and form part of a central administration, and for their armed forces to be integrated into a united ... force, falling under the central government. This would apply equally to the self-governing terri-tories. In terms of administration, we would end up with single depart-ments of health, education, etc at a national level.'

But, on the same day that this document was submitted, the ANC pre-sented a second submission effectively accepting the link between rein-corporation and a new regional system.[10] By then it had published its first regional policy discussion document, which suggested that South Africa be divided into 10 regions and which also seemed to hold out the prospect of entrenched regional powers. Its submission thus argued: 'When examining the ... effects of reincorporation, the context within which [it] will take place must be borne in mind. The restructuring of South African society will require the development of non-racial democ-ratic ... government at national, regional and local level. Of particular importance in relation to the reincorporation of the TBVC territories is the regional dimension.'

It also suggested a role for an interim government in establishing a new regional order. '... The establishment of an interim government in the near future should see the [TBVC] administrations brought under the ambit of this structure. This would be a transitional phase. Once elections have taken place for a constituent assembly, the task of final-ising issues such as the demarcation and powers of a new framework of regional government can be completed.' The suggestion that the assembly would 'complete' rather than begin the task suggested that key principles on the future of regional government would be dis-cussed before it met. This, together with the discussion document, suggested a shift in the ANC's position: its submission and the SACP's may not have contradicted each other, but there was a clear difference in tenor and emphasis.

The DP's position contained elements of those of both the 'major' par-ties. Its first submission, while at first glance dealing largely with logistics, linked reincorporation to the need for a new regional system into which the TBVC 'states' (and by implication the self-governing territories) would largely be collapsed.[11] It suggested that the easiest way of reincorporating the TBVC 'states' was to 'have them revert to the status of self-governing territories in the short run. In the longer term, all homelands and provinces would be reorganised into regions.' It suggested that TBVC 'states' under military rule could be placed under the control of an administrator, since there 'would seem to be little point in returning to representative government until the boundaries of new regions are worked out'. A moratorium should be imposed on land transfers between South Africa and TBVC territories 'until the regional question is sorted out'. SC3 would also 'need to decide how far to go in setting the framework for the development of new regional government at the financial and administrative levels', and how much attention to give to the form of interim government 'within which details of regional government will have to be worked out'. The theme is clear. For the DP, the mechanics of reincorporation could not be separated from the framing of a new regional government system; this is not surprising, given the DP's – and its predecessors' – long-standing commitment to federalism.

But a second DP document, submitted a month later, on 23 March, partly supported the ANC's revised position.[12] By this time WG2 had appeared to agree that the powers of regions be entrenched in the constitution and the DP presumably felt that, since regionalism was agreed in principle, it could move on to details. It argued that administration and finance in the TBVC 'states' should 'go through two stages of transformation'. The first would involve reincorporation as 'distinct entities'. (In a possible bow to TBVC sensitivities, it no longer insisted that they would become 'self-governing' territories, but suggested merely that SC3 examine this). More importantly, its proposals for the second phase suggested that aspects of reincorporation would have to be decided by an interim government rather than Codesa. It noted that: 'The progress which WG4 can make on it depends on decisions in WG2. There is little detail at this stage to work with. How far WG2 will go at the level of detail is itself uncertain.' It added that 'the working out of the second stage will take considerable time, certainly stretching beyond Codesa itself'.

So the change in status of TBVC territories from 'independent' to something else could be achieved immediately as long as they remained 'distinct entities'. To absorb them into new ones would take longer and would be the task of an interim government. WG4 should, therefore, discuss an 'accountable mechanism' to be set up by that government to deal with the legal, administrative and financial implications of 'the reorganisation of government functions'. This body would also deal with issues which WG4 had been unable to resolve; the DP expected these to be the civil service, the rationalisation of parastatals, the use of existing infrastructure, and a review of development priorities.

By the time these parties had revised their position, the TBVC 'states' had placed their own on the table. Bophuthatswana was most insistent on knowing what it would be expected to 'rejoin'. It consistently argued that reincorporation was just one of several options (including retaining 'independence'): 'every option which promises a better future, or [one] at least as good as the present situation, will be regarded as a feasible and realistic option for consideration,' it stated.[13] It argued that the 'average resident' in the territory enjoyed a quality of life and access to services which 'compared favourably' with any-thing in South Africa: 'there is appar-ently very little to gain administrative-ly and financially from reincorpora-tion'. Yet it did hold out the prospect of accepting reincorporation if Codesa agreed to its 'best case scenario' of regional government with maximum devolution of autonomy and powers. Its draft document would be refined once it had more details of a new con-stitution and its regional structures. Throughout Codesa, Bophuthatswana insisted that its reincorporation could not be assumed. But it also continual-ly held out the prospect of reintegra-tion if its terms were met in a new constitution. It was, in effect, testing the terms it might be offered for rein-corporation.[14]

Ciskei, too, attempted to argue that reincorporation was not a given, even though it did not (since it could not) advance arguments based on self-suffi-ciency. Instead it issued a declamato-ry call for federalism: 'The incorpora-tion of Ciskei is subject to the fact that the importance of a participatory model of democracy is not just that it gives us an alternative way of understanding democratic life, but also that it provides us with a ... model of nation-building under conditions of multi-ethnic and religious diversity ... Ciskei has opted for a federal constitutional model.'[15]

Transkei's Bantu Holomisa ... the territory insisted it would rejoin South Africa only after white rule had ended.

For Transkei and Venda, reincorporation did not seem to involve any weighing of economic and political consequences. The most important aspect seems to have been the political commitment to overturning their apartheid-derived status and rejoining a united South Africa. Although both submitted extensive documents on the more technical issues, nei-ther attempted to set conditions – with one exception: both indicated that they expected reincorporation to bring more state aid for develop-ment to overcome apartheid legacies in their territories. Venda said this was a major factor in its support for reincorporation.[16] Transkei, after arguing that the TBVC territories survived solely on budgetary transfers from Pretoria, added: 'It is therefore crucial that the TBVC states be reintegrated within an economic framework whose objective it is to stimulate balanced growth by [an] injection of capital into such backwaters ... which will have been absorbed into larger non-racial provinces.'[17]

But Transkei's position was curious in an important way. While seemingly concerned only with swift reincorporation, it had earlier also raised territorial claims: these advocated a 'greater Transkei' which would absorb Ciskei and other adjacent land.[18] Its claims sounded suspiciously like those of the Matanzima brothers, who had ruled the territory when it first accepted 'independence' and who did not expect ever to rejoin a united South Africa.[19] Why was it claiming land for a territory which, its own position assumed, would soon no longer exist? And why did the ANC – whose discussion document suggested a new region which seemed designed to meet Transkei's claims – feel a need to accommodate it? These questions did not affect WG4 debates, since the regional question was not seriously pursued. But it did raise issues to which we will return.

Ultimately all this came to nought: debate on this issue was joined in WG2, and there only inconclusively. But the positions staked out in WG4 were ironically more substantial than those in WG2: it was here that issues which were to threaten negotiations after Codesa 2 first emerged. WG4 was the only working group in which the strategic concerns of parties such as Bophuthatswana, Ciskei and the IFP (although it again played a muted role here) were the central issue. But even here the strategies of the 'big two' dominated.

By mid-April, a dispute which had been building in other WG4 subcommittees spilled over into SC3. In two submissions, on 21 and 28 April, the SAG insisted that the mechanics of reincorporation were a bilateral matter between it and the TBVC territories; its submission of 21 April argued that bilateral negotiations would be needed to end the 'sovereignty' of each 'state' and to arrange the transfer of its functions to 'constitutional structures compatible with the present or transitional or final new constitution, whichever may [then] be in force'. This would reduce Codesa's role in working out the details of reincorporation – and give the SAG a superior status to other Codesa parties.

This demand, which had already surfaced elsewhere in WG4, had little to do with the regional question. It stemmed from a deadlock in other subcommittees over the timing of reincorporation, a key strategic issue for the 'big two' which, rather than the concerns of TBVC administrations, had come to dominate WG4. And it was affected primarily by two issues: 'testing the will', and citizenship.

A one-sided table? The principle of reincorporation

The first signs of these conflicts emerged when the parties began discussing the principle of reincorporation. Formal statements at the second WG4 plenary on 6 February revealed multiple divisions within the group. One was between Bophuthatswana and those who took the desirability of reincorporation for granted; another was between those who insisted that reincorporation be decided by a popular vote, and those who replied that it was the right of each administration to decide. Among those who urged a vote, some insisted that all South Africans should decide, others that TBVC 'people' alone should do so. Moreover, the SAG and NP insisted that South African citizenship would be restored to TBVC 'citizens' only after reincorporation, while the ANC, SACP and DP rejected this link.

Three submissions are particularly vital: those of the two 'main' parties, the ANC and SAG, and that of Bophuthatswana.

In the ANC's view, the signatories to the declaration of intent had made their intentions clear; reincorporation was agreed, and WG4 should confirm this. 'Let us take that ... decision first before we do anything else,' it declared, and continued: 'All the signatories to the Declaration have committed themselves to ... a democratic and united South Africa. The vision of Codesa is to undo the divisions caused by the apartheid system. Part of the division ... is precisely the breaking up of South Africa at least constitutionally and legally into [separate] states ... Our view ... is that our country must be reunited. This implies the reincorporation of the TBVC states into South Africa, where they rightfully belong.'[20]

The SAG replied by declaring itself above the debate. It would accept reincorporation if, after a 'democratic test of the will' among their 'citizens', the territories wanted it. But if they wanted to reject it without testing that will, the SAG would accept this too.[21] So a test was needed to accept reincorporation, not to reject it. This, of course, gave TBVC administrations a veto. Bophuthatswana seemed eager to exercise one. Its submission claimed the territory was not a creation of apartheid, but had long predated it. It therefore repeated that it would surrender 'independence' only if offered something as good or better.[22] Its 'first prize' was internationally recognised 'independence' with enlarged boundaries and strengthened confederal ties with its 'neighbours' – failing that, the status quo. Next best was federalism; regional governments would have to enjoy more than powers delegated by the centre.[23]

Despite this attempt to project Bophuthatswana as a key party with a veto over change, the real importance of its submission lay in the conflict it sparked off between the 'major' parties. This was prompted by minutes which themselves suggested that the territory had no veto. Bophuthatswana was the only party at the 10 February plenary to reject the principle of incorporation. In accordance with procedural rules agreed by the DMC, the minutes recorded that 'sufficient consensus' had been reached on this principle, and simply noted Bophuthatswana's dissent.

At the next meeting, the SAG vehemently rejected this use of 'sufficient consensus' in WG4. This working group, it insisted, was 'unique': unless the SAG and TBVC administrations agreed on an issue, 'sufficient consensus' could not exist. The TBVC territories were independent and could not be forced by Codesa to change their status. Bophuthatswana, of course, endorsed this view,[24] which denied Codesa's right to decide on reincorporation at all.

Inevitably, the ANC alliance reacted angrily. The SACP replied: 'It is unfortunate that [this] ... creates the impression that the TBVC parties and the [SAG] are the main protagonists on this issue, and is tantamount to calling on the co-conspirators of the bantustan policy to express themselves while sidelining those parties who have long voiced their opposition to this apartheid policy.'[25] The NIC/TIC delegation added: 'The future of the TBVC states is the concern of all South Africans. [It] ... cannot be relegated [to] discussions ... among the government and TBVC states.'[26]

Nor was the ANC alliance alone on this issue. The DP noted that Codesa was convened to discuss a *South African* constitution: once they were included, the TBVC territories had, by implication, been classed as part of a unified South Africa. The SAG and Bophuthatswana, it implied, were refusing to be bound by one of the key assumptions behind Codesa.

Debate dragged on for weeks, and the issue was eventually referred to the DMC. It rejected the SAG view: no party in any working group had special status, and certainly none had the power to veto agreements; special circumstances would, however, be noted where necessary.[27] The SAG, which was formally committed to the Codesa process, accepted this. Bophuthatswana, which was not, did not: it insisted on a right to special treatment and to be exempt from any agreement it rejected.

Nevertheless, the ruling meant that WG4 could now begin discussing the 'how' rather than the 'whether' of reincorporation. There were three possible routes. The first was unilateral action by the SAG. This was the opening position of the SACP, which argued that the territories were not sovereign; they had merely been given powers by the SAG, which could revoke them. But it was later to change tack, arguing with other PF parties that unilateral action was untenable since it would return the territories to a country still ruled by the NP.

The second possible route was the direct opposite: reincorporation could be initiated by TBVC administrations. But, besides the fact that one was refusing to do this, the other three were administered by unelected governments whose right to act on behalf of TBVC 'citizens' was not established. So the third option, that the 'people' could decide the issue, was readily accepted by WG4.

But this agreement itself raised difficult issues. Which people would decide? All South Africans? Only TBVC 'citizens'? Only those who lived in the territories? And how would opinions be tested – by a referendum, opinion poll or election? This key question was delegated to SC1. And, whoever 'the people' were, what if they had not decided by the time transitional structures were established? Millions of voters would remain 'citizens' of another state and would not legally be entitled to vote. This raised the citizenship issue, which was referred to SC2.

Who are the people? Testing the will

SC1's brief asked it to 'consider testing the will of the people concerned regarding reincorporation or otherwise ... by acceptable democratic means'. It initially made rapid progress: only Ciskei, which felt that a test was superfluous (and of course Bophuthatswana, which still rejected reincorporation in principle) did not agree that 'the people' should decide the issue;[28] there was also broad agreement that a referendum would be the best method. Despite an IFP objection the NP, ANC and other delegates agreed that this poll should be conducted nationally among 'the people concerned' without reference to race or ethnicity.

But this 'agreement' masked crucial differences on who 'the people concerned' were. The SAG insisted that this referred only to TBVC voters, who had a right to decide whether they wished to 'rejoin' South Africa: their votes would be counted separately to determine this. This meant that TBVC voters alone would decide; the only mystery was what purpose would be served by allowing anyone else to vote.

The ANC and its allies again reacted angrily. '... To embark upon ... testing the will of the people in each TBVC state *separately*,' it said, 'is to condone the crime which was committed by apartheid.' It was 'also tantamount to perpetuating racist and ethnic solutions – which is what apartheid is all about. The ANC does not accept such an alternative.'[29]

Having thus boldly flung down the gauntlet, the ANC alliance then almost immediately appeared to accept that which it had vowed to resist. At the SC1 meeting of 9 March, Moorcroft drafted a summary of his understanding of proceedings so far; with one or two reservations, the meeting accepted it. It agreed that, when Codesa reached consensus on the constitutional principles under which the new South Africa would be governed and presented these to the people of South Africa for approval, it would be time to put them to the TBVC 'states'. It would then follow that rejection of the principles by the people of one or more TBVC 'states' would also indicate rejection of reincorporation. And, to identify the will of the TBVC 'states', it would be necessary to count their votes separately.

The ANC, SACP and NIC/TIC put it on record that they would not accept a referendum in which votes were counted separately according to racial or ethnic criteria, but, despite the fact that this completely contradicted the agreement, neither they nor the rest of the group seemed to see this as a rejection of the 'deal'. They had therefore apparently accepted an agreement which allowed separate counting, delayed reincorporation, and gave TBVC voters the veto the alliance had earlier rejected. (Nor does the agreement seem to have decided who TBVC 'people' were – residents or 'citizens'.)

On that note SC1 postponed further meetings until it had met SC2 to discuss progress on citizenship. This, it claimed, was necessary to establish who was eligible to vote in the referendum – a puzzling view, since SC1's agreement implied that all TBVC voters would vote in the referendum; they would presumably be eligible whether or not they were citizens.

In the event, the issue was never addressed. At the joint meeting on 24 March, Moorcroft presented the summary agreed to at SC1's last meeting. At this point the 'agreement' fell apart. The ANC, SACP and NIC/TIC now would not accept the separate counting of votes – the minutes noted that: 'while it is well within their rights to do so, the ANC and SACP have changed their positions entirely on the testing of the will. If there can be no separate counting of votes in the TBVC states, there can be no testing of the will of [their] people. The upshot is that the very terms of reference of SC1 are called into question.'[30]

With that SC1 deadlocked: no further meetings were held. The stalemate seemed to be a monument to Codesa's inability to settle conflicts between its parties. The ANC alliance had declared a position which directly contradicted the SAG view, yet the difference seems to have been neither debated nor negotiated. Instead an instant 'agreement' was reached which obscured rather than settled differences: it collapsed almost immediately. The culprit seemed to be Codesa's imperative to reach 'consensus' even where there was none – only a week before this meeting the DMC, reaffirming the principle of sufficient consensus in all Codesa's deliberations, had noted: 'All participants were encouraged to return to their task with a positive spirit and not to create variations of interpretation that will create, rather than solve, problems. *The point of departure should be to seek ... consensus rather than pointing out the differences*' (our emphasis). But the deadlock was also prompted by ANC negotiating strategy, since its negotiators *did* accept the agreement and then changed their position at the first opportunity. Joanne Yawitch, an ANC member and NIC/TIC representative in SC1, said later that its consent to a national referendum, despite separate TBVC vote counting, was a 'pragmatic' decision: 'Our priority was to ensure ... that all South Africans would participate in a constituent assembly, regardless of whether their governments had decided on reincorporation.'[31]

In other words, reincorporation, and who would decide on it, was secondary to the far more important goal of ensuring that all South Africans – in particular ANC supporters in the TBVC territories – voted in a single referendum. The agreement could in this view also be seen as a symbolic victory over Bophuthatswana, since, if its 'citizens' took part in a *national* poll, its claim to be sovereign was undermined. But why did the ANC alliance then change its stance? Because it feared that Bophuthatswana and Ciskei might use separate counting as a lever for a more decentralised constitution than the ANC wanted?[32] Or because its negotiators realised quickly that they had agreed to something their constituency would never accept? The answer is not clear. What is clear is that the deadlock was followed by a change in Transkei's position which complicated the issue even further.

Transkei, having first accepted the need to test the will of its 'citizens', now rejected this, claiming that it had received a new mandate from its citizenry. It claimed to have been in constant touch with 'the Transkei people' throughout the negotiation process. After De Klerk's celebrated speech of February 1990, it said, it had formed a committee of 159 organisations to canvass opinion on reincorporation; these were overwhelmingly in favour. When Codesa was launched, it claimed, further meetings were convened to give the Transkei delegation a clear mandate. And a meeting of the organisations on 13 April 'overwhelmingly resolved that a referendum was no longer a requirement for Transkei to join the new apartheid-free South Africa'.[33] Transkei therefore demanded immediate restoration of South African citizenship, and announced its intention to participate fully in all transitional arrangements. It was not demanding immediate reincorporation – only immediate citizenship for its 'people', an important difference to which we will return.

Now Ciskei too changed its stance. In an attempt to insure itself against reincorporation on terms that didn't suit it, it argued that a test of the will *was* necessary – but only after a new constitution was agreed: 'Reincorporation of Ciskei ... can only take place when the new South Africa has taken shape and the people of the Ciskei know what they are going to rejoin,' it declared. This decision could be taken only in a 'free and fair election', held when a new constitution was clearly formulated, which should include the boundaries of regions and the 'entrenched rights' of a federal structure. Ciskei voters would therefore be ruled out of elections for the constitution-making body, so strengthening the prospects of the NP. But Ciskei's shift was not an attempt to bolster the NP; it reflected an emerging alliance with Bophuthatswana and the IFP, prompted by fears that the NP was striking a deal with the ANC which would ignore their concerns – particularly by not securing cast-iron guarantees on federalism.[34]

The ANC's Dullah Omar ... framed key clauses of the final report in a deal with Pik Botha.

Opposition to a 'test of will' was now emerging on both sides of the spectrum. For Transkei – and Venda, which now insisted on full rights to participate in shaping South Africa's future – the issue was inclusion in transitional arrangements. Ciskei and Bophuthatswana's position would prevent that, perhaps denying the ANC a substantial voting bloc.[35] This deepened the deadlock over reincorporation. But this, the issue with which WG4 was ostensibly concerned, was secondary now to the size of the voters' roll in the first election. If reincorporation was not agreed, TBVC voters would take part only if their citizenship was restored before it occurred.

Who are the South African people? Citizenship

The opening SAG and ANC positions on this issue seemed to confirm a difference of principle on the nature of the TBVC 'states'. The SAG, which saw them as sovereign entities, insisted that citizenship could only be restored after a decision by each one to reincorporate; the ANC, which saw them as artifical creations of apartheid, argued for immediate restoration. But, since both saw eventual reincorporation as inevitable (see below), the difference was simply over timing.[36]

This was crucial, since it would decide who would participate in constitution-making and transitional arrangements. In a submission dated 9 March the ANC insisted: 'It is necessary for parties in Codesa to state where they stand ... Are you in favour of restoring South African citizenship immediately and thus making it possible for the people of the TBVC states to participate in the process of constitution-making and transitional arrangements? Or are you advocating a process which will ... risk depriving [them] of their right to participate ... That is the central issue ...' For the ANC, all parties were bound to ensure that TBVC 'citizens' did participate: they had agreed to this by accepting WG4's terms of reference, which acknowledged 'the need to provide for the ... democratic participation of all the people in the TBVC states in ... drawing up and adopting a new constitution as well as in all possible transitional arrangements'.

The SAG clearly did not feel bound by this clause. It insisted that only South African citizens could participate in shaping the new South Africa. And, while it had granted dual citizenship to white foreign nationals with residence rights to enable them to take part in the 17 March referendum, it rejected dual citizenship for people born on South African soil but technically citizens of a TBVC 'state'.[37] At the joint meeting of 24 March, it insisted that citizenship would be restored only after the 'test of the will' – and then only 'in due course'. The ANC and SACP claimed this was a change of position,[38] since the SAG was now refusing to accept the agreed purpose of SC2. The SACP added that the term 'restoration' was chosen deliberately, because citizenship had been ilegitimately taken away from people. Therefore, it should immediately be restored.

The SAG position left the ANC alliance with few options. If it wanted all TBVC 'citizens' to vote in the first election, it would have to agree to the separate ballots – or referendum with separate counting – which it had rejected. Nor would its problem be solved if the SAG dropped its insistence on a test and agreed that TBVC territories who wished to could rejoin South Africa immediately: Transkei and Venda insisted that they would rejoin only after white rule ended.

The two administrations had made this clear in SC3's discussions on participation in transitional arrangements. Ciskei and Bophuthatswana rejected this, since it would compromise their 'sovereignty'. The SAG agreed, saying it would not accept participation of another government in an interim government.[39] The other two territories wanted to participate in pre-election arrangements – but rejected reincorporation until there was an elected interim government or constituent assembly.[40]

If this was a stand of principle, it was hard to understand. The PF parties insisted that TBVC 'states' were not sovereign in the first place; why should they place conditions on undoing something which they insisted ought not to have been done? The issue was one of strategy, not principle. Transkeian 'independence' in particular was very useful to the ANC. It still could not be entirely sure that a settlement would be achieved, and until it was, Transkei provided a sympathetic enclave for MK guerrillas who might be needed if negotiations collapsed. Until agreement on the end of white rule was assured, there was no advantage to the ANC in reincorporation of Transkei. The ANC alliance therefore sought to secure South African citizenship for TBVC 'citizens' before reincorporation – the demand raised by Transkei in SC1. And, since the SAG refused to accept this, progress in WG4 was blocked.

Deadlock – and deal

WG4 now called in the rapporteurs to suggest a way forward. It was clear there was an impasse; restating the differences would resolve nothing. Their report began with a concession to the SAG position: they suggested that the decision on reincorporation be left to the government and people of each 'state', and that each make its own arrangements for 'testing the will'. It then rejected the demand for a 'one-sided' table: Codesa should formulate steps to be taken to effect reincorporation, and should supervise any bilateral dealings between TBVC administrations and the SAG. But the crux of the report was its recommendation that South African citizenship should be restored immediately, and that TBVC administrations should participate in transitional structures before an election.[41] Despite the gloss, it boiled down to an unqualified endorsement of the ANC's strategic goals.

Inevitably, the report 'caused a storm'.[42] After the meeting at which it was submitted, Daan Schoeman, a key Bophuthatswana advisor, approached DP advisor Simkins for his view on the report. 'Well, it's clear the rapporteurs are in the ANC's pocket,' said Simkins. Alfred Nzo, nominal head of the ANC delegation, overheard this and immediately demanded a retraction, claiming it impugned the neutrality of the rapporteurs. Simkins shrugged this off, gently rebuking Nzo for listening in on 'gentlemen's conversations'.[43]

According to one rapporteur, they had tried to soften the report since it seemed 'a little bald'. They had therefore padded it with motivating clauses and detailed reasoning before presenting it to WG4.[44] But the tactic backfired: the reasoning behind the report caused as much offence to delegations outside the PF as the more substantive clauses.

In motivating the suggestion that TBVC administrations should themselves decide by what means the wishes of their 'citizens' should be tested, the rapporteurs argued that, 'when independence was granted, the SAG left it to the government of the territory concerned to decide whether its people wanted independence. The same principle should apply here.' It would also be 'constitutionally anomalous' for the SAG to 'decide what the people of the TBVC state really wanted' or to test 'the wishes of the people in an independent state'. Finally, Codesa's structure assumed that TBVC governments spoke on behalf of their people. 'There is no reason to deviate from this premise when one particular aspect –

reincorporation – is being considered.' The rapporteurs were using apartheid's logic to justify a 'solution' which neatly fitted ANC strategy.

The report's critics had a field day with this reasoning. Ximoko led the assault in a closely argued statement drafted jointly by the most overtly anti-ANC delegations – the NP, IFP, Bophuthatswana, Ciskei, Dikwankwetla, Solidarity and the NPP. It was framed at a caucus which delayed a WG4 plenary on 4 May.

The statement urged that the report 'be rejected as unfactual, speculative in part', based in part on unwarranted assumptions.[45] In response to the claim that the TBVC administrations should decide how to test the will of their citizens, it retorted: '... to the extent that the governments of the TBVC states do not have a clear democratic mandate to resolve this issue, they cannot arrogate to themselves the right to speak on behalf of their citizens on the matter of reincorporation'. The need for a democratic test, it said, 'goes far beyond the ambit of the debate on the future of the TBVC states but goes ... to the very heart of that for which Codesa stands. Can Codesa afford to compromise on an issue so fundamental?' This argued in effect that, although TBVC territories were sovereign – and might even, to the NP camp, be representative – they had no clear mandate from their 'citizens' to reincorporate and were therefore bound to seek one (just as, presumably, De Klerk had sought one from white voters to continue negotiations).

It continued: '... The imperfections of the process whereby independence of the TBVC states was originally contrived have been raised by those who would disclaim the legitimacy of these states, yet according to the report this process is now being advanced ... as a valid precedent to determine how Codesa should deal with ... possible reincorporation. There can surely be no more anomalous position than that ... constitutionally *independent* states should participate in the writing of the constition of a neighbouring constitutionally independent state (the RSA) as the TBVC states are in fact doing via Codesa.'

The riposte pointed to the obvious inconsistencies in the report: TBVC territories were held to be 'independent', but their 'citizens' were to participate in (transitional) government in 'another state'. But it also showed its own inconsistencies. The NP, which had earlier suggested that TBVC administrations had a mandate to *reject* reincorporation, now insisted that they did not have one to accept it: only a test of the popular will would do. In WG4 both principle and consistency were at best secondary; strategic position was all.

The Ximoko document then added two riders which seemed to end any chance of agreement. Firstly, it proceeded to interpret the Declaration of Intent in a novel way: it did not, it said, preclude continued TBVC 'independence'. (This may have been literally true: the declaration talked of an 'undivided' country, but did not say where its borders would end. But all Codesa parties clearly believed it was a commitment to reincorporation – hence Bophuthatswana's refusal to sign.) Then it queried SG1's abortive 'agreement'. Linking the 'test of the will' to a vote on constitutional principles ran the risk of pre-empting WG2's discussions, it said (since WG2 might decide against a vote). It insisted on an adequate and separate test.

The wheels very nearly came off completely at this point. Inyandza tabled a document supporting the rapporteurs' report, almost certainly on behalf of the PF.[46] The SAG did not comment on either document; the DP remained strictly non-aligned. But WG4 had polarised sharply into two camps. Recalling this juncture months later, some participants remember wondering whether WG4 could possibly survive this impasse and reach agreement on anything. But at 15h30, after an adjournment which allowed both the ANC and the NP to reconsider, WG4 reconvened. Both parties then presented concise new position papers which were to provide the basis for an imminent agreement.

The ANC proposal declared that restored citizenship was not a pre-condition for participation in interim arrangements: in effect it backed down on its demand for immediate restoration but in a way that gave it what it wanted all along – TBVC people would participate, even though they were not citizens. Secondly, it declared, 'interim … arrangements will impact on the administrations and territories of the TBVC states in the same way as … on the SAG and its territory'. Therefore the SAG and all the TBVC governments would be equally answerable to the interim government, and none would have special rights. For the ANC this was crucial: if the SAG and the TBVC 'states' were equally subject to the interim authority, reincorporation was no longer a bilateral matter and the SAG had no veto over it.[47]

The SAG began by agreeing to the TBVC territories' participation in preparatory councils (see WG3), if these were advisory only. If they were given executive powers, participation would only be feasible if they became 'international councils', exercising the same powers in South Africa and the TBVC 'states' simultaneously; 'the people' of each 'state' would also need the chance to 'express themselves' on reincorporation before an interim constitution was agreed or through their participation in the envisaged election – in which votes would be counted separately to show support or rejection of reincorporation. The SAG said it remained committed to 'testing the will' but would not insist on a referendum: 'Any other reasonable, fair and meaningful process can be considered.' Hence the suggestion that an election would be enough.

This was a major retreat: Bophuthatswana delegates concluded that the SAG had abandoned them for a 'deal' with the ANC.[48] In the guise of a 'condition' for TBVC participation, the SAG had moved towards meeting a key ANC proposal: that the pre-election arrangements apply equally to the SAG and TBVC administrations. It did ask the ANC to compromise by agreeing to a separate counting of votes, but made a large concession in return – the referendum would become an election. TBVC 'citizens' were South Africans again since they would vote in its first non-racial election, even before reincorporation was decided.

After the statements were read to the meeting a task team was appointed, consisting of the SAG, ANC, TBVC 'states' and Ximoko. It met at 17h00 when a tentative agreement was drafted, probably because Pik

Botha was absent. At 10h30 the next day, with Botha now present, it met again and rapidly reached final agreement. Thirty minutes later the plenary reconvened; consensus was declared, and at 13h00 the meeting adjourned for lunch.

The key clauses of the final report, which reflected a deal between Pik Botha and ANC delegates Matthew Phosa and Dullah Omar, declared that:

- All delegations had no objection in principle to reincorporation.
- TBVC 'states' would participate in transitional arrangements as proposed by WG3, on the understanding that these would impact on TBVC governments and territories in the same way as on the SAG and the RSA.
- The people of the TBVC 'states' would take part fully in constitution-making and transitional arrangements, including elections. Participation would be arranged in such a way that their votes in a national election would signify support for or rejection of reincorporation. The result would be 'a sufficient test of the will of the people'.
- After the 'test of the will', South African citizenship would be restored to the citizens of all TBVC 'states' who would have been South African citizens but for 'independence'.

Fancy negotiating footwork did not secure Bophuthatswana's consent: it reserved its position on paragraphs 2, 3 and 4. This exempted it from the agreement but gave it the right to participate in interim arrangements. Not surprisingly this stance prompted great antipathy among some WG4 parties. But its stand seemed quixotic. For, while the first three clauses merely summarised what had been agreed, the fourth destroyed Bophuthatswana's bargaining position. By declaring that citizenship *would* be restored after the test of will, it assumed that the test could have only one result. If Bophuthatswana still insisted that reincorporation was not inevitable, none of its presumed allies still did.

WHEELS WITHIN DEALS: STRATEGIES IN WG4

It should be clear by now that WG4 was anything but predictable. At stake were issues of principle which had great symbolic importance for the parties; at times, however, they took positions which might have been expected from their opponents. The ANC at times used the logic of apartheid; the NP and its allies denied that TBVC 'leaders' were representative. We have suggested the reason; WG4 was about wider strategic goals first, and the principle of reincorporation second.

The ANC wanted what it had to have – the Transkei and Ciskei vote in constituent assembly elections. More generally, since it was likely to win a sizeable chunk of the vote in the other two territories too, it needed to ensure that 'citizens' of all four participated in the transitional phase.[49] It opposed separate tests of the will not because it expected votes against incorporation – which it assumed most 'citizens' of all four wanted – but because this would delay the process. Principle was not irrelevant: a poll in which votes were counted separately would seem to preserve a vestige of apartheid. But even here strategy mattered: a national poll would reduce the impact of regional votes against reincorporation, if there were any.

The NP/SAG was of course likely to benefit if TBVC votes were excluded. But this was clearly not a non-negotiable issue; nor perhaps was it something it really expected to win. It was also eager not to alienate potential 'homeland' allies by ignoring their concerns entirely. This was closely related to a symbolic issue: having insisted for longer than a decade that TBVC territories were independent, the NP may have been reluctant to simply brush this claim aside, if only because this would make it seem an untrustworthy ally. But all this was secondary to the need for a settlement with the ANC – hence the final compromise, which contributed to precisely the outcome the NP wanted to avoid, namely alienating 'homeland' allies.

Its strategy, according to several participants, was to retain its allies while striking deals with the ANC. Bophuthatswana's constant attempt to assert its interests were, from this perspective, inconvenient. Despite apparent SAG support for its position, Pretoria had conceded the principle of reincorporation and clearly expected TBVC territories to do so too: only timing was at issue. At one point an NP submission warned that 'were any TBVC state to decide not to be reincorporated, it would have to seriously consider [the] effects … The RSA would undoubtedly, in the interests of its own citizens, have to re-examine its financial relationships with such state, particularly if [it] claimed to be economically viable.'[50] In other words, the territory which claimed to be viable should remember who provided the financial iron lung which kept it alive. The final agreement confirms that the SAG never saw continued 'independence' as an end in itself, but rather as a bargaining chip.

The ANC's strategy was complicated by the fact that two TBVC territories were its allies, and they, too, were not eager to reincorporate immediately. Transkei had also raised claims which suggested that, despite its stated enthusiasm for a post-apartheid order, it did not expect its elite's vested interests to disappear with a settlement. The ANC could not afford to simply ignore them. Neither administration had been elected, and their support was at best untested. But a blanket TBVC rejection of reincorporation would weaken its position at Codesa. And, as we have suggested, Transkei's administration had offered the ANC strategic advantages it needed – hence perhaps its interest in a separate Kei region in return. Since it could not brush aside its allies the ANC was forced, despite rhetoric to the contrary, to treat them – and so all TBVC territories – as legitimate.

So WG4's 'straightforward' task was affected not only by the strategic goals of the 'major' parties but the interests of TBVC administrations which, on both sides of the divide, conflicted at times with those of their 'major' allies. While the strategic goals of the major parties were dominant in WG1, the ANC's strategies were partly affected by Transkei's interests, since it clearly had something to offer the ANC (free activity in its territory) and may well have expected something in return.

In the end, the divisions were largely suppressed by Codesa's emphasis on consensus. This produced an agreement, but ensured, as in other working groups, that real divisions were at best partly addressed. Rapporteur Geoff Budlender insists that a 'fundamental problem' which 'bedevilled the whole Codesa process' was that 'when disputes arose, there was no structured mechanism for resolving them'. In his view this was compounded by the fact that 'tiny irrelevant groupings' wielded the same formal power as the 'central' ones. 'Then there was this great drive to reach consensus – indeed, there were structural imperatives to do so. So parties were driven to come up with clever formulations, phrasing statements in a way that could accommodate everyone's perspectives. The problem was that different people attached different meanings to the words, which later led to disputes about some parties "reneging" on agreements – when it was just a different understanding of what had been agreed.'[51]

The DP's Errol Moorcroft ... chaired SC1.

That the pressure for consensus obscured important differences is clear; that smaller parties wielded undue influence is less so. While they had distinct interests in WG4, these, with the exception just noted, did not affect the outcome of its discussions.

The 'lesser' parties in WG4 played a fairly minor role – with the surprising exception of Gazankulu-based Ximoko. Fairly early it tabled a strongly worded criticism of Bophuthatswana's insistence on special treatment. Then, at the end of May, it led the critique of the rapporteurs' report, aligning itself with Bophuthatswana and the NP camp. This suggests that it did have independent interests. Gazankulu, situated in the far north-eastern Transvaal, has close ties with Mozambique, and is probably home to more Mozambican refugees than any other part of the country. After Bophuthatswana, it, of all the SGTs and TBVC 'states', most needs to retain porous borders, given the close family ties between Shangaan people on either side of the border. Its interests may lie in maximising its autonomy from a central South African authority – which would explain both an alliance with the 'federalist' group, and a measure of independence from it.

The IFP's role was limited to repeated attempts to steer discussion away from any talk of the future of the SGTs: on several occasions it reminded participants that the terms of reference mandated WG4 to discuss only the future of the TBVC 'states'. That apart, it contributed little and clung close to the SAG position. Since it was already beginning to forge an alliance with Bophuthatswana and Ciskei, this was curious: perhaps Buthelezi's absence again ensured that it preferred to pursue its strategy outside the convention. Bophuthatswana's role has already been discussed. Formally, it retained its independence to the end. But the deal ignored its concerns – and the NP's warning suggested that its continued independence would be bought at an unaffordable price. It almost certainly knew this and was seeking the best possible terms for reincorporation, not to avoid it entirely. If so, its concentration on WG4 weakened its hand, since the strong regionalism it wanted was debated in WG2.

Ciskei came to WG4 unprepared, and presented unsophisticated arguments. Its key advisors were English-speaking conservatives, not well informed on the nuances of the debate. One observer comments that its delegation seemed to be 'making it up as it went along'. And, while Ciskei had common interests with Bophuthatswana, an alliance was not formalised for some time.

The ANC went out of its way to humiliate the Ciskei delegation: when a steering committee was chosen it pointedly did not support any Ciskei nominee, although it later consented magnanimously to a Ciskei presence. Underlying this was its administration's claim to 'represent' part of the ANC heartland – and the fact that its military had once seemed to be an ANC ally, only to 'switch sides'.

WG4 was less of a multi-sided table than it seemed. The 'smaller' parties' influence was not as great as they believed; as in other working groups, the outcome was largely dictated by the strategic concerns of the NP/SAG and ANC.

ASK A SIMPLE QUESTION …

WG4 was, with WG3, the only working group which felt it had completed the task Codesa had assigned it. It did – if its brief was to resolve the differences between the 'major parties' over the timing of reincorporation. This it did by agreeing that all South Africans could vote in the first election. That it should have had to labour so long over so 'simple' an issue may seem bizarre: both the NP and ANC acknowledged that TBVC 'citizens' were South Africans. But Codesa had by now shown that nothing in the South African transition was simple, and WG4 confirmed this.

But if WG4 was meant to find an efficient and conflict-free way of managing reincorporation, it achieved little. It did not prevent the two 'states' which set terms for 'rejoining' the country from later joining an alliance which sought to threaten the entire process. And all logistical questions were referred to two expert commissions – at an unspecified future time.

It is debatable whether WG4 was bound to offer the TBVC leaderships any concessions. Only one was an elected government – and it presided over a territory in which, opinion surveys insist, its support is minimal.[52] The territories are indeed creations of apartheid whose sovereignty is arguably not even assumed by their own elites.[53] Since, as the NP itself implied, their major support base is the South African fiscus, their claims to influence may be less obvious than they seem.

But, as later events have shown, one question raised by some TBVC delegations – that of the powers of regional government – remain important. The IFP has made it so, but ANC allies may also make it so in future – witness Transkei's land claims. WG4 may have been a better forum to resolve this issue than WG2, since it was here that regional interests concentrated their forces. Admittedly, the future of SGTs was not addressed partly because the IFP was determined that they should not be. But the issue was not forced by placing it on WG4's agenda.

Furthermore, WG4's failure to address administrative issues does leave important questions unresolved. TBVC territories do have civil services and security forces; even if they disband, the question of the future of their personnel will have to be addressed. WG4 ducked these issues by proposing that two commissions be appointed to examine questions which differed little from those in its terms of reference. Had it concentrated first on resolving the political issues only it could conceivably have reached agreement earlier, leaving time to tackle these questions more thoroughly. It may therefore have tackled both too little and too much. One problem was its terms of reference, which seem to have been drafted in a fairly arbitrary way: the DP's proposals were accepted virtually without change.[54] And the way in which issues were raised and addressed was, says Simkins, 'like a Nile delta: it was all very swampy, with people getting lost about where they were. The territory was so poorly divided up that it made administration cumbersome and disorganised.'[55]

The talks were also unable to make much progress because, beyond their immediate strategic interests, none of the key players really knew what they wanted. SC1 and SC2 deadlocked because the interests were spelt out clearly; SC3 and SC4 proceeded because they were not. The final report was not a detailed plan for reincorporation; its substance amounted to a single page. To achieve more it would have needed definite guidelines from WG2, in particular. It did not get them. But these points assume that WG4 was an attempt to find solutions to agreed problems. It was not. It was another attempt to resolve the NP–ANC divide on a particular issue. It may have succeeded at the cost of alienating 'smaller' parties who were later to force their way into the debate in other ways.

One key question remains: what is the status of WG4's agreement? Its report was not ratified at Codesa, yet presumably remains binding. But the terrain has shifted so decisively that key sections of the agreement may now be redundant. Despite WG4's labours, the fate of the TBVC territories may have been settled elsewhere.

The missing
53 per cent

If some groups were over-represented at Codesa, one was sorely under-represented; women comprise 53 per cent of the population but made up only a handful of convention delegates. It was veteran politician Helen Suzman who pointed this out publicly amid the many ritual addresses at Codesa 1.

She was, according to participants, not the only person concerned about this absence. They say Codesa's management committee received letters from individuals and groups throughout the country, insisting that a specific women's voice ought to be heard in a national negotiating forum. Other sources suggest that the pressure for womens' interests to move onto the convention's agenda came primarily from the few women delegates at the World Trade Centre.

Whatever the source of the demands, Codesa's mainly male delegates responded to them by providing for a Gender Advisory Committee, constituted as a subcommittee of the management committee, whose brief was to examine Codesa's terms of reference and the minutes and decisions of the MC and working groups to advise the convention on their 'gender implications'.

The NP initially opposed this, arguing that Codesa's terms of reference dealt implicitly with women's interests – on the grounds, presumably, that any agreement reached at the convention would automatically extend rights to women.[1] But its later acceptance of the initiative meant that for the first time the idea that women had specific political interests and concerns had forced its way onto the formal negotiation agenda.

And, while the GAC was smaller than Codesa's working groups – it initially comprised one delegate from each party only, later expanded to include an advisor with speaking rights from each – and did not enjoy the same status, it too was expected to produce a report, reflecting the consensus of all Codesa parties, to be debated at Codesa 2.

The GAC was another test of the various parties' ability to bridge social divides, albeit in a different way. The women delegates were drawn from different parties and were therefore divided by all the issues which separated male participants. But they also, in the view of some analysts, shared something which the men did not – a common experience of being relegated to a secondary role. Did this bond allow the GAC delegates to find a common purpose which escaped the working groups? As with so much else at Codesa, this question remained unanswered.

Limited time, limited task

The GAC may have been a breakthrough for women's interests, but it was a qualified one. Firstly, it was only on 6 April, little more than a month before Codesa 2, that the GAC convened: it met from Monday to Wednesday each week until the plenary. In that time it had to find a procedure and formulate a report. It began life late because it was a sub-committee of a management committee for which it was a low priority. The MC began sitting only in January and was under pressure to address a host of issues left over from Codesa 1: its chief concern was the smooth running of the working groups, not the GAC. So the committee's late start suggests that, while women were now on the agenda, they were not near its top.

Secondly, the GAC set itself a limited task: to find ways of ensuring maximum participation by women in the transition. It did not seek to address ways of combating gender inequality in the new order which the negotiations were meant to produce. Some analysts suggest that this worked to the GAC's advantage. As the NP's response suggests, Codesa was not enthusiastic about giving priority to women's issues, and would have preferred not to address the question if it was able to avoid it.

By focusing on the transition rather than women's rights *per se*, and by stressing the mechanics of ensuring women's inclusion in a process which Codesa had convened to discuss, the GAC, they say, made it harder for the convention to ignore gender. It may also, they suggest, have made it far easier to reach consensus within the group, which might have been impossible if the future of women in the political order was on the agenda.

GAC participants however suggest that to have done more would have been to exceed its mandate; focusing on the transition was in any event all that was manageable in a few weeks. It focused on recommending changes to the working groups' terms of reference which aimed to ensure that nothing was agreed which would entrench inequality or obstruct women's full participation in transitional arrangements. For the rest, it could do no more than highlight issues which 'needed development'. The time constraints ensured that the GAC was forced to resort to formulations which read like asterisks in the margin of a large text – it had to assert principles without examining their content. For example it advised WG2 to draft, as a constitutional principle, a document outlining a set of ideals on gender 'which should be accepted by a constitution-making body as a document to be used by the courts to assist women in claiming and exercising their rights under the constitution and a bill of rights to ensure gender equality'.[2]

Thirdly, only a few delegations seemed familiar with the issues which faced the GAC. Participants say even government representatives conceded that the level of awareness of gender issues within the NP and SAG is very low. They add that some participants made 'no more than token appearances on behalf of their parties', while others, such as the Venda and Bophuthatswana representatives, 'rarely bothered to attend'. Only the ANC, DP and SACP participants seemed familiar with the main themes on the GAC's agenda, a problem compounded by a low level of support by many of the delegates' parties.

It was, they add, the SACP and DP contributions which allowed the GAC to complete its task under severe time pressure. The two parties' delegates, Sandra Botha and Gill Noero (also one of the GAC's chairs) for the DP and Janine Quince, Zo Kota-Mthimunye and Fiona Wallace for the SACP, were decisive. The low level of awareness among many members of the GAC, participants suggest, provides a more accurate index of

The DP's Helen Suzman, with NIC/TIC delegate Cassim Saloojee, right, and other DP delegates ... alerted Codesa to the absence of women.

the national tenor of debate on women's issues than the fact that the GAC was convened at all.

All of this meant that the proceedings of the GAC did not result in a tough bargaining session between contending parties; therefore, it also did not test the question of whether women could find each other across the party divides.

Nevertheless it was not exempt from the adversarial, point-scoring style of the working groups. The SAG and ANC caused a three hour delay with a lengthy argument about the definition of political prisoners; then the SACP dug in on an aspect of the land question that had little bearing on gender. In both instances – and in several others – it was clear that gender sensitivities were not necessarily a priority in daily debate; like all Codesa working groups and committees, the GAC was often reduced to another forum for posturing. This accounts at least in part for an outcome it shared with most working groups – the vagueness of some of its proposals.

Nevertheless, the parties did reach agreement and complete a report whose significance and impact is still a matter for debate.

A crack in the glass ceiling?

The GAC's recommendations are recorded in a slim report prepared for Codesa 2. Working item by item through Codesa's terms of reference and the agreements reached by the working groups, they outline a set of principles which aim to help maximise women's participation in the transitional phase and lay the basis for addressing inequalities later. The report's main theme was that, unless greater sensitivity was shown to how Codesa's resolutions affected women, a large part of the population would be 'sidelined' by the transition. To prevent this, it proposed that:[3]

- 'non-sexism' be added to all references to non-racism and democracy in agreements;
- special efforts be made to include women in all National Peace Accord structures. More representative security forces, with stricter codes of conducts regulating their conduct towards women, were needed;
- women's 'particular vulnerability' to intimidation through forms of sexual harassment or political patronage should be recognised, since this could threaten or deny women's political, social or economic rights;
- special efforts were needed to encourage women's participation in constitution-making and all future elections as voters, campaigners and representatives. The TEC (WG3) should include women. Special mechanisms should be created to promote participation and representation of women in local government;
- The proposed media commission (see WG3) should include 'gender conscious persons'; help ensure media access to women; monitor and discourage 'sexist' material; encourage 'non-sexist and non-discriminatory'

publications; encourage the participation of women on all media bodies; and organise radio and television programmes which educate women about the democratic process and their right to participate in it.

The GAC did not entirely ignore longer-term issues. It was concerned that a clause in the constitution guaranteeing the equality of all citizens would not ensure women's rights – indeed, that it could be used to frustrate them .[4] It therefore proposed that a justiciable bill of rights should be attached to the constitution, with a 'qualified' equality clause; the bill or some other document attached to the constitution should specify women's particular rights, and so ensure that the equality principle was not used to obstruct women's rights. It also proposed some form of rights and protection for children. All references to 'people' or 'persons' in the constitution should, it urged, be replaced by 'men and women' or 'men, women and children'.

On the land question, no agreement could be reached because the divisions which surfaced in working group discussions intruded here too. The DP proposed that 'WG3 suggest an urgent commission into legislation which prevents women's access to land ownership ... and that the results ... be immediately embodied in legislation'. The SACP insisted on linking this to an immediate moratorium on the sale and transfer of state property to individuals or corporations,

The ANC's Frene Ginwala ... proposed that the GAC's work should continue.

an idea which the NP rejected. Significantly, on a key issue which separated the parties, the common interests of women did not override those of their parties.

Unlike the working groups, the GAC survived Codesa 2. Its report concluded with a proposal that it should continue its work after the plenary and undertake a more systematic survey of discriminatory laws in need of repeal or change. Although its proposals were not discussed amidst the rhetoric of Codesa 2, Frene Ginwala of the ANC, one of the few women delegates with speaking rights at the plenary, proposed that its work should continue, which Codesa 2 accepted.

It did in fact continue to meet until Boipatong (see part 4), when the ANC, SACP and Transkei delegations withdrew. In this period it reviewed the reports of the working groups, and set up technical committees to deal with discriminatory laws[5] and develop a position on the role of traditional leaders.

More than a 'toothless dog'?

How much did the GAC achieve? Informal responses to its report seem to have been positive, although some male delegates to the working groups did not quite see the point of it. Said one participant: 'I think they respected the work, but could not find a use or value for it.' Nevertheless some participants believe that, had Codesa 2 not failed, the report would have ensured a breakthrough for women's concerns. ANC delegate Mavivi Manzini argues: 'If we had been on the podium, we could have got most of the recommendations through because they were not in contradiction at all with the decisions of working groups; it was simply that the groups were taking decisions and not taking into account the gender implications.'

Assessments of its contribution, made after the breakdown of Codesa, vary widely. Sheila Gastrow, author and an official of Idasa in Natal, commented at a public forum some months later that 'some men told me it was a complete failure'.

The SACP and MK's Thenjiwe Mthintso has described the GAC as 'a toothless dog'. It would be easy to see the GAC's recommendations as a set of fairly vague proposals, tolerated rather than endorsed by the Codesa parties, which are likely to have little or no impact on the transition. And, as noted above, its mandate and the limited participation by key delegations such as the NP's and the government's ensured that it did not become a concerted attempt to find common ground across the divide.

Gill Noero fiercely contests these appraisals. 'The GAC did not fail,' she argues; 'Codesa 2 did. The GAC had no opportunity to present its proposals, and it is unfair to criticise the committee as useless and powerless because it only had advisory powers.' She notes that it could not have had greater powers since it would then have been able to 'override the decisions of the mandated working groups'. Given its constraints, she believes the GAC chalked up substantial achievements. Some of its proposals were indeed more specific than those of working groups which did reach 'agreement'.

But, as Noero acknowledges, the failure of Codesa 2 means that the GAC's influence remains untested. Manzini notes: 'The GAC did much work in filling the gaps at Codesa, but at the moment we cannot say it is a success or a failure; all the work of Codesa is in limbo.'

Gastrow's and Mthintso's comments may reflect more on the constraints which the GAC faced than on the work of the committee itself. The former, Noero acknowledges, were formidable. The GAC was 'under-resourced in terms of access to influence in the MC'; it was 'marginalised' and its concerns on the whole were disregarded. 'Working group delegates did not generally understand what the GAC was doing, and often our GAC delegates did not explain,' she says.

Regardless of the quality of its work, then, the GAC was not necessarily the breakthrough for women which its appointment had seemed to suggest. The convention does seem to have seen its work as less than a priority. Even if, as Manzini suggests and Noero implies, its report would have been accepted by the plenary, this might not have guaranteed that the parties and the mechanisms they established to manage the transition would have taken more than cursory notice of women's concerns.

In the medium term, GAC participants believe, there is widespread support for a women's 'desk' or ministry in a new government which would emphasise women's demands for equality. They accept that the GAC's short life, tight mandate and limited progress ensured that it was not the forerunner of such a desk – although they believe that it might have been had Codesa 2 succeeded.

Nevertheless, senior GAC participants suggest that it may have contributed to a momentum which will still be felt. Its chief achievement was to implicitly shift the transition debate from who is eligible to participate, to who is able to do so (since it implied that formally allowing women to take part did not mean that they would be able to do so in practice). GAC members, participants note, are active within their parties and will surely try to influence the way in which they frame their positions. An election monitoring commission might find it hard to ignore the concerns expressed by the GAC. And there will, they add, be new opportunities for the issues discussed by the GAC to be raised again as multi-party negotiations resume. They accept however that the future of the GAC's recommendations may depend largely on the influence of individual GAC participants in their parties.

Critics and participants disagree about the GAC's achievements and impact. But they do agree that, despite the symbolic importance of its appointment, its brief history shows how far the country's major political actors are from giving gender discrimination and equality sustained attention.

PART 3
The aftermath

Back to
the streets

For a while after the collapse of Codesa 2 the parties kept alive a hope which was to prove a fiction: that the management committee would hold together what had been torn asunder in Working Group 2.

Again, this assumed that the deadlock was a problem of technique: a smaller, 'more business-oriented' body might focus the parties' minds, isolate the issues, and resolve them. But the problem was more deeply rooted. The convention's failure went deeper than the unwieldy number of participants, or the way in which meetings were handled. The gulf between the parties was then too great, trust between them too low, and their expectations of the concessions they could wring from each other too high for agreement. Pressure to agree quickly led either to vague 'deals' which could not stick or, as in WG2, to collapse.

That is why assembling in a smaller committee the same parties which had clashed in WG2 simply moved the conflict to a new forum. The MC's discussions perpetuated both the acrimony of the Codesa 2 plenary and the convention's penchant for avoiding central issues. Instead of tackling the constitutional questions which divided the parties, the committee fell to arguing over the ANC alliance's claim that the government was tapping its telephones at Codesa. The MC did not deadlock. But as events outside the World Trade Centre overtook it, it simply petered out.

For the next four months the parties which had sought a concord at Codesa engaged each other in a test of strength which, despite the later resumption of negotiations, is not yet over. For one of them that test had become inevitable even before Codesa deadlocked: the ANC had by then virtually committed itself to using popular power rather than elegant argument or subtle negotiation strategy to secure a settlement.

MOVING THE MASSES

The tripartite alliance's pre-Codesa 2 summit (see WG2) had hinted that 'mass action' would be used whatever happened at the plenary. What did happen removed any doubt.

At the end of May the ANC gathered for a conference whose chief aim was to agree on detailed policy on all those issues on which governments are expected to hold firm views: much of the debate centred around the economy, social policy and the like. The chief purpose was to show that the ANC was preparing itself to govern; the meeting moderated many of the movement's positions, turning some from wistful wishes into the germ of a government programme.[1] But it also gave delegates who had been remote from, and disenchanted with, negotiations for most of Codesa's life a chance to discuss the stalemate. Predictably, the frustration which had built up as the convention talked, surfaced on the conference floor. The regions, which had, as we have seen, remained silent during Codesa even when they were asked to respond, were now voluble. The result was a position more militant than the ANC's stance at the World Trade Centre.

The conference appointed a negotiations commission to frame a strategy. In a clear sign of its mood it chose as chair Ronnie Kasrils, an SACP and former MK militant who had been barely visible at Codesa[2] and whose enthusiasm for negotiation was at best qualified. The commission stressed the link between negotiation and 'mass struggle', and the conference formally endorsed a 'mass action campaign' which was to begin two weeks later, on 16 June, anniversary of the 1976 Soweto disturbances.

The campaign was, according to ANC secretary general Ramaphosa, to be a 'rolling' action; it would rely on continual but limited actions rather than a single mass event. The trade unionists who had devised it, however, expected it to culminate in a general strike in August.[3]

The ANC's Ronnie Kasrils ... became a key figure in the 'mass action' campaign.

To march is to rule?

Ramaphosa's public announcement of the campaign suggested that 'mass action' had a dual purpose. Firstly, he declared, 'if negotiations and mass action have not always been mutually reinforcing elements of our struggle, they now need to be so'. This suggested the first aim: 'mass action' could win negotiating gains which talking alone could not. In this case, Ramaphosa said, the main goal was to pin the government down to specific 'time frames' for the transition to majority rule, so ensuring that the ANC did not become trapped in an eternal interim government.

But he suggested too that the campaign would revitalise the link between the ANC's grass roots membership and the negotiation process, and help prepare the ground for a future election campaign.[4] This implied that 'mass action' was also needed to enhance the internal organisation and cohesion of the ANC alliance; to rally its supporters, invisible during the months at the World Trade Centre, behind it. This need partly explained why mass mobilisation may have been inevitable regardless of events at Codesa 2: at a briefing on 19 June, Mac Maharaj explained that the turn to 'mass action' was not solely a response to the breakdown at Codesa.[5]

The campaign germinated well before the second Codesa plenary – in late February, when the central committee of the Congress of South African Trade Unions (Cosatu) unveiled a plan of action for the second half of the year. On 8 March, just nine days before the white referendum, Cosatu announced plans for 'mass action on an unprecedented scale, including a possible general strike' if an interim government was not in place by the end of June. It also declared that it would organise marches and demonstrations on budget day, 18 March, to highlight demands for the establishment of an economic forum and an end to 'unilateral economic restructuring'.[6]

The announcement was out of step with the mood of the times. The ANC, fearful of a strong right-wing vote in the referendum, had placed a moratorium on utterances which might frighten whites into the 'no' camp. It had issued statements promising job security to civil servants, reassuring whites about the future of the negotiating process, and calling for a 'yes' vote. Cosatu general secretary Jay Naidoo's assertion that the referendum was 'irrelevant to the negotiating process' since the government had been brought to the table 'by mass action on the ground' (implying that whites would, presumably, be forced into more concessions by more of the same) seemed to signal a rebellion against ANC strategy. Government, business and liberal opinion-formers saw the statement's timing as bloody-minded and foolish; the ANC maintained a discreet silence.

But, as we argued earlier (WG2), the denunciations which followed Cosatu's statement ignored the dynamics behind it. Cosatu leaders presumably knew that it would take more than a press statement to frighten white voters into rejecting negotiation: only if the unions turned their words into deeds before the referendum might they affect the vote. And it was precisely this that Naidoo's statement prevented. He was reacting to some in Cosatu who did not agree that the referendum was 'irrelevant'; they saw it as a provocation, since it gave whites a veto over negotiations, and they had wanted action during the pre-referendum campaign. By insisting that the poll was meaningless, union leadership was saying that there was no need to mobilise against it; the action could be organised at Cosatu's convenience, and since it would take time to prepare it could wait until after the vote. And it may have been no accident that the first salvo in the campaign would be fired the day *after* the poll.

But the fact that the leadership needed to use clever footwork to prevent action before the referendum simply confirmed that there was strong pressure for it within Cosatu. Nor were leaders and work-place shop stewards divided on the need for mobilisation; both were concerned about the development of a negotiation process which they believed had lost its way.

There was firstly much unhappiness within Cosatu at the ANC's failure adequately to consult its allies over important tactical and policy shifts at Codesa; Cosatu had demanded a seat at the convention, since it was the only alliance partner not directly represented, and it wanted a say in the compromises which were being made on its behalf. Secondly, and perhaps more importantly, it was alarmed by the seemingly cosy relationship developing between government and ANC negotiators, since it seemed not to be matched by any noticeable progress towards the goals the alliance had proclaimed: an interim government and a constituent assembly. And thirdly, it believed – along with some ANC figures – that the ANC negotiators, enchanted by the cordial atmosphere of the World Trade Centre, were rapidly losing touch with their grass roots and the mood within the country.

Behind these complaints lay the two reasons for action suggested by Ramaphosa's announcement. Unionists, experienced in labour bargaining, where negotiation is often accompanied by shows of strength (or the threat of them), believed that the ANC negotiators did not understand bargaining. There was no special magic at the table which allowed parties to win more than they were strong enough to gain; if they wanted to win concessions in negotiations, they needed to continue to show strength outside them. Like some key ANC alliance leaders outside the union movement, they argued that mass mobilisation was a key source of their strength; by discarding it during negotiations they were fighting with an arm tied behind their backs. Negotiation did not remove the need for mobilisation; on the contrary, the two complemented each other – by 'demobilising the masses', the ANC was playing the game by the NP's rules. If the alliance wanted victory, it needed to mobilise: 'victory' was not just a settlement, but attainment of the interim government and CA to which it was committed.

There were some within the alliance who went further than Cosatu and its allies. They saw mobilisation not simply as a route to more favourable compromises, but to the government's demise. They pointed to eastern Europe where the people, marching in the streets, had caused the government to fall: the same was possible here, they insisted, and so the 'Leipzig Option'[7] was born. But this was a minority position – even within the SACP, which was sometimes wrongly identified with it. For the main stream 'mass action' was a negotiation tactic, not a revolutionary weapon.

For some who rejected the 'Leipzig' formula it was more than that.[8] With Cosatu, they suggested that Codesa-type negotiations were becoming an elitist exercise, removed from those the negotiators claimed to represent. The 'masses' who had led the fight against apartheid and

forced the 'regime' to negotiate were now being pushed aside. Some might see the answer to elitist negotiation in regular report-backs by negotiators to their constituencies and the citizenry. Within the ANC alliance, unionists and activists steeped in ideas of mass democracy insisted that this was not enough – mere communication would simply allow the leaders, with their greater hold on information and their eloquence, to control the process. The 'people' must force their way in by using their greatest weapon, their numbers – and they could do so only by taking to the streets.

Cosatu's Sam Shilowa, Jay Naidoo and John Gomomo announce the 'mass action' campaign, including a possible general strike, at a press conference on 8 March 1992.

These ideas were not entirely new. They had been circulating for some time as pressure for action built through Codesa; ANC negotiators who were unconvinced by the argument had presumably been able to stave it off with promises of gains at the table. When they returned empty-handed, they were left without ammunition and the pressure became irresistible.

Nor were some ANC heavyweights simply giving in to pressure from below. Leaders such as Ramaphosa might have harboured doubts about the image of a democracy – or even a negotiation process – in which the prime form of decision-making was the mass march. But they did see the dangers of losing touch with their constituency during a difficult transition which would, they hoped, culminate in an election. Just as the NP had solidified its camp by holding a referendum, so they believed the ANC needed to secure the loyalty and commitment of its supporters through mass mobilisation.

In the days before the policy conference, momentum towards 'mass action' may have been unstoppable. But Cosatu took no chances. Shortly before the conference it restated its plans for a mass campaign timed to

begin a month later; it would, it said, include
marches, demonstrations, boycotts and a stayaway lasting 'at least three days'. It repeated its
timetable for a quick transition, and added a
shopping list of demands aimed at alleged government corruption and covert security operations.[9] Cosatu delegates were also much in evidence at the conference when it adopted what
was in essence the union federation's campaign.
This is not to say that Cosatu 'imposed' the decision; it found no shortage of willing listeners and
supporters. But, as the best organised section of
the alliance, it arrived with detailed plans and
the muscle to implement them; it was hardly surprising that the gathering should make use of
most of its work.

The campaign began with rallies on 16 June,
whose success was hotly debated. The alliance,
pointing to the mass stayaway from work on
that day and the thousands of people who
attended meetings, pronounced the campaign's
opening a success. The government, aware that
there was always a mass stayaway on 16 June
and that there would doubtlessly have been one
whatever the ANC conference decided, replied
that the meetings were attended by a fraction of
the population in the regions where they were
held; this, it suggested, meant that the 'masses'
were less than enthusiastic about 'action'.[10]

The exchange was revealing, for it illuminated
the key obstacle facing those who claimed to be
able to move the authorities through popular
power. Rallies or demonstrations in any society
draw only a fraction of the population; organis-

ers who attract some 30 000 people to a stadium in a township of one
million people may be doing very well. The size of the crowds did not
show that the alliance lacked popular sympathy, merely that there is a
limit to the number of citizens who will take part in demonstrations,
however much they sympathise with a cause. And that of course was
the Achilles heel of a strategy which claimed to be able to force the NP
into conceding the alliance's demands through sheer weight of popular
numbers.

To the barricades

Almost immediately, the 16 June rallies were overshadowed by an event
which is remembered as a more decisive influence on negotiations. On

Funeral of victims of the Boipatong massacre, 29 June 1992.

the night of 17 June, shack-dwellers in Boipatong township in the Vaal Triangle were massacred by raiders assumed to be IFP-supporting hostel residents; claims, as yet unproven, that they were aided by police added to the already widening gap between the parties. In protest, the ANC formally suspended negotiations which, despite the campaign, had never officially ended. Some critics insist that it used Boipatong as a pretext since it was, tragically, not the first massacre, not even the first in which police collusion was claimed. But in the climate already created by negotiation's growing distance from the concerns of ANC activists, an incident of this sort was bound to have consequences which might have been avoided at a calmer time.

On 22 June Nelson Mandela announced the formal suspension of talks, and the following day the ANC executive presented the government with 14 demands it wanted met before negotiations could resume.

145

The central ones called for an interim government and rapid movement to an elected CA. Others suggested that the violence was the government's doing, and that it should end it before talks could resume. The ANC demanded an end to 'the regime's … campaign of terror against the people'; It insisted also on the implementation of agreements reached a year earlier on security measures at hostels (which were seen as IFP fortresses) and the carrying of weapons by IFP members – the government's failure to act, it implied, showed collusion between it and Inkatha. It urged the repeal of 'all repressive legislation' and an international inquiry into Boipatong.[11]

Inevitably, in the charged climate of that time, the government refused to meet any of the demands. Instead, a 'war of memoranda' began. It was only one example of the heightened verbal belligerence on both sides which was to last almost three months. Since the ANC's unbanning, it and the NP might officially live in one country. But they now talked at, not to, each other. Both held press conferences and issued heated statements as they vied for the attention of the world media.

Some of the flavour of the contest is offered by an exchange of letters between De Klerk and Mandela in July. De Klerk responded to the 14 demands thus: 'Contrary to the ANC's accusations the government has not, and will not, plan, conduct, orchestrate or sponsor violence … against any political organisation or community. The lie that the government is sponsoring and promoting violence remains a lie no matter how often it is repeated.'[12] He continued: 'The fundamental difference between the approach of the ANC and the government regarding the purpose of negotiations lies … in our commitment to constitutionality and a transitional government as soon as possible: and … in the ANC's insistence on an unstructured and immediate transfer of power before a proper transitional constitution is negotiated.'

In reply, Mandela accused De Klerk of 'falling into the NP trap of finding communists to blame for what is happening in the alliance'. His claims about the nature of the divide between the parties were, Mandela declared, 'indeed a novel description of the purpose of negotiations'.[13]

Until September there was no sign that the government would move
on the ANC demands. The ANC pressed ahead with 'mass action', and the
verbal war continued. To be sure, Boipatong did not fuel an outbreak of
mass fury – except perhaps in the Vaal area itself, where its result was
near-anarchy, not disciplined 'mass action'. But it did add to the militant mood among activists, adding impetus to the campaign. Several

Wreaths laid at the
scene of the shoot-
ing at Bisho, Ciskei,
7 September 1992.

union-organised lunchtime factory and street marches were staged during July, along with sit-ins at various state offices around the country.
The action was designed to climax on 3 August with the beginning of
what was initially described as an indefinite general strike.

But if Cosatu had criticised the ANC for failing to find a balance
between negotiation and mass mobilisation, it was not about to err in
the opposite direction. No sooner had the ANC suspended negotiations

than Cosatu began talks with the South African Employers' Consultative Committee on Labour Affairs, the business community's national representative on labour issues, which were to bring the two within a hair's breadth of an embryonic social contract. Their talks merit a closer look, for they have important implications for our theme.

Hard bargaining for a soft deal

Initially, informal contacts revolved around an attempt to agree on the modus operandi for a day of mourning for the Boipatong dead, scheduled for 29 June. Besides direct Cosatu/Saccola contact, negotiations also took place in some industries, notably mining. The prospect that this would become the first stayaway in the 'rolling' campaign was defused when Saccola, the South African Chamber of Business and the Chamber of Mines each issued statements sympathising with some form of dignified show of mourning. The stayaway was thus restricted to the Vaal region, and the unions marked the day with local lunchtime gatherings. By now, however, business and labour – the country's two most organised interests, who shared a long bargaining history – had begun to consider combining their forces to break the deadlock which less seasoned negotiators had caused. Saccola, through key negotiator Bobby Godsell, said there had been exploratory union–business contacts 'over whether business and labour can do something to break the political deadlock'.[14]

These talks were born of more immediate concerns than a mutual desire to save national negotiations: employers' first need was to avoid the threatened strike. This they hoped to achieve by offering a gesture which might nudge the politicians out of stalemate; a joint business/labour stand might be influential, could break the deadlock, and offer a more effective way of meeting the concerns behind 'mass action' than a costly stayaway. And, in an attempt to meet Cosatu's fears of exclusion from economic decisions, business negotiators also offered a commitment to collaborate with unions on tackling poverty and underdevelopment. Employer negotiators were not simply managing a crisis. They were also trying to make a virtue of necessity; business too had an interest in speedier progress towards a political settlement and co-operation with labour on the economy. But, for much of their constituency, averting the stayaway was the priority.

The result was a Charter for Peace, Democracy and Economic Reconstruction. It contained commitments to combat violence and suggested methods for doing so; programmes for alleviating poverty and beginning economic reconstruction; and a commitment to a rapid transition to democracy. The economic clauses were the first evidence of something of which both sides had begun to talk but which until then had seemed a distant idea: a negotiated economic strategy – or 'social contract' – between business and labour.[15] The political clauses endorsed labour's concern for quick movement towards a settlement. More significantly, they offered business support for positions which seemed closer to the ANC's than the government's.[16]

Like the political negotiators, business and labour had constituencies which were not convinced of the need to compromise. Some unionists saw the stayaway as a necessity which could not be negotiated; some business leaders and entrepreneurs resented making concessions 'in the face of threats'. But, unlike the Codesa parties, both had long since learned that they could not compromise without the consent of those for whom they spoke. Cosatu convened an internal meeting in which, after heated debate, the views of the larger unions – such as the miners and textile workers, who favoured a compromise – prevailed; one of its largest unions, the metalworkers, reportedly abstained. Saccola returned to its constituency with as much seriousness but less success – partly because Cosatu had imposed conditions for a compromise which employers were unable to meet.

Business negotiators could not persuade their constituency to accept the accord unless Cosatu called off the stayaway. But in exchange Cosatu required a shutdown of the economy, including the public sector, for one day on 3 August. As a private employer body, Saccola could not deliver a public service shutdown. Equally importantly, as a loose confederation of employer organisations it also could not offer a blanket undertaking that the entire private sector would close for a day, although several major corporations were apparently willing to make this commitment themselves. According to its senior officials, Saccola's task was made far more difficult by a developing public perception, shared by many in business, that the charter and a 24-hour shutdown would signal that business was siding with the ANC alliance against the government.

The government itself was fully informed of developments by Saccola and was sympathetic, with reservations – based precisely on some unease that labour and business might be 'ganging up' against it. But even its tentative approval was enough to prompt an angry attack – aimed at De Klerk in particular – from Buthelezi, who accused the government of yielding to the ANC alliance's 'political blackmail'. This does not seem to have influenced the outcome, but the government's reservations ensured that, while it might welcome a business/labour deal, it would not throw in its lot by shutting down the public service. Parts of business also seemed to worry at the prospect of being seen to back the ANC, and so the offer to shut down for a day finally remained restricted to a few major companies.

Some business leaders, in last-minute attempts to salvage the accord, tried privately to convince their Cosatu counterparts that an undertaking by several prominent companies to close on that day would have a snowball effect, thus meeting Cosatu's needs. But Cosatu's leaders, already divided over the wisdom of negotiating away the protest, would not accept that half–measure, and the stayaway duly began on 3 August.

At first glance these negotiations seemed to confirm what Cosatu leaders had implied when they complained about ANC bargaining strategy: that labour negotiators on both sides could teach their political counterparts a thing or two. Both clearly understood a great deal about the use of power to achieve compromise and the need to 'sell' agreements to supporters. Both drove a hard bargain, but knew that, even in the midst of deep conflict, a bargain might always be there for the making.

Yet the talks may also have shown the limits of labour bargaining as a way of dealing with political divisions. The negotiations foundered partly because they assumed that business as a whole had a united interest in compromising with the unions to end the negotiations deadlock; but the idea of 'business as a whole' is dubious. The political divide within white society runs through business and, while some of its leaders saw merit in a deal which would protect business interests even if this weakened the government's negotiation position, others shared the government's perspective. Business and labour might show the way to a more sophisticated approach to negotiation, but they could not become a substitute for the political parties and movements. More importantly, the reaction of that part of business which resisted the deal showed that political divisions ran perhaps too deep for the sort of bargaining strategies to which business and labour were accustomed.

From the union perspective, the threat of a stayaway did extract concessions from business but the possibilities were not endless; faced with terms they found unpalatable, many businesses preferred to ride out the storm. After a decade of negotiating experience, business was far more adept at compromise than the government – nor was it faced with an apparent threat to its survival, as the government believed it was at the constitutional talks. If 'mass action' could not achieve union aims here, its success in the constitutional arena might be even more limited.

This raises a more general point. Union tactics may work in industry because, however rough bargaining becomes, the two sides are forced to live with each other. The disputes are often crucial, but they do not challenge the survival of the parties. In South Africa's constitutional negotiations – certainly at the time Cosatu and its allies employed 'mass action' – far more was at stake. The dispute concerned who would rule; if one side was to be forced to capitulate, it would need far more than the limited pressure used in labour disputes to defeat it. The degree – and the length – of mobilisation needed to move the government were, as events were to show, beyond the ANC alliance.

To the brink and back

The alliance hailed the stayaway as the most effective ever, although it is not clear that this claim was justified. It was reduced from an initial 'indefinite' action, to one week (in the early days of July), to two days. And a rough assessment suggested that in most unionised work places arrangements were made to work in lost production at weekends and after hours. If it was designed to pressure business and government to yield to the 14 demands, it failed.

The stayaway may have been a triumph of solidarity, mobilisation and organisation, but its practical effects were limited. Having first threatened an action which was to shut down the economy until the government yielded, Cosatu, recognising that the costs to workers were too great, sought to achieve its aims through a negotiated agreement and then settled for a symbolic action.

ANC march to Union Buildings, Pretoria, 5 August 1992. In the foreground are Thabo Mbeki and Essop Pahad.

Despite this, the 'rolling action' continued to roll for a while longer. The stayaway was followed by marches through the week in various cities, reportedly drawing some 200 000 people. The main one in Pretoria, which ended at the Union Buildings and was addressed by Mandela, will probably enter the annals of 'struggle' folklore.

But it was also a curious anticlimax. It was the culmination of a seven-week campaign, yet it was unclear where the action would – or could – head next. Mandela captured the new circumstances with a speech that forsook the aggressive rhetoric that had become standard on both sides. A week earlier, on his return from an overseas trip, he had publicly taken issue with the small group within the alliance who favoured the 'Leipzig Option'. The aim of 'mass action', he said, was not insurrection. It was to force concessions from the government which would permit a return to negotiations. At the Union Buildings he told the crowd he did not wish to gloat. And, addressing both the government and his own supporters, he said it was urgent that negotiations be resumed. 'History will not forgive any of us,' he declared, 'if the search for face-saving formulae prevents us from finding the correct responses which allow negotiations to be successfully resumed.'[17]

The significance of these remarks would become clear soon. Two weeks later, on 22 August, Ramaphosa and Meyer met officially for the first time since the suspension of negotiations. And on 3 September, the ANC published a draft Transition to Democracy Bill which spelt out in precise detail a proposed transition. It reiterated many ANC positions, among them an elected CA with a limited life, and a popular referendum to break the deadlock if it could not agree (the proposal which, in Delport's view, sank WG2). But there were also concessions: an interim constitution, and a 55 per cent majority requirement for the referendum.[18] This was not enough to meet the NP's concerns; but the ANC's collective mind was once again clearly turning to negotiation.

Bungling at Bisho

Nevertheless, the campaign would not pass without another upheaval. Now the focus shifted from the centre to the periphery, from Pretoria to the 'homelands'. Mass mobilisation had done all it could to weaken Pretoria. But it could still, some in the ANC believed, be applied to its 'allies' in Ulundi, Mmabatho and Bisho who, it complained, continued to bar it from their territories, so preventing the free political activity which was essential to the transition.

There were two reasons for this new emphasis. Firstly, the move from Codesa to the streets allowed ANC regions to initiate their own actions. Two of the most militant, Border and Natal Midlands, were near 'homelands' (Ciskei and KwaZulu) which they saw as intolerable holdovers from the apartheid past and from which they were effectively barred by 'homeland' security forces. The campaign seemed an ideal chance to shift the balance of power in their region towards the 'people'. Secondly, some alliance intellectuals, having recognised that mass action was not going to bring Pretoria to its knees, genuinely appear to have believed that the 'Leipzig Option' could work against the 'weaker' governments in the 'homelands'. Three days before the first planned salvo in the campaign, a march on the Ciskei capital of Bisho, Raymond Suttner – head of the ANC's department of political education, a key SACP strategist and a march organiser – suggested that the action could trigger a change in allegiance by Ciskei soldiers and public servants, so collapsing the 'homeland' administration. His intelligence was, in hindsight, horribly flawed.

The rulers of the territories seemed to take the 'Leipzig Option' very seriously indeed: they reacted aggressively to march plans, and vowed to stop them. Oupa Gqozo, military ruler of Ciskei – the first target – carried out that threat outside Bisho on 7 September. On the day he was due to attend a meeting of government allies called to discuss a common commitment to federalism,[19] Ciskei Defence Force soldiers opened fire on the march, killing 28 people. While threats to march on Ulundi and Mmabatho continued, the marches did not materialise. After Bisho the ANC leadership would not countenance further adventures; regions which planned new 'mass action' in the 'homelands' were offered sympathetic statements – and a thinly veiled message to desist.

The Bisho killings were yet another milestone, ironically giving new impetus to negotiation. Condemnation of the Ciskei soldiers was mixed with criticism of key ANC activists – Kasrils in particular, the former 'negotiations commission' chief, was seen to have led marchers recklessly into a trap and was branded, not only by the NP camp, as a threat to the negotiation process. The costs of 'mass action' were becoming prohibitive, and senior ANC leaders concluded that talks would have to resume in earnest. On his visit to the site of the shootings the following day, Mandela said that the country's political leadership had to pull it out of its quagmire.[20] That remark, one of his close associates said at the time, meant that the ANC wished full-scale negotiations to resume as soon as possible. Less than three weeks later, the government and ANC met and signed the 26 September Record of Understanding, which was to prompt renewed negotiations.

Did the ANC return to the table because 'mass action' had achieved some of the goals Codesa could not, or because it hadn't? Conventional wisdom in ANC circles still has it that it was the campaign which drove the government towards a more realistic stance and so made negotiations possible once again. This ignores Mandela's own eagerness to stress the damaging effect of 'mass action', primarily on the national economy: he said that the ANC's desire for a quick return to the table was partly prompted by an assessment of the state of the economy by Finance minister Derek Keys, presented to ANC economics chief Trevor Manuel. The presentation made such a deep impression on Manuel that he immediately conveyed it to Mandela.[21] Also, the 'mass action' campaign had reached its limits even before Bisho. Despite impressive support for the stayaway and for some of the protests during the campaign, the 'masses' were not available to be mobilised perpetually; they had lives to lead and were not willing to be permanently 'empowered' by marching through streets and staying away from work without end.

Indeed, some ANC negotiators may have known all along that the campaign would reach a dead end. Having repeatedly parried claims that 'the masses' could achieve what talking alone could not, they may have resigned themselves to waiting for it to run its course before inevitably resuming talks;[22] they may also have expected to resume bargaining with a freer hand, since the 'alternative' would have been shown to be no such thing.

Others might have seen the campaign not as direct pressure on the government but as a way of renewing the bonds between ANC leaders and constituents, giving the movement a firmer base from which to negotiate. This it may have done; but while the precise effect which mass action had on government thinking cannot be measured, there is little doubt that the ANC returned to the talks because, after Bisho, it had nowhere else to go.

Despite the trauma and tragedy which it brought, the campaign was probably inevitable; the ANC's assessment of its own strength and the government's weakness during Codesa was so inaccurate that it was necessary for it to discover the limits of the alternatives to negotiation. And the campaign may have allowed an ANC strengthened by shows of mass support to begin making the compromises from which it shrank at Codesa.

But although there is no hard evidence that it was the campaign which shifted the government, there is little doubt that something did. Events after Codesa's collapse forced it too to moderate its equally unrealistic assessment of what it could win: it too needed to bump up against reality before it could frame an

approach which might produce a settlement. A return to talks was only possible after Bisho because the government was shifting towards compromise too.

BEGINNING TO BEND

While the ANC was taking to the streets, the NP was fighting a war of its own. The furious exchange of memoranda was, we noted earlier, merely one example of heated NP rhetoric – invariably matched by similar ANC ripostes – resembling the style of the dark days of 'total strategy', not the dawn of negotiation. The government lost no opportunity to blame

EC and UN observer
in Katlehong,
Sharpeville Day,
21 March 1993.

the ANC for the breakdown in talks or any other mishaps, including the state's inability to perform its most basic duty – maintaining law and order. It insisted repeatedly that the country's prospects would only improve when the 'liberation' movement saw reason. The answer lay not in meeting ANC demands, but in the ANC recognising reality.

Some saw in this a quixotic attempt to beat the ANC in the battle for public support. The government seemed to be fighting an early election campaign which it expected to win; a perception actively encouraged by ministers such as Pik Botha.[23] Indeed, at times it sounded as if it believed it could do without the ANC entirely. Within months however it signalled what its power-sharing strategy had already confirmed: that it could not do without its former adversary. Not only was it back at the negotiating table, but it was making substantial concessions to hasten a settlement. What prompted this seeming reversal?

The world is watching

Boipatong's most direct political impact was felt not in the streets, but in the offices of foreign politicians and diplomats. The sense of crisis it engendered resolved an issue which Codesa's WG1, due largely to NP resistance, had failed even to discuss until the final day of its existence – it triggered international involvement in the transition.

While South African politicians are often wont to insist that world opinion is a secondary audience in the negotiation process, their actions and words belie this claim. It was, as we have noted, influence and pressure from abroad which began the negotiation process; throughout it, the protagonists continued to bargain with one eye on the foreign audience.

As the world climate changed from unprecedented identification with the ANC to even-handedness in some cases and growing sympathy with the NP in others, it was the latter which looked particularly hard at foreign opinion. When in 1991 policemen were found to be secretly funding the IFP, government ministers hastened to assure the press that they would find a response to satisfy world opinion;[24] sentiment at home seemed relatively unimportant.

Since Codesa convened, the country's major trading partners in particular had been eager to maintain neutrality, supporting the process rather than any of the parties; this was in itself a welcome shift for an NP used to foreign vituperation. The 17 March referendum had created much greater foreign enthusiasm for the NP and its white constituency. Hardened NP rhetoric after Codesa's deadlock may have had little to do with an attempt to tilt at windmills by seeking an election victory – its chief aim may have been to paint the 'liberation' movement as the 'spoiler' in foreign eyes, so strengthening the NP's bargaining position and perhaps forcing the ANC back to the table on NP terms.

But the suspension of negotiations after Boipatong had the opposite effect. The massacre markedly changed foreign perceptions. Evidence that the attackers were IFP supporters; previous evidence of covert government support for Inkatha; and a growing view that the government bore a major share of the blame for Codesa's failure combined into a serious setback for the NP, and De Klerk in particular, in the courts of world opinion. Now ANC charges that De Klerk was guilty of at least sins of omission in his handling of the violence began to gain credibility.

The ANC – which had always been enthusiastic about an active international role in the process – seems to have seized the opportunity. It used its relationship with the OAU to raise the deadlock in negotiations at the UN. The government, which previously would have ignored any UN 'interference' in South Africa's internal affairs, was no longer in a position to do so; it did not attempt to frustrate a UN role. On 15 July, all 19 Code-sa parties addressed the UN Security Council, which then adopted a res-olution expressing concern at the breakdown and calling on the secre-tary general to appoint a special representative to investigate the vio-lence and recommend ways of ending it.

Foreign minister Pik Botha, who by now was willing to support the appointment of a special representative (former US secretary of state Cyrus Vance), labelled the resolution a defeat for the ANC since it called for a resumption of negotiations and took a non-partisan position on the causes of violence; Mandela had strongly argued that the government was to blame.[25] ANC International Affairs director Thabo Mbeki's view, though, was that the ANC had achieved what it set out to do[26] – secure a UN role in the transition.

Vance's mission led to the arrival of some 40 UN observers, and this opened the way for teams from the EC and OAU. Contrary to Botha's claim, it could be argued that international intervention signalled a swing of the pendulum. The absence of a role before then could be read as a signal that the government – with its negotiation partners of course – was well able to handle the transition fairly. The arrival of representa-tives of the world community would then signal that it was wanting. The UN's role since the breakdown of Codesa has been consciously non-parti-san. But its very presence reflected an NP concession – and a signal that it too was under pressure to show willingness to negotiate.

A far more direct sign of the changed signals the NP was receivng from abroad was a presentation to the Africa subcommittee of the US House of Representatives by Herman Cohen, US under-secretary of state for African affairs, on 23 July in which he outlined the most comprehen-sive US position yet on negotiations. Cohen was at pains to appear even-handed. He called on the government to fully investigate the massacre. He told the ANC that 'mass action' should not seek to overthrow the state, that it must be conducted peacefully, and that undisciplined ele-ments must be curbed. But the crucial section of his presentation dealt with a future constitution: it was a direct attack on the NP's position on a minority veto.

'All sides must recognise the right of the majority to govern, while assuring that all South Africans have a stake in their government,' he said. But no side could insist on 'overly complex arrangements intended to guarantee a share of power to particular groups which will frustrate effective governance. Minorities have the right to safeguards; they can-not expect a veto.'[27]

Like the UN, the US has also remained non-partisan. But Cohen later repeated his warning, suggesting that federalism was a far better safe-guard for minorities than enforced power sharing; he and US ambassador Princeton Lyman have also taken issue with other NP positions, such as a warning by De Klerk that violence would have to end before an elec-tion could be held (this, they said, was an invitation to use violence to prevent a poll).[28] The shift has been almost indiscernible at times. But, together with UN involvement, it has marked a decline in the government's and De Klerk's world stature – the end of a two-and-a-half year honeymoon. And, as the world community became more impatient, and seemed to blame the NP at least as much as the ANC for the stalemate, so the NP hope that irritation would be aimed at the ANC waned and the need for government concessions before a return to talks became clear.

On 23 and 24 July, around the time that Cohen was addressing the House of Representatives, the cabinet held a *bosberaad* (deliberation in the bush). The day after this meeting, Meyer called an off-the-record briefing of journalists in Pretoria. Without offering detail, he said the cabinet had devised ways of resolving the constitutional impasse on three key issues: a constitution-making body, a transitional executive, and an interim parliament. The ANC dismissed

The SACP's Joe Slovo ... article opened the door to compromise on power sharing.

these unsourced reports as too vague to be worth a response; they certainly did not offer it enough credence to call off its stayaway, planned for the following week. But in hindsight the cabinet's rural gathering may have been a critical event at which the government recognised the need for concessions on constitutional issues which would narrow the gulf between it and the ANC.

It would be simplistic to insist that changing world opinion alone forced the NP to moderate its position – as simplistic as the claim that mass action was the sole pressure. But that it was a factor – and an important one – seems clear. One other key factor is so obvious that it is usually barely noticed.

Not on speaking terms

As the ANC returned with zeal to what it knew best – mass action – it seems not to have noticed that its most potent weapon may have been not what it did after Codesa's collapse, but what it refused to do after Boipatong; its refusal temporarily to talk may have been far more effective than action in the streets.

The clue lies in statements by NP negotiators Gert Myburgh[29] and

Roelf Meyer,[30] explaining why the government made concessions to the ANC in September. This was, they said, necessary to bring it back to the negotiating table.

For the NP, despite its rhetoric after Codesa, events since February 1990 assumed one overriding reality – that a settlement with the ANC was essential. At issue was only the terms and the timing. As the stalemate continued, foreign investment remained blocked, by uncertainty as much as the (waning) effect of sanctions; the economy continued to stagnate; and public confidence, in the NP's camp as well as the townships, continued to erode. The NP was not defeated and need not return to the table at any price; but if it needed to pay a price to return it would do so.

Indeed, even as the level of angry rhetoric on both sides rose, the government pressed for talks. On 2 July, in reply to a memorandum from Mandela, De Klerk denied government complicity in violence and called for a summit between the two – while packaging the invitation in an attack on the ANC, accusing it of bowing to 'SACP radicals'.[31]

At that stage the invitation might have been rhetorical, an attempt to woo world opinion, since Mandela was in no position to accept the offer. (He replied: 'It appears that we are all agreed that South Africa faces a serious crisis. When it comes to charting a way out ... however , it is clear that there are hardly any points of convergence.')[32] But De Klerk's response also contained a hint of concessions, whose importance was to become clear later. He hinted that discussion on the fate of political prisoners could be reopened, and announced that the government was considering new regulations which would deal with the bearing of 'cultural' weapons. And he also invited discussion on international involvement in the transition – an issue which, as we have seen, his negotiators deliberately evaded throughout Codesa and which the NP was, two weeks later, to concede.

This was then the first – albeit vague – attempt to woo the ANC back to the table: 'The government will do whatever it can,' he declared, 'without departing from its principles and ideals, to get negotiations, both bilateral and in Codesa, on track again.'[33]

The NP's strategy after Codesa was not an attempt to do without the ANC, but to decide the terms on which it would have to live with it. The longer the stalemate continued, and the less the ANC seemed inclined to return without concessions, the more likely it became that the government would make them.

But, just as the ANC's return was speeded by changing government positions, so was the government's changed by new ANC signals. When the ANC did respond after Bisho, through for example Mandela's call to '[pull] South Africa out of the quagmire' (see above), De Klerk renewed his offer of a summit, which Mandela accepted. The ANC leader then gave an extremely conciliatory interview to the *The Star* newspaper[34] in which he whittled the ANC's 14 demands down to three – the release of political prisoners, action on hostels and dangerous weapons – and implied that Kasrils and other zealots would be reined in.[35] This helped the NP make a decision, albeit one it knew it had to make.

By September, both sides had faced a sobering encounter with reality which weakened some illusions which deadlocked Codesa. They no longer believed that negotiation could avoid severe compromise, or that they had alternatives to treating with each other. Less than three weeks after Bisho, and only 11 days after Mandela's *Star* interview, the summit was held – and it quickly produced an agreement which restarted negotiations.

BACK TO THE TABLE

The agreement – known as the Record of Understanding – was in the view of many commentators and politicians, including some in the NP, a dramatic victory for the ANC. All three demands spelled out by Mandela in his *Star* interview were met.

Primary among them were the release of nearly 400 prisoners (see WG1), among them Robert McBride and other prominent figures as well as young people convicted of crimes such as public violence. The parties agreed that 24 hostels would be fenced in and patrolled by police; a retreat from the government's insistence that the two parties could not agree on securing hostels, since this needed consultation with all affected parties.[36] The government undertook 'within weeks' to 'prohibit countrywide the carrying and display of dangerous weapons on all public occasions'.[37] The document also made important symbolic concessions to the ANC's latest position spelled out in the Transition to Democracy Bill: the elected constitution-making body could have either one or two chambers, it would have a 'fixed time frame', and it would also have 'adequate deadlock-breaking mechanisms'.

Mangosuthu Buthelezi at Shaka Day rally, 27 September 1992 ... announced the IFP's withdrawal from negotiations.

The Record of Understanding created a widespread belief that the government had conceded most ANC demands; this impression was half true. The government had made concessions – indeed, symbolically, at least, had made most of them – but so had the ANC; its key security demands may have been met, but not all the remaining ones were (see note 11). Of the three which were conceded two were never implemented, as a result of IFP resistance: the government had apparently decided to ignore this in its eagerness to win the ANC back to negotiation, but confronted with IFP mobilisation (see below) it changed tack again, albeit without meeting serious ANC resistance.

The agreement in principle to 'time frames' and 'deadlock breaking' did not commit the NP to the ANC's proposed referendum. And, in a continuation of a venerated Codesa tradition, key issues remained unresolved: these included the majorities which would decide a new constitution, the way in which deadlocks would be broken – and indeed whether the assembly would have one chamber or two.

And it soon became clear that the NP was not the only party which had been sobered by the post-Codesa trauma. Only days after the Record of Understanding the ANC signalled that it was about to make a concession which would give the government what it had sought since February 1990.

The first sign was an article prepared for the SACP journal *African Communist*, which was 'leaked' to the press in advance.[38] It was written by SACP chairman Joe Slovo, who suggested that strategic realities might force the ANC to offer the government 'sunset clauses' in a new constitution which would entrench power sharing for a fixed period. It might also have to offer guarantees on regional government and amnesty for security officers, and honour the contracts of civil servants, either by keeping them on or compensating them.

While Slovo insisted that the ideas in the article were his alone, insiders suggested that he had written it at the behest of the ANC executive;[39] he had, it was argued, taken sole responsibility because a call for substantial compromise was most likely to be effective if it was made by the alliance party whose 'militant' credentials were strongest. That the Slovo article was a stalking horse for an ANC leadership position seemed to be confirmed when his arguments soon appeared in an ANC document, *Negotiations: A Strategic Perspective*, offered for adoption to its national working committee.

On 18 November the committee formally adopted the document, although not without fierce disagreement between Slovo and his supporters on the one hand and ANC Information and Publicity director Pallo Jordan on the other. Jordan, expressing the position of the more militant regions and activists, saw this approach as a betrayal of the ANC's 1969 position which had called for the destruction of the apartheid state. Slovo appeared to be arguing for the retention of that state in its most obvious forms by suggesting that its bureaucracy and security forces would remain in place to create a breathing space in which majority rule would be introduced gradually. But the ANC leadership had read the strategic writing on the wall and persuaded the committee to read it too.

A Strategic Perspective[40] argued that the 'liberation' movement's limited capacity, the government's ability to 'endlessly delay', the cost to the country of protracted negotiations and the need to 'prevent a further consolidation of the counter-revolutionary forces' demanded a 'swift negotiation process'. The 'democratic revolution' would proceed in phases in which 'the balance of forces' might force the ANC to 'make certain compromises to protect and advance this process'.

Arguing for a government of national unity, it declared: 'The objective reality imposes a central role for the ANC and the NP in the transition. The ANC is the custodian of the peace process, while the NP is the party in power. In this process it may be necessary to address the question of job security, retrenchment packages and a general amnesty ... as part of a negotiated settlement. These measures will need to apply to all armed formations and sections of the civil service.' Crucially, it added: '... We also need to accept ... that, even after the adoption of a new constitution, the balance of forces and the interests of the country ... may still require us to consider ... a government of national unity.'

In a foretaste of things to come, the document suggested that bilateral agreements between the government and ANC could be reached and then broadened in a multi-party forum. This set the stage for negotiation on the compromise which months of manoeuvring at Codesa had failed to achieve. While the document was seen by some as a betrayal of the ANC's historic mission, it had brought it closer to power than any other decision in its history.

In a sense, the NP concessions in the Record of Understanding and the ANC's in 'A Strategic Perspective' confirmed what several commentators had noted since the Codesa 2 deadlock; that, although they did not sit across a table, the parties had continued to negotiate by making demands, counter-demands and compromises.

Now the process for which Ramaphosa and Meyer may have sought to lay the ground in the last days of WG2 began. The government and ANC, meeting in a series of bilateral talks, began to hammer out details of a settlement. By March 1993 they appeared to have agreed on a transitional executive which would prepare the way for an elected interim government and constituent assembly, taking decisions by a two-thirds majority.

A deadline would be imposed on constitution-making, but no new election would be held once a new constitution was agreed; the interim government would rule for at least five years, probably until 1999, and would comprise all parties which won more than an agreed share of the vote. The principle of autonomy for regional governments was also reportedly agreed.[41] Some analysts suggested that the NP had secured a place in government until at least the end of the century, and the regionalism it had demanded; in exchange it had made a host of concessions – on decision-making in the assembly, limits to the life of power sharing, and other issues. In sum, the purported agreement was the compromise which Codesa had not been ready to achieve.

But while the 'bilaterals' were a sharp departure from Codesa's approach, in one sense they continued it. The compromise had been achieved by the two 'major' parties only. No sooner had the Record of Understanding been signed than they were reminded, more forcefully than at Codesa, that there was a third party too.

THE THIRD PARTY

The Record of Understanding convinced the two 'main players' that multi-party negotiations would succeed only if they reached understandings, if not agreements, in advance. There was a logic to this – much of the time spent at Codesa hearing long presentations by smaller parties who, having expounded on their position, showed no great desire to move from it, could perhaps be used more productively. Bilateralism's supporters also suggested that, once the 'main parties' reached an understanding, the others, most of whom were more or less closely allied to them, would probably go along. And confidentiality in bilateral talks reduced the scope for positional bargaining. The Record showed, they believed, how much could be achieved once they dispensed with the myth of a multi-party forum.

All this assumed a two-sided table, with 'minor' parties lined up behind the ANC or NP. But the IFP insisted that the table had three sides; it reacted to the Record with ferocity. It argued, with some justification, that two of the security issues on which the parties had agreed – hostels and weapons – affected it too. And, not for the first time, it began to fear that the ANC and government were cooking up a deal which it would be expected to accept, and which would exclude it from power in the new order. Ever since February 1990, that fear surfaced whenever the ANC and the NP negotiated on fairly cordial terms. The IFP denounced the Record of Understanding, and refused to be bound by it. At a Shaka Day rally, at which King Goodwill denounced the agreement as an attempt to 'wipe us off the face of earth as Zulus', Buthelezi announced his party's withdrawal from negotiations.[42]

This forced a partial revision of the Record, particularly on securing hostels. (In the face of threats from residents to tear fences down 'with our bare hands', the government declared that the agreement would be enforced gradually; the ANC agreed). When Buthelezi insisted on leading marches, brandishing 'cultural weapons' in defiance of the Record, the police did not act, despite threats to prosecute. On both issues the risks of acting against the IFP, forgotten in the haste to conclude the Record of Understanding, seemed to have been recalled. And the ANC and government became careful to present their 'understandings' as proposals which would be put to other parties, not firm agreements. Both the NP and ANC also convened bilateral meetings with the IFP.

But this was not enough to convince the IFP that it was being treated as an equal in a triumvirate; soon it added a new condition for its return to talks – the disbandment of MK, the issue it never raised in WG1.[43] Its fears could not be dismissed purely as paranoia. True, both the NP and the ANC had decided to bend over backwards to ensure that, in form at least, it received equal treatment. But, while far more significant a player than most of the other 16 parties, it is not seen as an equal by the 'big two'. In his 1993 New Year's address De Klerk warned obliquely that negotiations would have to go ahead even if all groups did not partici- pate; the ANC, while stressing that it would like the IFP to join the train, added that it would leave the station even if it did not. Both seemed to assume that, while IFP participation was desirable, they would not pay any price for it – and that, if they created enough momentum towards a settlement, it would be forced to join the ride for fear of being labelled a threat to national progress.

The IFP's response was to gather an alliance about it – the Concerned South Africans Group (Cosag). It was formed in early October by the IFP, the CP and the governments of Ciskei and Bophuthatswana, in response to the Record of Understanding. This ad hoc group was bound by a common interest in opposing an exclusive ANC/NP deal, and a need for a decentralisation of power which would limit a national government. It doubted the NP commitment to federalism, suspecting it would trade it for power sharing if needs be.

The IFP, reacting to eyebrows raised at its link with the white right, repeatedly insisted that Cosag was not an alliance and that it had limited objectives. And, not long after the group was formed, it began distanc- ing itself from the CP in particular. But the IFP – naturally the leading force within the group – seemed willing to use Cosag to achieve short- term strategic goals; if necessary, to block the progress of negotiations.

Nor was Cosag the only string in its bow. In December it unveiled a 'federal' constitution for Natal/KwaZulu and demanded a referendum in the region on the document; if voters favoured the proposal, the IFP in- sisted, it would become non-negotiable. Analysts pointed out that its constitution did not see the region as part of a united country; it amounted almost to a charter for an independent region.[44] Two aims seemed to lie behind it. Generally, it hoped to cement an alliance with powerful white interests in Natal, such as the business community, which had endorsed federalism. Specifically, it sought to drive a wedge into the NP, some of whose Natal leaders seemed eager to embrace the IFP plan.

Its hope seems to have been partly realised – one Natal NP MP has joined the IFP, while surveys indicate a sharp growth in IFP support among whites at the NP's expense. The costs of the 'major' parties' strat- egy seemed to be rising prohibitively. For the NP it was counted in a loss of support; for both, in the prospect of a powerful lobby which, unlike the NP and ANC, hinted that it did have an alternative to compromise – an exit from the country.

By March 1993 there was evidence that the danger might be overstat- ed. Organised Natal business did not endorse the IFP's plan – it warned that an independent region had no chance of economic survival.[45] There were also signs of strain within the IFP, some leaders reportedly favour- ing a return to 'mainstream' negotiations.[46] When on 5 March the Codesa parties, strengthened now by the presence of the PAC and the white right

The CP's Ferdi Hartzenberg, left, Ciskei's Oupa Gqozo and Bophuthatswana's Lucas Mangope at Cosag's founding conference, 8 October 1992.

wing, met to discuss a new multi-party conference, the IFP was there too: participants found its delegation leader, Frank Mdlalose, surprisingly conciliatory.[47] And continued attempts to include the IFP in bilaterals with the 'major' parties held out the prospect that two-sided talks could guarantee progress even when the table had three sides.

But the consequences of the 'two-sided' approach remain uncertain. Firstly, even if resumed talks in 1993 do produce a settlement, with or without IFP consent, the issue may not be resolved. If the IFP can disrupt a settlement it may try only well after one is agreed. Secondly, the IFP's plans remain uncertain. While full autonomy for Natal/KwaZulu is a chimera, it could continue to hold out for it in the hope that the NP and ANC will shrink from the threat of continuing violence (and, in the NP's case, a further loss of support) and meet most of its terms.

On the other hand, it may choose to settle for second best and seek a compromise. If it does, it would have to limit its goals. Copious survey evidence and the IFP's own strategy suggest that it is not an equal partner; it lacks the support to claim a significant share in power anywhere but its Natal stronghold, and even there its appeal may be overestimated.[48] And it would probably have to accept strong regional government, rather than the quasi-independence it has demanded.

Its choice – and the outcome – may depend on the third uncertainty; the likely effect if it is relegated to a secondary role. Is it blustering when it gives veiled warnings of endless turmoil if it is not granted equal status, or does it enjoy the power to frustrate whatever the other two decide? We will ponder this in our final section. But by early 1993 this question, rather than the divisions between the NP and ANC, had become the key for those weighing our chances of a smooth transition.

UNCERTAINLY INTO THE UNKNOWN

On 5 March, as the parties with their new recruits gathered again at the World Trade Centre for a planning conference which sought to chart a new course to a multi-party settlement, many lessons seemed to have been learnt.

Andries Beyers of the Afrikaner Volks- unie greets the ANC's Cyril Ramaphosa at the multi-party planning conference, 5 March 1993.

They seemed, after the turmoil of 1992, to have learnt more about their strengths and weaknesses and those of their partners. Behind closed doors in the months before the meeting, some of them seemed to have narrowed the divide which doomed Codesa. They had learnt, too, the danger of promising too much and delivering too little: the proceedings were not televised, for fear of raising expectations too soon. They also appeared eager to avoid some pitfalls which had dogged Codesa; despite ANC promises that the old forum would be resurrected, they resolved to discuss a new name (in deference to the newcomers, who had vowed never to join Codesa). More importantly, they insisted that the new forum would be less elaborate; it would concentrate on reaching agreements more than on reassuring those outside that it was doing so.

It seemed possible then that Codesa and its aftermath had been a bitter, tragic but necessary lesson, and that having learnt it the parties could go on to negotiate a settlement.

And yet ... part of the malaise which afflicted Codesa seemed to linger. The 'historic' compromise between the NP and ANC, the Record of Understanding, had proved less portentous than it seemed. Of the agreements which had been tested – those on security – only one was implemented, and that in a way which for a time caused as much conflict as it resolved.[49] The 'understanding' between them left open key questions, such as the role of a transitional executive, over which they were still divided at the turn of the year. And, in an uncomfortable echo of Codesa, the planning conference reached agreement by the simple expedient of shelving every contentious issue.

While a settlement seemed likely, it was not then assured. And even if it was achieved, the signs suggested that the divisions it sought to heal, and the parties' reluctance to bridge them, might remain for many years to challenge the attempt to build a new nation on the failures of the old.

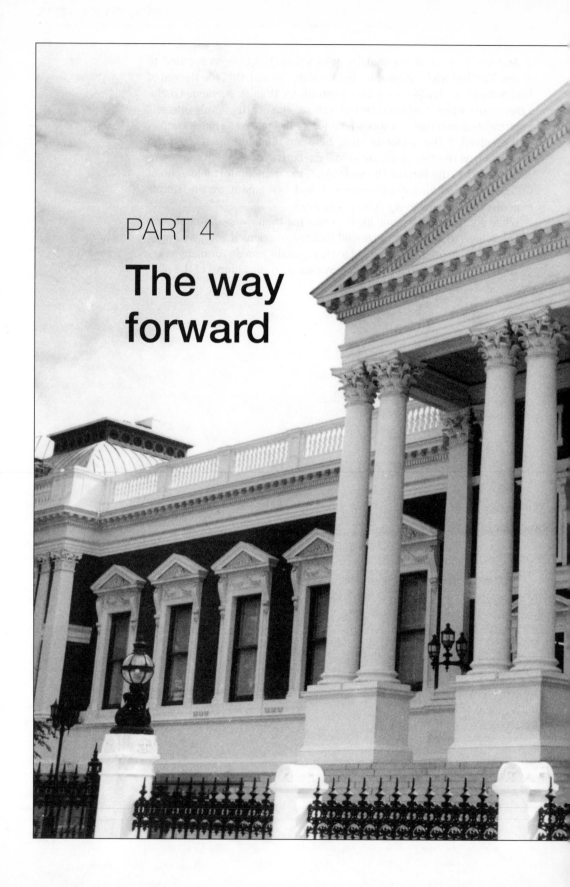

PART 4

The way
forward

Slow walk
to freedom

Since the hosannahs of February 1990, South Africa's search for a settlement has proceeded amid alternating waves of euphoria and despair. For much of the second half of 1992, despair was in vogue. But as the parties left the World Trade Centre on 6 March 1993, after agreeing to restart multi-party talks, Ramaphosa in particular sought to rekindle the flame of euphoria: the resumed talks, he said, lit 'a torch of hope'.[1]

This time the response was more muted. If Codesa and its aftermath did nothing else, it prepared both a wary press and public for the possibility of new false dawns, of further stalemates and diversions. Perhaps when new problems emerged, they would be less likely to provoke 1992-style despair. But if the restarted talks did produce a settlement, even the wary seemed unlikely to resist the temptation of a new burst of euphoria.

Just how warranted is the gloom and elation? Is a negotiated settlement possible? More importantly, is it possible to reach an agreement that will last? If it is, will it heal the divisions which brought the parties to Codesa in the first place, and will it begin the progress the convention promised?

These questions are more pressing to South Africans than an autopsy of the convention which collapsed for a time. But one more look backwards may be needed if we are to look ahead.

RELUCTANT NO MORE?

We have argued that the Codesa parties were reluctant reconcilers. Are they no longer so? That they have resumed talks is no evidence of this, for they have talked reluctantly before. Even if they reach a settlement this may be no evidence, since they might settle reluctantly, only to find after they have done so that the problems they meant to resolve are still present. That too they have done before – at Groote Schuur, Pretoria, and perhaps in some of Codesa's working groups.

A preliminary skirmish

In principle, Codesa was not meant to be a constitutional convention at all. It was supposed only to prepare the way for one. But with the Zimbabwean and Namibian models in mind, it was seen widely at home and abroad as South Africa's 'grand negotiations' – a local version of the Zimbabwean Lancaster House talks. It was therefore overloaded from the outset with expectations that it would chart the course to a new political order.

Those hopes were not confined to outsiders: the expectations outside the World Trade Centre were at least partly shared by those within. The NP hoped Codesa would settle as much as possible, leaving only minor details to an assembly. The ANC insisted that the real constitution-making lay ahead, and it wanted the convention to agree on a quick route march to majority rule. Both expected to leave the convention with their chosen future assured.

But our account of WG2's deadlock suggests that, by the time the parties began working round the clock to settle, some of their strategists had already decided that Codesa could not succeed; its deadlock seems to have been something of a relief all round. By then, both 'major' parties may have known that a pause in the search for a settlement was needed. The reason, as we have suggested, lay not in the convention's presumed flaws but in the reality that the parties were not yet ready to agree. They went to the table misreading what they could win and what their opponents would concede.

The wrong signals may have begun flashing when F W de Klerk made his celebrated speech on 2 February 1990. It was interpreted by many as a concession speech, an acknowledgment of the inevitability of majority rule. But it was not the product of a blinding flash of insight on the way to Damascus, or of a realisation that the costs of resisting rule by the majority had become too high. Contact with the ANC, publicly by academics and business leaders, privately by government emissaries who saw Mandela, had begun during the P W Botha era when majority rule was on no government planner's agenda.

Even then the ANC's unbanning and an attempt to reach agreement with the 'liberation' movement was clearly the final goal: it was obstructed for a time by Botha's reluctance to take risks, or indeed to take any step unless he was sure that he remained in full control. De Klerk's contribution was to do what many in the NP knew had to be done before it was forced to do it. And he did that partly because a changing international climate suggested that unexpected gains could be reaped if the deed was done then.

A surrender to majority rule was not what the NP had in mind. Analyst Lawrence Schlemmer notes that De Klerk, like NP strategists before him, worked with a consociational model of democracy in which power would be shared by contending blocs. To be sure, he favoured a new version which seemed more equitable. Power sharing would be real rather than a sham; while earlier NP versions saw power shared by racial blocs, De Klerk's suggested sharing it between parties.[2] This difference in approach made a settlement possible in principle, while the 1980s version of NP thinking did not. But it was still a continuation of, not a departure from, the NP's attempt to retain a share of power on the best possible terms: indeed, some senior government sources claim that its contact with Mandela in prison had led it to believe that this is what the ANC was prepared to accept.

In February 1990 De Klerk was engaged in the politics of opportunity. His strategy was based on gaining the initiative, on rallying and maximising international support for his side of the bargaining table, on confusing his opponents and making a quick run for the goal, and on the premise circulating in a Broederbond document that the greatest risk was to take no risk at all. Beyond that, everything remained vague: it is doubtful that government planners and strategists had the time to think through the potential consequences of this strategy by the time it was implemented. Implicitly it was an act of faith in the NP's strength to sustain its interests through the period of political 'adhocracy' which would follow.

The effect was to help create a period of immense turmoil: the NP's traditional constituency was thrown into confusion overnight; the UDF, the internal standard bearer of the ANC tradition, had to absorb not only leaders released from prison but the exiled community as well; the IFP's constituency became directly threatened by the political appeal of an unbanned ANC. The cornerstone of the established political ethos – the portrayal of the ANC/SACP as the country's enemy – had been removed, leaving little in its place besides a conviction that fancy footwork would manoeuvre the ANC into accepting an offer – power sharing on NP terms – which it would prefer to refuse.

Analyst Lawrence Schlemmer ... outcome will be a 'grand coalition' of the major parties.

From the perspective of those outside the circle of NP strategists it seems that, although the government had been contemplating the prospects of unbanning the ANC for some time, there was an almost breathtaking lack of planning and vision when it actually came to implement the decision. Even at Codesa a senior government negotiator is reported to have replied in answer to a question about the NP's vision for South Africa: 'it doesn't have one.'[3]

Another effect was to create expectations of negotiations which they could not possibly meet. Analyst Joe Thloloe captures something of this: 'De Klerk missed a golden opportunity in 1990. If he had said, "I intend turning this country into a democracy within the next seven years, and these are the steps I am going to take to get to that point", he would have had the support of the majority of South Africans. At the moment he has aroused so many suspicions on all sides that even if he now said, "this is my programme or vision", nobody will believe him.'[4]

But De Klerk did not then intend turning the country into a democracy in seven years. If democracy is a synonym for majority rule it is not clear even now whether his party intends that (see below). From that 'fateful' 2 February until the end of Codesa and beyond it was engaged in a tactical manoeuvre, not a considered strategy for a smooth transition to a 'full democracy'. It was this that many failed to read.

Whether the ANC read it is unclear. Certainly, its response was equally surprising when we recall that it had long rejected the South African state's claim to sovereignty. Given its suspicion of the NP, it would not have been unreasonable to expect it to set detailed conditions for its return – and for negotiations – and to insist on bargaining these with Pretoria from outside the country before abandoning exile. By returning almost unconditionally, it implicitly accepted that the government would play host to the negotiations and would to some extent be able to set their terms.

Two theories suggest themselves. One is that conditions in exile were becoming so difficult that the prospect of establishing itself again on South African soil overwhelmed any thought of a more carefully planned response. The ANC was also playing the politics of opportunity – taking immediate advantage of an open door through which to get its people back into the country. If negotiations were to fail, it would then be in a much stronger position. The second theory is that the ANC misread the terrain to which it was returning. While its suspicion of the NP remained deep, it seems to have believed that the government was more vulnerable than it really was and that it (the ANC) merely needed to return home to claim the prize it had sought for decades.

Both explanations may reflect part of the truth. But the consequence is clear: when the ANC leadership emerged from prison and exile the divide between it and the NP remained as wide as ever, but both sides assumed that they could quickly make the other cross it on their terms. Their constituencies believed this too: many in the 'establishment' camp assumed that the ANC had come back to join the existing order; many in the 'liberation' fold believed that the exiles and prisoners had returned to take the NP's surrender.

Had the parties negotiated the terms under which the ANC was to return before it did so, much turbulence and disillusion might have been avoided; the groundwork may also have been laid for more workable negotiations. But they did not, and so events leading to Codesa – vague agreements between the parties which turned out to bind them to little, slow progress towards a settlement which had seemed almost assured, and mounting conflict – did as much to disrupt the transition as to advance it. When Codesa finally met, the parties still faced each other with the expectation that they could outmanoeuvre the other behind closed doors and then emerge from the cloisters to present their prize to their waiting followers. The convention therefore worked in an insulated cloud above the heads and beyond the reach of society. There was little synchronisation between the political leaders at Codesa and their structures on the ground, including those which had been created specifically to deal with the conflict between them, such as the Goldstone Commission and the National Peace Accord.[5]

The ANC came to Codesa expecting to achieve agreement on an elected assembly which would have a relatively free hand in writing the new constitution.[6] While it might have been aware that it was not dealing with a defeated enemy, its strategists believed that any obstruction from the government would be unsustainable because it would face irresistible international pressure. The government came to Codesa expecting to co-opt the ANC as junior partners into a transitional government of undefined duration, and during whose reign a new constitution could be negotiated according to principles determined in a multi-party forum loaded in its favour. As Codesa wore on, both parties, political analyst and former politician Frederik Van Zyl Slabbert notes, '... increasingly became aware of [its] artificiality as a negotiating forum; it wasn't power talking to power but rather a sort of debating society where you could go through endless agendas. I don't think there was any real intention of coming out there with a deal that could stick.'[7]

It was not of course that they didn't want a deal. They simply did not understand what was needed to achieve one. On the ANC side, Slabbert adds, 'power for Mandela was a simple exercise of, "you've got it, now give it to me". The ANC did not therefore have a realistic appraisal of the strength and tenacity of the South African state. Only after the mass action campaign had run into severe obstacles did it begin to realise that it could not force a quick settlement on the government.'

On the government side, 'the solidarity of the boardroom was confused with the political reality out there,' notes Slabbert. 'Pik tells you that he and Thabo [Mbeki] sat down together and it was all over – finished – we negotiated; and the next thing that happens is that it all falls apart'.[8] This belief that a neat deal engineered across a table would solve problems which had divided the society for decades failed to appreciate that ANC leaders did not exercise the same sort of control over their constituency as the NP was used to exercising over its own. It also overestimated the NP's own control: parts of the civil service in particular were no longer simply acting as its compliant instrument with which it could do as it chose. It ignored the reality that a settlement would have to bind deeply divided forces and interests, which would not bury their suspicions simply because negotiators instructed them to do so.

With the wisdom of hindsight, the Codesa breakdown now seems both inevitable and necessary. Both 'major' parties, having sparred for months on the basis of flawed assumptions, had a strategic need to withdraw from negotiating in the spotlight of expectations and amid the competing agendas of numerous parties.

Besides its failure to win quick ANC compliance, the government was not then prepared to enter into an agreement which would result in multi-party control over the state too soon. The SACP's Jeremy Cronin offers a conspiratorial explanation: he believes that an early multi-party interim government would have threatened to expose South African military activities in Angola's September 1992 elections. He claims too that Military Intelligence was monitoring the Namibian and Angolan elections as a 'dress rehearsal' in preparation for an inclusive South African election which it intended to manipulate.[9] Both theories are of course hotly denied by government representatives. A less dramatic explanation is advanced by ANC strategist Joel Netshitenze: 'The NP was not ready to clinch a deal – given the state of the security forces and the administration, and given the exposures since Codesa 2, one can understand that they were not ready to subject these to multi-party control.'[10] In other words, the security establishment and civil service had too many skeletons in their closets and were in any event in no state to be handed over to multi-party control.

The reality may have been more mundane. A settlement would have entailed an election, probably within a year. The NP had not begun to wage an organised electoral campaign in black communities. Having discovered that negotiation was not as simple as it had believed, it also lacked the confidence to move rapidly to a quick settlement. It had, University of Stellenbosch political scientist Philip Nel believes, entered negotiations with too much self-confidence; overwhelmed by long-forgotten international diplomatic successes, it believed it could determine the agenda, win crucial concessions from the ANC, and settle on its own terms at Codesa.[11] But during Codesa it began to realise that negotiations would be more complex than that.

Sociologist Heribert Adam suggests that government strategy had banked on a longer, more drawn-out process. The multi-party context of Codesa held some surprises for it and opened divisions within the cabinet between 'hard-liners' led by Kobie Coetzee, who advocated caution, and 'soft-liners' led by Roelf Meyer, who wanted bolder action aimed at winning a settlement.[12] Stellenbosch analyst Willie Breytenbach argues that the government went for a high-risk win at Codesa, but lost.[13] All these explanations stress a similar theme: the NP, its early expectations dashed, needed a breathing space in which to re-evaluate strategy.

The ANC, which had been under such pressure to reach agreement that it insisted that WG2 work through the night until it achieved a settlement, was also probably relieved to withdraw. It believed that, the longer negotiations dragged on, the less favourable would its situation become.[14] But it needed to regroup – and, as important, to return to its constituency. During Codesa, Cronin recalls, the ANC had 'showered' its branches with briefings but this, together with the SABC's interpretations of events at Codesa, had merely overwhelmed people who believed that negotiation was not delivering results. Mass action allowed leaders to resume contact with their constituency.

These more immediate concerns simply flesh out our theme: that Codesa failed because it was not underpinned by the strategic realism on either side which could have allowed it to succeed.

Sadder, but wiser

Against this background, the key question is whether the events which followed made the 'big two' any more aware of the requirements for a settlement than they were when Codesa 2 collapsed. Public perceptions – and most analysts – believe they have.

In the period when negotiations had formally broken down, all the fault lines in South African society and politics which had been papered over during Codesa became evident, revealing the potential for prolonged instability well into the future. Revelations about alleged military and police conspiracies and 'dirty tricks'; exposes of ANC violence and torture in its detention camps in exile; increasing violence and crime; all pointed to the danger that the centre, over which both adversaries hoped to rule, might come apart, leaving them little over which to reign. The threat was emphasised by apparent loss of government control over elements in the military, and the ANC's matching loss of authority over its self-defence units. The NP's control over its 'allies' loosened as political calculation drove some towards Cosag. The economy, already severely battered, was a continuing victim. The centre seemed to be unravelling and the possible consequences were all too clear. This realisation, together with severe international pressure for a settlement, served to concentrate the parties' minds on a compromise.

Analyst Joe Thloloe ... 'De Klerk missed a golden opportunity in 1990'.

Besides the sobering experiences we have mentioned earlier, Slabbert notes that Bisho provided the ANC with 'a salutary lesson of confronting a fairly weak element of the state which could simply turn around and put an end to mass mobilisation'.[15] Cronin, from a very different vantage point, suggests that 'mass action' brought the ANC alliance's grass roots into negotiations for the first time, perhaps bringing home its necessity: 'Because leaders had to be on the ground in 1001 places to negotiate around the National Peace Accord, this for the first time translated negotiations down to grass roots level.'[16]

For Slabbert, the ANC document *A Strategic Perspective* is the most compelling evidence that the movement has fully committed itself to a negotiated transition – because it recognises that 'an approach that aims to secure a negotiated surrender from the regime will entail a protracted process with tremendous cost to the people and country'.[17] Its stress on a government of national unity because all parties need to commit themselves to maintaining stability during the transition marked a watershed, he believes, because it meant that the ANC was 'beginning to address the problem of sharing responsibility for stability during the transition, and without consensus on stability, there will not be a transition. You can look at any transition – that's the turning point.'[18] Further evidence was its concern to meet its opponents on the future of the civil service and on regional government. Netshitenze confirms this: 'Having taken stock after Codesa, the ANC realised that it was necessary to specifically address the issues of the civil service and the future of regions, even separately from discussions on constitutional issues.'[19]

As for the NP, despite its attempt in early September[20] to warn the ANC that it could negotiate without it if necessary, the turmoil had shown again that its major opponent was indeed indispensable if international approval was to be retained and social order preserved. In late November De Klerk announced a timetable for negotiations: bilateral talks to be completed by February 1993; multilateral negotiations to be reconvened by the end of March; agreement on a transitional constitution by May; legislation establishing a transitional executive council and electoral commission to be passed by June; and elections in March or April 1994. Whether or not the schedule was met (and this then seemed unlikely), the government's willingness to set dates to the transition gave it a sense of purpose, almost inevitability, which was lacking until then.

All this suggested that the nightmare which followed the breakdown of Codesa instilled a sense of humility, sobriety and realism in both government and ANC leaders, and impressed upon them the dangers of delaying a settlement.

But what of other parties? The IFP and its allies seemed not to have reconciled themselves to settling for second best. Some seemed not even to have settled for what was conceivable – Bophuthatswana still waxed enthusiastic about independence, and the CP continued to devise ever new boundaries for a whites-only state. Not only did the IFP begin to imply that its participation in negotiations was not guaranteed, but it too began to play the mass action card, organising marches to defy the Record of Understanding. The PAC seemed unaware of the new mood of realism. The NP–ANC *rapprochement* coincided with attacks by its Azanian People's Liberation Army on white civilians, which prompted marches by the white right: in early January two break-ins, one at a weapons store in Welkom and the other at an SADF armoury near Kimberley, pointed to growing right-wing militancy.[21]

Despite these disturbing signs, analysts detect a convergence among these parties as well. The evidence was that, except for the fringes on both sides, all parties were, amid the inevitable bluster, beginning to drag themselves reluctantly towards the centre. The IFP, drawn partially into the charmed circle by its own series of bilaterals with the 'big two', rejoined negotiations, despite its threat to stay out until MK was disbanded. So did the CP, albeit reluctantly. Five of its MPs, sensing that the traditional right-wing agenda was a cul de sac, left the party to form the Afrikaner Volksunie (AVU) which began to advocate non-racial federalism (albeit with one Afrikaner region) rather than racial partition. The

PAC too joined the talks: and, despite its continued public refusal to dis-avow Apla actions,[22] the attacks tailed off – for a while.

The mobilisation by most of those outside the ANC–NP bilaterals seemed therefore to be last reluctant reflex kicks against a reality they knew to be inevitable. The leaders of the two 'major' parties' negotiating teams had indeed seemed to create a new momentum which left other parties with little option but to join or face life on the peripheries, pursuing unattainable dreams.

To the altar this time?

In March 1993, as the most inclusive array of negotiation partners yet[23] prepared for a new multi-party attempt to negotiate a new order, it seemed likely that the two 'major' parties, chastened by the events of 1992, would indeed reach agreement on the shape of a new order. Most of their differences seemed to have been resolved in the bilateral talks of the past few months.

The reported parameters of the agreement, detailed in the previous section, appeared to be that a transitional constitution would be written by a multi-party conference while the existing parliament, stripped of the racial 'own affairs' departments, would govern alongside an expand-ed cabinet and a transitional executive council. They would prepare the way for the election of a constitution-making body and a transitional government which would rule for about five years, during which time a final constitution would be framed. The new government would com-prise all parties which gained an agreed portion of the vote.

This 'understanding' was more detailed than any of the 'agreements' reached since negotiation began. Most of the issues which divided the 'big two' at Codesa had been resolved by concessions on both sides. Their accord seemed to support the new conventional wisdom that the trauma of 1992, together with the resort to bilateral talks, had indeed moved the country to the threshold of the settlement which had eluded Codesa.

Yet the expectation that a settlement between the 'main' antagonists had been achieved, seemed premature. Firstly, senior government con-stitutional planner Gustav von Bratt noted in early March that two major areas remained unresolved.[24] The first was the manner in which the post-election interim government would be constituted. No agreement had been reached on the percentage of votes required for parties to join the cabinet. The government, which had presented itself persistently as the champion of minority rights, was reportedly pressing for a high per-centage which would exclude smaller parties. The ANC, the standard bearer of majority rule, wanted a low one which would include them; this was one difference between NP 'power sharing' (between two or three parties) and the ANC's preferred 'government of national unity' (inclusion of several parties).

The reason for this peculiar reversal of roles, it was claimed, was that the government, having secured the power sharing it wanted, preferred an arrangement between itself, the ANC and the IFP only; the ANC wanted to dilute NP and perhaps IFP influence by including other parties.[25] Even in the new mood of reconciliation the battle for position continued; tactics, not principle, was all. A related issue was the manner in which cabinet members would be chosen. The ANC wanted the majority party to choose them from lists submitted by other parties; the government preferred minority parties to appoint their own members.

The second unresolved issue was more substantial – the powers and functions of regions. The parties had reportedly agreed to leave these to a constitution-making body, a prospect which alarmed many in the NP,[26] let alone in the IFP, which insisted that this key issue had been left to a body likely to be dominated by the ANC. This claim seemed a little hasty: since decisions were to be taken by two-thirds majority, parties which wanted strong regions were likely to wield a veto. But the failure to settle so crucial an issue raised the spectre of new deadlocks when the parties tried to agree on a new regional system.

Equally importantly, some issues which the parties claimed were settled, seemed less than cut and dried. Publication of the NP/ANC 'understanding', together with a statement by a government representative insisting that the ANC had endorsed 'power sharing',[27] triggered dissent within the 'liberation' movement. This prompted an ANC national executive committee meeting which rejected 'power sharing' in favour of a 'government of national unity'. To some the difference seemed semantic, and the ANC's protestations an attempt to soothe ruffled activists. But to others, the difference seemed more deep-rooted. In an attempt to satisfy aggrieved 'militants', the ANC's NEC stressed that decisions in the cabinet would be taken by simple majority.[28] This was not 'power sharing', since minorities could be outvoted repeatedly. The NP, eager to retain the appearance of consensus, did not react aggressively; but again the prospect of future disagreement seemed real. The arrangement for a transitional executive also seemed open to damaging conflicts about 'interpretation'. It still did not seem to spell out how precisely parliament would govern alongside the executive, and did not take WG3's agreement much further.

More generally, the ANC's constituency problem, reflected in the partial rebellion against 'power sharing', was matched by deep misgivings within the NP about apparent compromises. That the parties (rather than some of their negotiators) had indeed resigned themselves to a power-sharing compromise was not at all assured.

These factors raised at least the possibility that final agreement might again elude NP and ANC negotiators; certainly, they suggested that the transition might not be as smooth as De Klerk's timetable assumed. But a new stalemate seemed unlikely, if only because the events of 1992 had shown 'bitter-enders' on both sides the likely consequence of a new deadlock – a fresh spiral of mounting violence, despair and economic decline.

Less clear was the commitment of those outside the bilaterals. The IFP, we have noted, was not necessarily convinced that it had no alternative to a compromise. While clearly a minority party, it does appeal to Zulu-speaking people with a strong traditional and ethnic identification – and a sense that they are deprived because of it. How many of them there are is a matter for debate, but that they are willing to act aggressively in support of their values is not. Another potentially important source of IFP power is the Zulu chieftaincy. Under the KwaZulu administration some chiefs have flourished; their control over land[29] and their links to Ulundi give them great power to reward supporters and punish opponents – they are directly threatened by changes to the current order.

The IFP's strength is also reinforced by conservative white interests in Natal who would much rather ally themselves with Buthelezi than face ANC 'domination' from the centre; exposés in 1991 suggest that the IFP might be able to rely on the support of sections of the white security establishment. It also commands the Kwa-Zulu police and civil service. This set of interlocking interests, if mobilised into active opposition, could in theory pose a grave threat to a transitional government which the IFP refused to join.

A full grasp of the IFP conundrum is not possible without an understanding of Buthelezi's personal political history. He was himself a member of the ANC and originally organised Inkatha with its support; the ANC had seen the movement as a source of anti-apartheid mobilisation at a time when virtually all opposition activity was suppressed. But the ANC's attitude towards Buthelezi hardened as it became clear that he saw himself as an independent actor, not necessarily bound by ANC policy and strategy. At the same time his refusal to accept 'independence' for KwaZulu or to negotiate on the government's terms during the 1980s ensured that he retained an often hostile distance from P W Botha's government.

Analyst and former politician Frederik Van Zyl Slabbert ... ANC has committed itself fully to a negotiated transition.

Buthelezi therefore found himself in a very awkward position: Slabbert notes that he was 'between the carpet and the floorboards, because Botha would not talk to him and after the ANC's 1985 Kabwe conference it began to target him, having adopted the peoples' war approach'.[30] Buthelezi has therefore developed deep suspicions of the other parties and is unlikely to relinquish his independence easily. An analyst suggests that his belligerent and imperious approach stems from the ANC's unwillingness to recognise his role in its unbanning, and his perception that De Klerk has abandoned the IFP in the face of ANC pressure.[31]

Thloloe strikes a similar note, arguing that Mandela missed an important opportunity after his release – had he then wooed Buthelezi, he suggests, the latter would not now be threatening to derail the transition.[32] Be that as it may, recent political history, both before and after 1990, has ensured that Buthelezi and his party are unlikely to entrust their future to either of the 'big two', still less to agreements reached between them.

For much of the transition, it seemed that the IFP was holding out for a prominent place in a unity government. But by March 1993 there were signs that its strategy had shifted: strategist Walter Felgate suggested that it planned to stay out of the transitional executive and enter the interim parliament as an opposition party.[33] Its goal would then narrow to winning a federal system, which would give Natal/KwaZulu enough power to counter or dilute the writ of central government. NP concessions to the ANC on this issue therefore ran the risk of alienating the IFP and ensuring that it waged war on, rather than joined, the transition. This was of course a danger which faced the ANC too, but, as we noted earlier, the stakes for the NP were higher since it also ran the risk of losing more supporters to the IFP.

We will return to this issue. At this point we need only note that there were signs that IFP participation in – or at least agreement to – transitional arrangements did seem possible as multi-party talks resumed. On the one hand, the ANC appeared to be shifting ground on the regional issue, opening the way for a compromise.[34] On the other, the apparent softening of the IFP position suggested that it was aware that the transition's failure could mean a debilitating dead end for it too. And if it was resigned to negotiating a compromise, it was difficult to see how its allies in the Bophuthatswana and Ciskei administrations could stage a 'last stand' on their own.

Finally, despite the real danger of resistance from both white right and black 'left', a settlement did not depend on the acquiescence of parties representing these positions. Codesa had proceeded on the assumption that a stable agreement could be achieved in the face of their opposition: as the PAC, CP and AVU moved closer to negotiations, the belief among other parties strengthened that they needed the process more than it needed them.

Glib promises of a smooth transition as the 'big two' marched purposefully to settlement, dragging the others in tow, seemed overstated as the parties prepared to resume multi-party negotiations in April 1993. Despite this, domestic turmoil and foreign influence still seemed likely to nudge them towards a settlement, sooner or later. But the problems noted here would not then disappear. Indeed, they might only begin.

HOLDING THE CENTRE

Three years into a difficult transition, in which fractious parties repeatedly promised a reconciled society while continuing to behave as if they saw negotiation as a new theatre for a decades-old war, it was difficult to see into a future in which the centre would indeed hold.

To dismiss the possibility of that future would be illogical, despite the seeming welter of evidence pointing away from it. Transitions are always uncertain and, in a divided society, the stakes are unusually high. The travails of the first three years could yet prove to be a temporary trauma which may quickly subside as the uncertain becomes set. A post-settlement government will be so different from anything we have known that it may be rash to predict its course. It is at least possible to imagine a multi-party government willing and able to curb the opponents of compromise, ensure order without eclipsing democracy, and steer the country to a common future.

But if this was possible, it was hardly certain – or perhaps even likely. And, since a settlement could well be greeted by yet another wave of euphoria (albeit more muted than that of 1990) it is as well to examine some of the pitfalls ahead.

A fretful forced marriage

If a settlement is achieved, the outcome will inevitably be a 'grand coalition' of the major parties. This, Schlemmer suggests, may either take the form of 'stressed power sharing', in which the parties continue to compete as they share power, or a 'co-operative alliance', in which they at least share responsibility for key issues such as stability and economic growth. 'It will probably start with the first, while parties are in a competitive mode for elections, and move towards the second, as the establishment orientations of a new elite begin to consolidate.'[35] But an arrangement which expects parties still deeply suspicious of each other, still representing constituencies whose divisions often seem deeper than those between their leaders, to take joint responsibility for order and efficient government faces obvious perils.

The first challenge will be posed by the nature of the coalition itself. If it 'turns out to be (or is seen to be) a thinly disguised victory for one side,' argues one analyst, 'then stability – and democracy – may be out of reach, no matter how vigorously the new administration commits itself to making the settlement work'.[36] In other words, if the arrangement is, or seems to the parties' constituencies to be, an ANC government adorned with a few faces from other parties or – which is more likely – a continuation of the old order with ANC participation, it may not endure.

Even if the coalition does balance the contending interests it is unlikely to be free of conflict, and this may damage its effectiveness. The temptation to blame coalition partners for the inevitably unpopular decisions which the transitional government will have to take, will severely test the leaders' commitment to their partners. If leaders cannot resist this temptation, 'the power-sharing arrangement could face stresses so acute that it will either collapse altogether or limp along while society fragments into warring factions'.[37] Heavy demands will be placed on the leadership abilities of its key figures if it is to avoid this.

The danger is heightened by the possibility that, whatever details are recorded in a settlement, the parties may hold very different expectations of the intended life span of a joint government. By early 1993, the NP seemed to have reconciled itself to five years of power sharing, followed by majority government. Perhaps. But, for an NP still deeply

suspicious of majority government, a five-year breathing space seems slim protection against the perils it fears ahead. Some NP strategists have indeed suggested that majority rule may be inevitable after a 'buffer period'.[38] But they have proposed 10 years, not five, as a minimum period, and they may be a minority within their party. While evidence is lacking now, it seems reasonable to suggest that the NP may nurse strong hopes of extending power sharing beyond its agreed life span.

This would obviously require the agreement of its partners, and it may be banking on making itself so indispensable during the first five years that it will persuade them that it and its constituency are as necessary to stability as they were when the arrangement began. Nor is it inconceivable that the ANC would accept this proposal when and if it is made (presumably towards the end of the 1990s). But that does not alter the reality that the parties may be entering a power-sharing arrangement with very different expectations: one of laying the ground for a five-year 'transfer of power', the other of cementing longer-term power sharing. The divide between them would be little different from that when Codesa began. If differing expectations crippled the first round of negotiation, it takes little imagination to suggest what they might do if imported into a government.

The SACP's Jeremy Cronin ... 'mass action brought grass roots into negotiations for the first time.'

A 'grand coalition' implies that the major parties accept joint responsibility for the stability of society. But even if the political leaders accept this, they may be unable to maintain the loyalties of their constituencies as they take decisions which run directly counter to the expectations of those they represent. Stability might be maintained only by an authoritarian style of government – or not at all. Since neither the NP nor the ANC are steeped in democratic tradition, there is a real danger of a reconciled governing elite becoming increasingly isolated from a discontented and fragmenting society.

The danger is heightened since the idea among ANC constituencies that 'mass action' is an essential ingredient of democracy may remain alive after a settlement. If the new government takes unpopular decisions, it could face fresh bouts of mobilisation from trade unions or civic associations once the likely 'honeymoon' period is over.

On entering a government of national unity, the ANC might lose much of the romantic appeal which it enjoyed as a 'liberation' movement. Were it ruling alone it might bring enough credibility to prevent deferred expectations from triggering mass mobilisation. But the NP's presence in the government might ensure that authority remains a target and that mobilisation will continue: action against mass activity is likely to be resented by people whose expectations of 'liberation' are not likely to coincide with the possible. For those who stand to gain directly by the ANC's accession to power, and for the majority who are tired of violence and long for a return to normality, a government able to maintain order will come as a relief. But there will be many activists for whom this will not be so, and they could find a willing audience among the unemployed and homeless.

In theory, the PAC is ideally situated to lead the dissent. There are some who believe that it already has more support than the IFP, but is badly organised: 'The PAC has more ideological support than organised support, especially among the youth.'[39] But its ability to take advantage of disaffection with a transitional government is questioned by analysts, including some who are sympathetic to the PAC.[40] They suggest that its lack of effective organisation – and, perhaps, a public perception that it is ineffective – will limit its potential, whatever a joint government does.

But there is still a prospect of a threatening challenge to a unity government. Some individuals in the ANC, such as Winnie Mandela and Harry Gwala, and branches such as Natal Midlands are clearly disenchanted with power sharing. The prospect of a reincarnated version of the UDF, bringing together a range of groups to the new government's left and mobilising against it in much the same way as the old UDF did against the NP government, cannot be excluded. The SACP's old programme of action – the two-phase revolution – does provide for an attempt to achieve 'socialist transformation' once a democracy is secured. Whether this is still its strategy in practice rather than theory is not clear. But there clearly is support within it for the idea that the fight for 'liberation' should not end once universal franchise is achieved.

Whether or not a power-sharing government faces an organised challenge of this sort, it is likely to be a fragile arrangement, with repeated tensions between the parties. It will also face threats from within the NP constituency which might pose more direct problems. A nervous security establishment and civil service, imbued with the ideology of anti-communism and still operating within the 'total onslaught' paradigm, contemplates a deeply embittering fall from its status as an elite within an elite: it could prove to be less than co-operative.

But some analysts believe that a joint government can endure and provide a centre of stability. Cronin argues: 'The ANC would prefer to govern alone, but in practise this is not possible. Sharing power will probably involve bickering over policy formulation and implementation, but it will have the advantages of continuity and expertise.'[41] Schlemmer goes further. He acknowledges that power sharing will be subject to great stress and that it would be unrealistic to predict harmony within the government. But the forces holding the society together, he argues, are greater than those tearing it apart; just as the parties have repeatedly pulled back from the brink when they have faced the prospect of a permanent break in negotiations, so will they draw in their horns when tensions between them threaten to collapse a power-sharing government.

Fear on the fringes

In this view, pressure from right and left there will obviously be, but it is likely that the new government will command enough legitimacy and power to deflect them. On the left, even a well-organised opposition alliance would lack the muscle to seriously challenge the new government. Unlike the ANC prior to a settlement, it would not enjoy the legitimacy bestowed by disenfranchisement or presumed majority internal support. It would certainly lack international backing, including that of neighbouring states. Survey evidence also suggests that, while such a movement may express the aspirations of many South Africans, it would be hampered by a widespread belief that its goals are simply not attainable; it is this perception which accounts for the low support for more militant parties in opinion polls.[42]

On the right, white response to a post-settlement government is probably one of the most unpredictable questions; there are no real precedents on which to base predictions. Other African countries had white minorities before independence, which chose to leave rather than resist. But none compared in size with South Africa's white population, nor would even substantial white emigration change this. Slabbert has pointed out that the largest example of 'white flight' in Africa occurred in Algeria, where 800 000 people left;[43] even if double that number left South Africa about 2,5 million whites would remain. Many whites are already adapting to change, albeit reluctantly. Would enough resist to offer militant white leaders a fertile recruiting ground?

The evidence suggests not. Repeated threats by the CP and its allies to mobilise against the prospect of majority government have come to nothing – there have been no general strikes or tax revolts, relatively few marches or demonstrations. Enthusiasm for a military 'struggle' will be even slighter. Despite superior white access to weaponry, fighting a majority government would probably be futile – after all, if force was an effective way of dealing with majority aspirations there would have been no negotiation process at all. Fighting a power-sharing government buttressed by part of the current SADF would be far more unrewarding. And more than four decades of privilege and relative prosperity have made most whites unlikely candidates for an enterprise which would entail great sacrifice for a distant goal. In addition, right-wing political leaders are well aware that, even if the internal balance of power allowed a return to white control, it would be unsustainable in the face of intense foreign pressure.

This may explain why the trend on the white right was, in early 1993, to move towards accommodation, an attempt to carve out the best deal possible within a non-racial framework. The AVU's strategy is perhaps the best example. But the CP's apparent attempt to build an alliance with the IFP based on a shared interest in regional powers illustrates the point too.

All this is not to dismiss entirely the possibility of white right-wing dissent or disruption. Damaging violence does not require large numbers of supporters, merely a few individuals with access to weapons. A post-settlement government may have to live with isolated acts of right-wing violence, whatever is done politically. (The same may be true to the left of the ANC alliance.) It is also trite to point out that large-scale white disaffection among those who cannot emigrate could ensure continuing tensions, together perhaps with countless petty or not-so-petty acts of disobedience. A transition which makes no attempt to soothe fears among those to the right of NP negotiators will raise the costs of maintaining stability and creating a climate for economic growth.

More importantly, the real threat from the right may not be militant resistance led by current right-wing parties, but disruption from white civil servants, soldiers and police. On the first score, official obstructionism, together with revelations suggesting that some officials are more concerned with emptying the public purse ahead of political change than with administering the state, has already damaged NP credibility and strategy during the transition; it may create even more difficulties for a joint government. The ANC is aware of the problem and has, as we have noted, attempted to soothe civil service fears. It is conceivable that the problem will abate as the future becomes certain. But tension may also be just beginning.

Even in a power-sharing regime, the ANC will face irresistible pressure to accommodate its supporters in the new bureaucracy. While the problem may be addressed partly by retaining the incumbents and allowing the public service to swell (perhaps the most implausible promises made by politicians during the transition are those endorsing a 'lean public service'), the ANC will not be able to stay in government long unless at least some senior posts are transferred to black newcomers. White resentment within the service seems inevitable and, while sensitive management might reduce the problem, it will hamper the state's functioning and create new dangers of more determined disruption from within.

Some of the same considerations apply in the security establishment, but here the stakes are, for obvious reasons, higher: disgruntled troops and police have far more scope than public servants to do something about their disaffection. One of the most glaring gaps in the transition has been the failure to address the future of the security forces systematically, or to include the military and police in discussions on their future. But, even if this gap is filled, disruption from some in uniform may be yet another unpleasant reality which will face a post-settlement government.

What *is* becoming clearer as the transition proceeds, is that the right-wing threat, even from disgruntled security personnel, will probably be eminently containable unless the right can forge an alliance with a significant black force. It has also become clear that the right has, accurately, realised that its most significant potential ally is the IFP: Cosag's formation signals this on the political front, while revelations of collusion between elements of the security establishment and Inkatha raise the spectre that disaffection in Ulundi could provide military dissidents with an ally. So no discussion of the possibilities and perils ahead would be complete without a brief assessment of the IFP's options.

Wounded lion or noisy pussycat?

Whether or not the IFP decides to participate in transitional arrangements, it will not become clear until well after a settlement whether it is to be an ally of stability or a threat to it.

If it stays out it could seek to mobilise against the new arrangement. But even if it agrees to participate, prospects for a smoother transition might improve only marginally. IFP hostility to the ANC and deep suspicion of collusion between it and the NP may abate if and when it joins them in government, but this is hardly certain. It is possible to imagine a government in which the tensions of mid-1992 simply play themselves out within a national administration which is meant to be pulling the country out of its trough.

Clearly, these dangers would abate if the IFP's terms are met – but it is not at all clear what those terms are. As noted above, a prominent role at the centre has dropped down – or off – its list of priorities, to be replaced by strong regional government. But how strong? The IFP's public position, and private comments by some of its leaders, suggest that it will demand an arrangement which allows the central government to exercise only those powers which the regions grant it. If this is indeed its non-negotiable position, it is hard to see the other parties accommodating it: the ANC would not concede so radical a form of devolution, while even the NP would be hesitant. But if the IFP is merely holding out for a compromise on regional powers this should, as we have suggested, be possible.

The answer depends largely on how strong the IFP really is: if it does have alternatives to a compromise, it might well be prepared to pursue them. Here, opinions among analysts differ. One view warns that the IFP cannot simply be boiled down to an extension of Buthelezi's personality. Inkatha is buttressed, its advocates say, by the powerful array of forces mentioned above: tribal chiefs with immense power over their subjects, a significant body of traditionalist supporters, important white allies, and a police force. It also suggests that, while the secession proposal was a strategic manoeuvre by Buthelezi to back up his negotiating position, it remains a last resort which would have important support among elements of the Natal establishment.[44]

The contrary view suggests that the IFP's battalions are greatly overstated. The chiefs, it argues, hold sway over their subjects largely through patronage; their 'power' stems purely from their relationship with Ulundi. Analyst Paul Zulu argues that, were the IFP deprived of the wherewithal to buttress their patronage, it would be left with little intrinsic allegiance, since the chiefs would have nothing with which to reward supporters or punish opponents.[45] The army of traditionalist supporters is far smaller than it seems – hence the IFP's poor showing in the polls – and is also largely maintained by a steady supply of arms from potentates who would no longer wield power in a new order. The white allies may find the IFP a more palatable alternative than the ANC, but are unlikely to fight in a trench for its survival. Secession, in this view, is no option at all – it has been firmly rejected by Natal business, the province's NP leaders are not united in enthusiasm for it, and it would attract unremitting international hostility. It would be economically unviable, politically and militarily unsustainable.

The answer may lie somewhere in between. The IFP and its sympathisers have almost certainly overstated its power and disruptive potential: its 'exit option' would be extraordinarily costly and would hold out highly uncertain gains. Like the other parties, it may well be aware of this. On the other hand, the risks to the 'major' parties of pressing ahead without it are real since, stripped of alternatives, it may believe that it has little choice but to disrupt. While this would probably prove futile, that would not make it any less costly. And if the settlement does become a cartel-like arrangement between the NP and ANC alone, the IFP may find some unlikely allies on the left – the PAC, for example – if it resists. More immediately, the question of how much power the IFP has to disrupt the transition may remain moot since, for more pressing reasons, the NP may need to accommodate it; it is of course well aware of the IFP's poll gains among whites.[46] For this party, the IFP may be less a threat to the public order than to the coherence of the NP constituency. Analyst Oscar Dhlomo notes tensions within the Natal NP between those who might be willing to ignore Inkatha and those who 'feel that it is strategically dangerous to sideline the IFP'.[47] It is now common knowledge that these divisions run through the NP from the grass roots to the

Analyst and former politician Oscar Dhlomo ... 'Buthelezi cannot ignore the will of the people'.

cabinet. The more the NP appears to ignore the IFP and its concerns, the more it risks losing MPs, voters, and perhaps even ministers to the Natal-based party.

The key challenge to the 'major parties' may be to find a formula which accommodates the IFP but does not overstate its power. A form of regional government with which the ANC can live may offer that remedy. But it is worth noting that the problem would not even then disappear. We noted earlier that the assumption on which IFP strategy rests – that it would win a regional election in Natal – is hardly secure. Indeed, most analysts suggest that it is likely to lose.

Some argue that the IFP could then become South Africa's Unita. Buthelezi, they say, has so convinced himself that the IFP will win that a defeat would appear to be the product of fraud.[48] This claim may find sympathetic ears among right-wing parties, not only in Natal. (The same might be said of the western Transvaal, where Bophuthatswana is seeking an alliance with right-wing parties. But here resources to resist would be far scantier). Others insist this would not be a realistic option. Dhlomo argues that Buthelezi has committed himself to democracy over too long a period to ignore the 'will of the people', even if it expresses itself against him. 'If the IFP lost,' he argues, 'it could be hoist by its own democratic assertions.'[49]

In this situation, IFP options would be even further constricted by international hostility, probably supplemented by white distaste for a continuing war against a free election result. The seeds of war are well sown in Natal; there may well be some in the IFP and the security establishment (as well as among their opponents) who hope to see them bear further fruit. But on balance it does seem as if the IFP is not an intractable barrier to transition. If it does overplay its hand – by holding out for an 'unreasonable' degree of regional power, or by rejecting the outcome of a regional election – the other parties might find it easier to contain it than some analysts imagine. But if no serious attempt is made to ensure a role for minority parties or to address regional concerns, the prospect of an IFP-led challenge from the right will be very real.

THE LONG TRANSITION

South Africa's potential for instability during the transition rests on two fundamental factors: the complexity of the society itself, and the disorientation caused by the sudden change of all the rules of the political game. The first ensures that there are a host of interests, on both sides of the racial divide, which will be directly affected by the compromises which the parties make; but because the ANC may not control trade unionists, former guerrillas or activist youths, and the NP may not control business people, civil servants and soldiers or police, these interests will not automatically endorse compromises because the parties wish them to do so. On the second score, sudden change has scattered established political identities like sand in a whirlwind.

The memberships of all parties and movements find themselves subject to 'cyclonic' political forces: those once on the 'extremes' of their parties are being driven towards the peripheries of the newly forming political spectrum, while those 'moderates' in the centre of their parties are being drawn towards the gradually forming core of the new political establishment.

Change of this order cannot be expected without disturbance, and the country's troubled search for a settlement since February 1990 illustrates

IFP members demonstrate outside the National Peace Convention, 14 September 1991 ... no intractable barrier to transition.

this. As the parties seemed to edge towards a settlement in early 1993, it was becoming clear that the turbulence would not end when the agreement was signed. It was certain to be fragile, and buffeted by constant winds long after the ink had dried.

But despite the real dangers the threat of insurrection or civil war seems small. South Africa is not a Yugoslavia, in which ethnic groups clustered together in virtually self-contained and autonomous collectives were 'united' by the illusion of nationhood. South Africa's divide, Schlemmer suggests, is not about people's identities, but about how much power and what share of the wealth competing groups are to have in a common political system and economy; differences of this sort, unlike those in which identity is at stake, can be addressed by 'trade-offs' rather than endless conflict.[50] While racial distrust may run deep, the society is underpinned by an almost assumed sense of interdependence: blacks and whites share a common economy, are doomed to live with each other, and – most important – they know it. This is confirmed not only by observation but by opinion surveys showing for example that even most ANC supporters believe power sharing to be necessary,[51] and that many CP supporters believe that their party's policies are unworkable.[52] Many on both sides may well prefer a future without the other. But the vast majority know they cannot have it.

If that is a possible guarantee that the society will cohere, it is no assurance that it will soon become a stable democracy. American political scientist Dankwart Rustow has argued that democracies are usually born out of deep conflict between warring parties who accept it as a 'second best'.[53] This seems reassuring to South Africans, an indication that our divides are not as formidable an obstacle as they seem. But he adds a less comforting note: conflict, he suggests, can produce democracy only if the society has a 'sense of community' so deep that it is unstated, so much is it taken for granted. The sense of interdependence which South Africans share falls far short of this 'sense of community'. In societies which meet Rustow's criterion the parties, by accepting second best, may ensure first prize for their compatriots. Here, the society itself may have to accept second best too.

A unity government will take office amid severe conflict and economic stagnation. It will comprise parties who are still unsure whether they are enemies, opponents or partners, and many of whose constituents are still convinced that they are enemies. Like all interim governments its first task will be to ensure stability against challenges from right and left, some of which may emerge from its parties' own ranks; if it fails to act decisively to hold the centre together against these threats, it could collapse.[54]

That it will seek to do this democratically may be the best guarantee of long-term stability, but may be also too much to expect from parties – and a society – to which democracy is hardly second nature.

By early 1993 there were already whispers that the 'major parties' had agreed that their first priority was to impose order, in order to create a framework for investment; it seemed unlikely that they meant to do so entirely within democratic rules. By then, not even a first election was assured. The parties to the transitional executive could conclude that violence made a poll too risky and that order should be imposed before the people were allowed to decide. Given the risks in *that* strategy, the people might wait a long time. This outcome remained unlikely, if only for fear of foreign reaction. But, if a first election was not a foregone conclusion, a second one was far less assured.

Nevertheless, this did not mean that an authoritarian cartel was inevitable. It would not only face hostility from abroad: to impose such an option, the parties would need a high degree of coherence and sense of common purpose. In addition, they would have to be backed by strong organised interests, and the 'extremes' against which they acted would have to be relatively weak. Since the government itself seemed likely to be weak and the challenges to it strong, it seemed unlikely to try to imprint its divided will on society by force alone.

The likeliest outcome then was that the transition would continue well after a settlement. A partial democracy and partial stability seemed most plausible; while some who challenged the centre would be met by force, others would remain free to operate if only because there was little hope of suppressing them.

Within the centre itself many issues remained unresolved, and it seemed likely that the attempt to settle them would continue into the unity government. That there would be costs for efficiency seemed obvious. But the lack of alternatives made it likely that the parties would continue the transition rather than slide into the abyss. Negotiation as well as positioning for power would continue into the new era as the parties to the unity government continued to jockey and confront each other to win new victories, suffer new defeats, and make new compromises. Neither a balance of power nor a sense of common purpose needed to sustain a 'full' democracy seemed likely during the first years of the new arrangement. But this did not have to mean that they would never be created, simply that the task would be incomplete – and would continue.

In sum, if the 'transition' which 'began' on 2 February 1990 really began a long while before then, it will not end for a long while after the negotiation process has seemingly ended. If South Africa is unlikely to become another Lebanon or Yugoslavia, its journey to a consolidated democracy is at most halfway. The test will not be whether democracy and stability are achieved soon, but whether continued progress will be made towards them. If that is no cause for elation, neither is it one for despair.

Notes and references

PART 1: The road to Codesa

The reluctant reconcilers

1. See for example Friedman, Steven, 'The National Party and the South African Transition', in Lee, Robin and Schlemmer, Lawrence (eds), *Transition to Democracy*, Oxford University Press, Cape Town, 1991.
2. For these and other ANC statements on 'people's war' see Lodge, Tom, 'People's War or Negotiations? African National Congress Strategies in the 1980s', in Moss, Glenn and Obery, Ingrid (eds), *South African Review 5*, Ravan, Johannesburg, 1989.
3. For an extremely sympathetic account of De Klerk, see De Klerk, Willem, *F W de Klerk, The Man in his Time*, Jonathan Ball, Johannesburg, 1991.
4. See Lodge, Tom, *Black Politics in South Africa since 1945*, Ravan, Johannesburg, 1983.
5. For a fuller analysis see Friedman, Steven, *Options for the Future*, SA Institute of Race Relations, Johannesburg, 1990.
6. See Friedman, Steven and Narsoo, Monty, *New Mood In Moscow*, SA Institute of Race Relations, 1989.
7. 'Statement of the National Executive Committee of the African National Congress on the Question of Negotiations', Lusaka, 9/10/1987.
8. Mashabela, Harry, *Fragile Figures*, SA Institute of Race Relations, 1989.
9. For details see De Klerk, Willem, op cit.
10. The Harare Declaration, drafted by the ANC and endorsed by the OAU, had insisted that an appropriate climate be created before negotiations could begin. Among its conditions were the release of political prisoners and the end of emergency rule. These measures were needed, it said, to 'produce the conditions in which free discussions can take place'. See *Declaration of the OAU Ad Hoc Committee on Southern Africa on the Question of South Africa*, Harare, 21/8/89. The government countered with demands that guerrilla activity cease, and the two sets of conditions set the agenda for the early meetings.
11. According to police figures there were 17 088 'unrest incidents' in 1990; 12 more than in 1985. *Business Day*, 7/2/1991.
12. Rantete, Johannes, *Room for Compromise: The ANC and Transitional Mechanisms*, Centre for Policy Studies Transition Series, 1992.
13. *The Daily Mail*, 9/4/90.
14. Rantete, Johannes, *Liberation and Negotiation: The Pan Africanist Congress in the South African Transition*, Centre for Policy Studies Transition Series, Johannesburg, 1992.
15. PAC leaders arrived at a conference in Cape Town at which they planned to seek the mandate, to find delegates brandishing posters denouncing participation. So tangible was the opposition that they abandoned the attempt to seek a mandate and denounced the all-party meeting instead. See Rantete, ibid.

PART 2: Anatomy of a convention

From breakthrough to breakdown

1. The father of the head of the KwaNdebele administration, Prince James Mahlangu, for example, claimed royal status.
2. Dikwankwetla of QwaQwa, Intando ye Sizwe of KwaNdebele, Inyandza National Movement of KaNgwane, United People's Front of Lebowa, and the Ximoko Progressive Party of Gazankulu.
3. The Labour Party (House of Representatives), and Solidarity and the National People's Party (House of Delegates).
4. The Declaration committed participants 'to bringing about an undivided South Africa with one nation sharing a common citizenship, patriotism and loyalty ... amidst our diversity ...'
5. The stated NP position was that power sharing should be a permanent state. Some of its strategists did concede, however, that this was untenable; they foresaw instead a lengthy transition period of 10 years or more in which power would be shared. See Friedman, Steven, *The Shapers of Things To Come: National Party Choices in the South African Transition*, Centre for Policy Studies, 1992.
6. At a Federal Congress in September 1991 the NP adopted a complex plan which provided, among other elements, for joint rule by the three or five parties which received the largest share of the vote. See National Party, *Deelnemende Demokrasie in 'n Regstaat*, 1991.
7. ANC *Negotiations Bulletin*, no 6, 16/1/1992.

WORKING GROUP 1

Hard labour, scant reward

1. *Declaration of the OAU Ad Hoc Committee on Southern Africa On the Question of South Africa*. For details, see 'The reluctant reconcilers', note 10.
2. Act no 3 of 1953. Section 3 empowers the state president to declare a state of emergency; Section 5A, introduced in 1986, empowers the minister of Law and Order to declare 'unrest areas' in which the police may enjoy increased powers. The latter section has been used on several occasions since February 1990.
3. This agreement, reached after a summit between state president F W de Klerk and ANC leader Nelson Mandela, contained a paragraph allowing UN monitors to witness progress in securing hostels 'in co-operation with the Goldstone Commission and the national peace secretariat'. See text of Record of Understanding in *SA Barometer*, vol 6 no 20, 9 October 1992.
4. Transkei, Bophuthatswana, Ciskei and Venda, all of whose administrations had accepted statutory 'independence' and whose formal reincorporation into South Africa, demanded by the ANC and other anti-apartheid parties, was the focus of WG4.
5. A joint ANC/SAG working group established by the Groote Schuur Minute of 4 May 4 1990 and the Pretoria Minute of 6 August 1990 purportedly reached agreement on guidelines for the release of people who committed political offences before 8 October 1990. However, differences of interpretation between the two have never been fully resolved. The ANC effectively defines as a political offence any act carried out with a political motive. The government's interpretation is far narrower, although not consistent.

For example, it had refused to release Robert McBride who had planted a bomb outside a Durban beach front bar, killing three white people, on the grounds that his actions had led to the deaths of innocent people. But other prisoners convicted of murder had been released earlier, leading to accusations that the government was concerned with the race of the victims rather than the nature of the offence. The Record of Understanding, op cit, would later rather refer to them as 'prisoners … who according to the ANC fall within the guidelines defining political offences, but according to the government do not'.

6. Again, this issue was the subject of agreements which, at least in public, were subject to disputed interpretations. The published report of the working group established to consider this issue by the Pretoria Minute, released in early 1991, simply noted agreement that 'it was vital that control be exercised' over MK arms and 'cadres' within the country.

7. 'Terms of Reference for Working Group One: Position Statement by Bophuthatswana', undated.

8. The Bophuthatswana government did, however, request that its media be given better access to South African markets.

9. In the face of mounting by-election losses to right-wing parties, F W de Klerk called a referendum of white voters on 17 March in which he requested a mandate to continue the negotiation process. He received it – from 68,7 per cent of those who voted.

10. *The Star*, 17/3/1992.

11. In WG2's discussions, the NP explicitly insisted that the referendum had merely given it a mandate to negotiate its constitutional principles.

12. Minutes of the meeting of WG1, SG1, 11/2/1992.

13. Draft minutes of WG1, Addendum E, 6/2/1992.

14. Professor Karl Norgaard is a Danish jurist appointed at the time of the Namibian independence process to determine which Namibian prisoners were eligible for amnesty as political offenders. Norgaard drew on international extradition law – most extradition treaties exclude people charged with political offences – to frame his principles.

15. See note 5. McBride's sentence had then been commuted to life imprisonment; he was released after the Record of Understanding.

16. Draft minutes of WG1, Addendum E, 6/2/1992.

17. The act allowed the government to indemnify in secret any perpetrator of a politically motivated crime: its clear purpose was to provide indemnity for security force members who might have been guilty of irregularities. It was rejected by the House of Delegates, and the state president then instructed the President's Council, in which the NP has a majority, to break the deadlock, a measure which was integral to the tricameral system but had not been used since the administration of P W Botha. The government, accused repeatedly of 'indemnifying itself', insisted that it was merely implementing agreements made with the ANC.

18. Besides allocating voting rights – and power in central government – on racial criteria, the Act also established the 'own affairs' system which created racial departments of education, health and the like, which were still providing racially separate services at the time Codesa was in session.

19. Law Reform Project, 'Declaration of Intent – Draft Legislation Proposals', undated.

20. Minutes of the seventh meeting of WG1, SG1, Addendum D, 21/4/92.

21. Minutes of the eighth meeting of WG1, SG1, Addendum C, 27/4/92.

22. Minutes of meeting of WG1, SG2, Addendum C, 24/3/1992.

23. Minutes of meeting of WG1, SG3, 17/2/1992.

24. A commission appointed by the government to investigate the future of broadcasting, which had reported in September 1991. It was chaired by Christo Viljoen, chairman of the SABC board.
25. Working documents for Codesa 2, vol 1.

End of innocence

1. WG2's final session was tape-recorded; Delport, Ramaphosa and Ngubane's remarks are taken from that tape.
2. See Rantete, Johannes, *The African National Congress and Transitional Mechanisms*, Centre for Policy Studies Transition Series, 1992; Friedman, Steven, 'The National Party and the South African Transition', in Lee, Robin and Schlemmer, Lawrence (eds), *Transition to Democracy*, Oxford University Press, Cape Town, 1991.
3. The *Negotiations Bulletin* was circulated to all ANC branches and was marked 'confidential'. While it was clearly an internal document it is, of course, debatable whether a document circulated to branches throughout the country and meant for discussion within them can remain confidential in practice rather than intention.
4. ANC *Negotiations Bulletin*, no 6, 16/1/1992.
5. See note 10, 'The reluctant reconcilers'.
6. Welsh, David, 'Turning Point', *Towards Democracy*, Institute for Multi-Party Democracy, vol 1 no 1, 1992.
7. Welsh, *Towards Democracy*, op cit.
8. African National Congress, *What is meant by the term 'General Principles'?* Johannesburg, undated.
9. The two-thirds stipulation weakened the government's claim that the constituent assembly was to be a vehicle for 'simple majoritarianism'. But it represented no shift in position for the ANC; it had never taken a view on majorities required at the assembly, and support among ANC strategists for a special majority, influenced partly by the adoption of a two-thirds provision in the Namibian Assembly, had been evident before Codesa was convened. See Rantete, op cit.
10. Western Cape and possibly Natal. See Humphries, Richard and Shubane, Khehla, *A Delicate Balance: Reconstructing South African Regionalism*, Centre for Policy Studies, Johannesburg, 1992.
11. If 'homeland' support for regionalism was based on the expectation that non-racial regions would 'deliver' majorities for incumbent homeland leaders and their allies, their expectations were likely to be dashed in every region except perhaps Natal/KwaZulu. See Humphries and Shubane, ibid.
12. The wording of the principles is contained in the minutes of the WG2 meeting of 2 March 1992, point 4.4, page 3.
13. SAG submission recorded in ibid. 'Since a function cannot be performed without the necessary financial capability, fiscal competency must accompany the allocation of powers to the highest practicable degree.'
14. Ibid. The minutes record: 'The working group also noted the ANC's statement that the following concepts are neither implied nor rejected by clause 3 of the document: a) concurrent powers, b) overriding powers, c) the creation of metropolitan governments with a special status.'
15. This is a system similar to the present one: the regions might have education powers and functions, for example, but central government would still set the general policy which lower levels would implement.
16. National Party, *Deelnemende Demokrasie in 'n Regstaat*. As noted earlier,

it insisted that power be shared among the three or five parties which won the largest share of the votes; a collegiate presidency would be shared by these parties.

17. National Party, 'The Meaningful Participation of Political Minorities', submission to WG4, 25/2/1992.

18. African National Congress, *The Constitution, Minorities and the New South Africa,* Johannesburg, undated.

19. This term refers to the organisation of voluntary associations independently of the state. In the ANC view, minorities who do not win a direct say in government can still pursue their interests by forming independent associations partly beyond the control of that government.

20. ANC *Negotiations Bulletin,* no 7, 12/3/1992.

21. 'Statements by the Government on Proposed Transitional Arrangements', submission to WG2.

22. SA government, 'Proposals for Transitional Arrangements', submission to WG2 and WG3.

23. African National Congress, 'Body and Procedures for Drafting a New Constitution', submission to WG2, 30/3/1992.

24. Inkatha Freedom Party, 'Proposals of the IFP on the body and procedures for drafting a new constitution', submission to WG2, 30/3/1992.

25. Human Rights Commission, *Checkmate for Apartheid: Special Report on Two Years of Destabilisation, July 1990 to June 1992.*

26. Cronin, Jeremy, 'Codesa – What is De Klerk up to?', *Work In Progress,* 7/1992, pp 7 – 9.

27. This was fuelled by a display of bellicosity by Buthelezi at the signing of the National Peace Accord – which seems to have disturbed some NP decision-makers. Together with the demand that the king be seated at Codesa, this created the impression that the IFP had its own agenda which might not coincide with that of the NP.

28. 'Proposal by the SAG on Para 3.2 of the Draft Document', proposal to Codesa 2. A draft submission to Codesa 2 detailing agreements reached in WG2 but not making a choice on percentages was in fact drafted.

29. Despite subsequent NP claims that it could reasonably expect to win a majority in a non-racial election, interviews with NP leaders shortly before Codesa convened, revealed that none expected the party to win this ballot. See Friedman, Steven, *National Party Choices in the South African Transition,* Centre for Policy Studies, Johannesburg, 1992.

30. In the same set of interviews, a senior NP MP had foreshadowed the dispute by offering a different rationale for the special majority the party was later to propose: the NP, he argued, would have to accept that a party which only won say 20 per cent of the vote could not credibly demand a relatively long share of power. See Friedman, ibid. But evidence that the NP expected to win more than 25 per cent but less than 34 per cent came shortly after Codesa 2's collapse: an NP estimate of likely support among the various races conveyed to a member of the CPS research team revealed that it hoped to win around 30 per cent. A senior government source later confirmed that 30 per cent was the estimate which guided NP strategy.

31. Welsh, *Towards Democracy,* op cit. The suggestion that this proposal was partly 'at the behest' of homelands is consistent with the NP claim that it was responding to requests from these parties.

32. Statement by the ANC's Department of Information and Publicity, 13/5/1992.

33. Naas Steenkamp of Gencor, quoted by Finance minister and former Gencor chief executive Derek Keys, *The Star,* 4/2/93.

34. Former NIS chief Neil Barnard became the department's director general; he brought Maritz Spaarwater with him. Barnard was appointed by Viljoen; inevitably, he was retained by Meyer.

WORKING GROUP 3
Phoney peace in a phoney war

1. Minutes of the 10th meeting of WG3 held on Monday 27 and 28 April, 1992.
2. Interview, Ken Andrew, 17 November, 1992.
3. Its members drawn from WG3 were Andrew, Arthur Chaskalson (ANC), Maduna, Thabo Mbeki (ANC), Roelf Meyer, Velaphi Ndlovu (IFP), Fanie van der Merwe (SAG). Co-opted experts were: Halton Cheadle (ANC), Andries Cilliers (Ciskei), Francois Junod (Ximoko) and Dawid van Wyk (IFP). Minutes of WG3 steering committee meeting held on 6 April, 1992.
4. Interview, Dawid van Wyk, 12 February, 1993.
5. 'Shakeout', in *Towards Democracy*, Institute for Multi-Party Democracy, vol 1 no 1, 1992, p 14.
6. Interview, Jeremy Cronin, 13 November 1992.
7. Interview, Dawid van Wyk, 12 February 1993.
8. South African Government, 'Submission to Working Group 3', 23/3/1992. The government's second submission was dated 6/4/1992.
9. Interview, Jeremy Cronin, 13 November 1992.
10. ANC, 'Submission to Working Group 3', 30/3/1992.
11. For further details, see Rantete, op cit.
12. Telephone interview, Fanie van der Merwe, 9 February 1993.
13. 'Report of Working Group 3 to Codesa 2', May 1992, p 2.
14. 'Rapporteurs' Report on Interim Arrangements', tabled at the fourth meeting of WG3.
15. Interview, Joel Netshitenze (Peter Mayibuye), 15 December 1992.
16. 'Report of Working Group 3 to Codesa 2', May 1992, p 2, our emphasis.
17. 'Rapporteurs' Report on Interim Arrangements', tabled at the fourth meeting of WG3.
18. NPP, 'Submission to Working Group 3', 12/2/1992.
19. IFP, 'Submission to Working Group 3', 6/2/1992.
20. Telephone interview, Walter Felgate, 27 November 1992.
21. Interview, Ken Andrew, 17 November 1992.
22. Telephone interview, Walter Felgate, 27 November 1992.
23. Interview, Joel Netshitenze (Peter Mayibuye), 15 December 1992.
24. Interview, Ken Andrew, 17 November 1992.
25. On 31 January 1992, shortly after the start of Codesa, Jac Rabie, NP leader in the House of Representatives, introduced a motion of no confidence in the LP Ministers' Council. Six independents and one member of the Freedom Party voted with the 37 NP members in the House of Representatives to win the no confidence vote by 44 votes to 40.
26. Interview, Desmond Lockey, 18 November 1992.
27. Interview, Jeremy Cronin, 13 November 1992.
28. Interview, Ken Andrew, 17 November 1992.
29. Interview, Ken Andrew, 17 November 1992.
30. Eglin, Colin, 'Shakeout', in *Towards Democracy*, vol 1 no 1, 1992, p 13.
31. Interview, Ken Andrew, 17 November 1992.

WORKING GROUP 4

Rescrambling the egg

1. P W Botha speech to Orange Free State National Party Congress. See SA Institute of Race Relations, *Race Relations Survey 1985*, Johannesburg, 1986, p 29.
2. 'Citizenship' of TBVC territories was automatically conferred on any member of the 'ethnic group' for which the 'homeland' concerned had been created regardless of residence: people deemed to be Xhosa, Venda or Tswana were therefore TBVC 'citizens' even if they had been born and had lived their entire lives outside the territory. Only Bophuthatswana softened this by allowing individuals to renounce their citizenship and apply for South African citizenship. But this applied only if it was specifically requested, and there was no guarantee that South African citizenship would be granted. In 1986 the Restoration of South African Citizenship Act allowed all individual TBVC 'citizens' to renounce their 'citizenship' and claim that of South Africa. Anti-apartheid groups insisted that citizenship should be restored *en bloc* to all TBVC people.
3. The Congress of Traditional Leaders of South Africa – see 'The reluctant reconcilers'.
4. The Secretariat of the Economic Community of Southern African States. Founded by Pretoria and the TBVC administrations, it is charged with organising multilateral discussions between them on socio-economic and development issues.
5. Many participants believed that DP delegate Kobus Jordaan initiated the Secosaf proposal. He had links to the organisation through a family member, and insisted that its officials had the experience and sensitivity to act as rapporteurs.
6. National Party, 'National Party's Standpoint: Submission to SC3', 24/2/1992.
7. National Party, 'Submission to WG4, SC3', 23/3/1992.
8. African National Congress, 'Submission to SC3', 17/2/1992.
9. South African Communist Party, 'Submission to SC3', 23/3/1992.
10. African National Congress, 'Submission to SC3', 23/3/1992.
11. Democratic Party, 'Submission to SC3', 17/2/1992.
12. Democratic Party, 'Submission to SC3', 23/3/1992.
13. Bophuthatswana government, 'Submission to SC3', undated.
14. Senior officials responsible for strategy formulation in the Bophuthatswana government had, apparently, for some time been urging its leadership to 'keep (its) options open' on reincorporation. This advice dated from a particularly hostile speech by president Mangope in 1990 when, in Ian Smith-like fashion, he declared that his government would survive for a long time to come.
15. Ciskei government, 'Submission to SC3', undated.
16. Venda government, 'Submission to SC3', undated.
17. Transkei government, 'Submission to WC3', undated.
18. See Humphries, Richard and Shubane, Khehla, *A Delicate Balance: reconstructing regionalism in South Africa*, Centre for Policy Studies Transition Series, Johannesburg, 1992.
19. Ibid. An IFP analyst, Joe Matthews, claimed also that the ANC's initial proposal for a Kei region 'managed to ensure that the age-old dream of the Xhosas, to unite all Xhosa traditional lands between the Fish River and the Umzimkulu River, will be realised'. See Matthews, Joe, 'Inside Story', in *Towards Democracy*, vol 1 no 2, 1992. To be reprinted as 'Federalism in an African Context' in *Federalism and its Foes*, Centre for Policy Studies (forthcoming).

20. African National Congress, 'Submission to WG4', 6/2/1992.
21. SA government, 'Submission to WG4', 6/2/1992.
22. Bophuthatswana government, 'Submission to WG4', 6/2/1992.
23. Ibid. Appended to this submission was a lengthy 'historical perspective' on the origins of Bophuthatswana, intended to vindicate its claim to be a credible, independent state. Having traced the founding of the Crown Colony of British Bechuanaland in 1885, and detailed the 'betrayal' of the Botswana people by Britain in 1895 and at Union in 1910, the account described Bophuthatswana's independence in 1977 as 'a golden opportunity to regain the independence given away by the British Government in 1895'. Thus it cast itself in the same mould as Swaziland and Lesotho, and coupled this to a significant land claim – the outstanding remainder of the former British Protectorate, now part of the Cape Province.

   In trying to assert Bophuthatswana as an historically legitimate entity, this narrative focused on the area south of the Molopo River – the largest part of the territory. But nowhere did the document refer to any of the other parts of the territory dotted around the Transvaal and Orange Free State. This silence, apart from compromising its broader claims, raises questions about its contingency plans for the future. Was it seeking to consolidate its advantage in the western Transvaal, with the old Protectorate forming the core? Was it preparing to relinquish its claim to the other portions of the territory to achieve this – even though most of its 'citizens' live outside the former Protectorate? As a territory dispersed in seven disparate portions within the boundaries of another country, its claim to statehood during the apartheid era was somewhat bizarre. Any suggestion that this fragmentation could endure into a reconstituted South Africa was unlikely to be taken seriously.
24. 'Draft minutes of the fourth meeting of WG4', 17/2/1992, item 3.1.
25. South African Communist Party, 'Submission to WG4', 6/2/1992.
26. Natal/Transvaal Indian Congress, 'Submission to WG4', 6/2/1992.
27. 'Report on the meeting held between the Steering Committee of WG4 and the DMC on Consensus', 2/3/1992.
28. Venda saw no need for a referendum, but was prepared to participate in one.
29. African National Congress, 'Submission to SC1', 17/2/1992.
30. 'Draft minutes of the first joint meeting of sub-groups one and two of WG4', 24/3/1992.
31. Telephone interview, February 1992, Johannesburg.
32. Charles Simkins to Errol Moorcroft, 'Reincorporation of TBVC states', 24/4/1992.
33. Transkei government, 'Addendum to Transkei's Working Group 4 Input to Codesa', 21/4/1992.
34. The three parties had earlier met president De Klerk in Cape Town to assert their unease with the Codesa process. At this meeting Buthelezi presented De Klerk with a 16-page memorandum on behalf of the group.
35. Despite the stance of the two administrations, opinion polls suggest that the ANC could expect an overwhelming share of the Ciskei vote and substantial support in Bophuthatswana.
36. Charles Simkins to Errol Moorcroft, 'Reincorporation of the TBVC states', 24/4/1992.
37. Note that provision for dual citizenship for TBVC citizens on an individual basis already existed in of the 1986 Restoration of Citizenship Act (see note 2). TBVC citizens who reclaimed their South African citizenship were not required to renounce their TBVC citizenship. See South African Communist Party, 'The Restoration of Citizenship', memorandum submitted to SG2, 5/3/1992.
38. Note that the SAG's presentation was made on 24 March, just one week after De Klerk's referendum triumph. Was this indeed a change of position

by the SAG, bolstered by a new-found confidence in its prospects for the future? There is no conclusive evidence either way, but Moorcroft, chairman of SC1 and rapporteur, believes in retrospect that the SAG was taking a tougher position.

39. Minutes of WG4, 21/4/1992.
40. 'Report by rapporteurs – 21 April 1992'. Minutes of WG4, 21 April, Addendum G.
41. 'Working Group 4: Proposal by the Rapporteurs', 27/4/1992. Draft.
42. Interview with Geoff Budlender, Johannesburg, 12 December 1992.
43. Charles Simkins, interviewed in Johannesburg, 19 January 1993.
44. This document was entitled 'Second Report of the Rapporteurs', dated 27 April; their first report, dated 21 April, was a simple collation of standpoints.
45. Minutes of WG4, 4/5/1992, item 4.1.1.
46. Matthew Phosa, interviewed in Johannesburg, 19/11/1992.
47. Telephone interview, Dullah Omar, Cape Town, 25/1/1993.
48. A senior Bophuthatswana participant remarked in an interview that, at WG4, the SAG 'had been taken to the cleaners by the ANC'.
49. This would do more than reduce its share of the vote. It would also concede the principle of a united South Africa, and open the way to secession by Afrikaans and Zulu-speaking right wingers.
50. National Party, 'Submission to SC3', 23/3/1992.
51. Geoff Budlender, interviewed in Johannesburg, 22/1/1993.
52. See statistics quoted in Schlemmer, Lawrence, 'Natal: a special charter?' in Friedman, Steven and Humphries, Richard (ed), *Federalism and its foes*, Centre for Policy Studies, forthcoming.
53. Ciskei continues to favour its absorption into an eastern Cape region. Bophuthatswana's commitment to 'independence' is belied by its participation in a forum which is attempting to agree to a regional arrangement for the western Transvaal.
54. The DP's call for an investigation of customary law was however rejected.
55. Charles Simkins, interviewed Johannesburg, 19 January 1993.

THE GENDER ADVISORY COMMITTEE

The missing 53 per cent

1. Since the GAC's task was partly to help bring unorganised, marginalised voters to the polls, the NP's stance could have been seen as an attempt to prevent that. But is seems unlikely that this was its motive.
2. Report of the Gender Advisory Committee to Codesa 2, p 5, 2.1.4.
3. Report of the Gender Advisory Committee to Codesa 2, op cit.
4. In Canada, participants note, the equality clause has been used by men to challenge in court special treatment for women.
5. Shortly before Codesa 2, the GAC began a hurried survey of discriminatory legislation, largely through the contribution of Denise Bjorkman, then acting as an advisor to the IFP. This may have diverted attention away from the required focus on transitional procedures.

PART 3: The aftermath

Back to the streets

1. See African National Congress, *Ready To Govern: ANC Policy Guidelines for a Democratic South Africa, adopted at the National Conference, 28-31 May 1992*, Johannesburg, 1992.
2. Kasrils was an SACP delegate to WG1 but played little or nor role in its work.
3. Sam Shilowa, Cosatu assistant general secretary, in interviews with team member Patrick Bulger.
4. *Business Day*, 1/7/1992.
5. Briefing attended by team member Patrick Bulger.
6. *Business Day*, 9/3/1992. Cosatu complained that the government was unilaterally placing crucial areas of the economy outside the reach of political decision-making in an attempt to limit the power of a future majority government. The forum, which was designed to give the union movement a role in negotiating economic policy, was established in late 1992.
7. A reference to the East German city in which mass marches appeared to trigger the collapse of the government.
8. These positions were set out by the SACP's Cronin in a paper entitled 'The Boat, the Tap and the Leipzig Option'. The 'boat' referred to Codesa negotiators who did not want 'to rock the boat'. The 'tap' was the strategy of those who wanted to turn 'mass action' on and off to achieve bargaining gains; they saw it as a tactic only. Cronin rejected both these views as well as the 'Leipzig Option', advocating instead the position described in this paragraph.
9. *Business Day*, 27/5/1992.
10. Attendance at the main rally, addressed by Mandela, was estimated at 30 000. Police estimated total rally attendance around the country at 80 000; other estimates suggested 100 000–150 000. Even ANC opponents acknowledged that these were impressive figures, but they failed to match some over-ambitious claims before 16 June. *Beeld*, 17/6/1992; *Citizen*, 18/6/1992.
11. 'Statement by the National Executive Committee of the African National Congress', 23/7/1992. Some specific demands included the termination of all 'covert operations' by security forces; confinement to barracks of special security forces; and suspension and prosecution of 'all officers and security force personnel involved in the violence'. The hostel demands insisted that they be 'phased out', replaced with family accommodation, and that they be fenced, guarded and searched regularly.
12. Letter, De Klerk to Mandela, 2/7/1992.
13. Letter, Mandela to De Klerk, 9/7/1992.
14. *Business Day*, 25/6/1992.
15. See Friedman, Steven, *Another Elephant? Prospects for a South African Social Contract*, Centre for Policy Studies, Johannesburg, 1991.
16. The Charter urged the need to 'move as speedily as possible to a political settlement based on [universal franchise] elections'; it also endorsed an 'elected constitution-making body unfettered in its capacity' to draft a constitution. It stipulated principles by which this body would be bound, but only one of them, elected regional governments with 'adequate' powers, could be seen to reflect an NP demand. It also endorsed an independent elections commission. See *New Nation*, 31/7/1992.
17. *Business Day*, 6/8/1992.
18. *New Nation*, 4/9/1992.

19. In the event, Gqozo, alarmed by the threatened march, did not attend the conference and was in his office when the troops opened fire.
20. *The Star*, 9/9/1992.
21. *The Star*, 15/9/1992.
22. A few days before Bisho the ANC's NEC had met and formally rejected an immediate start to negotiations. A member of its negotiation team – also, interestingly, an SACP member – confided afterwards to friends: 'The comrades seem to have lost all touch with reality.'
23. Botha confidently predicted that the NP was within reach of winning the first non-racial election.
24. *The Star*, 25/7/1991.
25. *Business Day*, 7/7/1992.
26. *Business Day*, 10/8/1992.
27. Cohen, Herman J, 'The Current Situation': statement before the subcommittee on Africa of the House Foreign Affairs Committee, Washington DC, 23/7/1992, *US Department of State Dispatch*, vol 3 no 30, 27/7/1992.
28. Cohen signalled this position in his 23 July presentation: 'We oppose linking continued negotiations with an end to violence. This only gives extremist elements on both sides a veto over the process.' see *Department of State Dispatch*, ibid. At the time, this seemed to be largely aimed at the ANC which had broken off talks. Repeated later, it was aimed at the NP.
29. Interview with team member Alan Fine.
30. *Agenda*, SATV, 31/1/1993.
31. Letter, De Klerk to Mandela, 2/7/1992.
32. Letter, Mandela to De Klerk, 9/7/1992.
33. De Klerk to Mandela, op cit.
34. *The Star*, 15/9/1992.
35. Kasrils's judgment, he said, 'may not have been the correct one'. He noted that he and SACP chief Chris Hani, another key advocate of 'mass action', were loyal ANC members and added: 'If I were to say that ... this was the decision taken regarding future demonstrations, I will get their maximum support.' *The Star*, ibid.
36. De Klerk to Mandela, op cit.
37. Record of Understanding, signed by Mandela and De Klerk, 26/9/1992. The ban on weapons was subject to an exemption to be prepared by the Goldstone Commission. It has not been enforced since the Record was signed.
38. *The Star*, 1/10/1992. The article was entitled 'Negotiations: What Room For Compromise?' and it triggered a heated debate in the pages of *African Communist*.
39. According to these sources, the NEC mandated Slovo to write it as a means of testing support for compromise. This is supported by a senior SACP source who describes it as evidence of 'the party's constructive contribution to the ANC alliance'.
40. African National Congress, Department of Information and Publicity, *Negotiations: A Strategic Perspective* (as adopted by the national working committee on 18/11/1992).
41. *Sowetan*, 19/2/1993. This report quoted an 'understanding' reportedly reached between the two parties which held out the prospect of a senate (in the new constitution, not the assembly), which might offer a role for regional representatives who would enjoy a veto over any proposals which affected the regions.
42. *Business Day*, 28/9/1992.
43. *Business Day*, 5/10/1992.
44. It insisted for example that federal troops could not be deployed in the region without its consent. *The Star*, 2/12/1992.

45. Tony Ardington, president of the Sugar Association and Cedric Savage, managing director of Tongaat–Huletts, warned that the region could not 'go it alone' economically. *Business Day*, 18/12/92; *Finansies en Tegniek*, 11/12/92.
46. *Weekly Mail*, 29/1 – 4/2/1992.
47. Before the meeting, Inkatha had made several threats which seemed to herald an attempt to disrupt proceedings. It did not – and, when the CP tried to place obstacles in the way of progress to a new convention, it was rebuked by Mdlalose. *City Press*, 7/3/1993.
48. In a private discussion with team member Steven Friedman, an IFP leader noted that the party received regular confidential reports on voter allegiances in Natal/KwaZulu. 'The evidence,' he conceded, 'is not encouraging.'
49. Agreement on hostels was partly implemented; that on weapons not at all. Political prisoners were released, but the government also used the Record, in the teeth of ANC protests, to override parliament by passing the Further Indemnity Act (see WG1).

PART 4: The way forward

Slow walk to freedom

1. *City Press*, 7/3/1993.
2. Interview, Lawrie Schlemmer, 2 December 1992.
3. Interview, Ken Andrew, 17 November 1992.
4. Interview, Joe Thloloe, 16 February 1993.
5. Interview, Frederik Van Zyl Slabbert, 20 January 1993.
6. Interview, Pravin Gordhan, 7 December 1992.
7. Interview, Frederik Van Zyl Slabbert, 20 January 1993.
8. Interview, Frederik Van Zyl Slabbert, 20 January 1993.
9. Interview, Jeremy Cronin, 13 November 1992.
10. Interview, Joel Netshitenze (Peter Mayibuye), 15 December 1992.
11. Interview, Philip Nel, 19 November 1992.
12. Interview, Heribert Adam, 16 November 1992.
13. Interview, Willie Breytenbach, 18 November 1992.
14. Interview, Desmond Lockey., 18 November 1992.
15. Interview, Frederik Van Zyl Slabbert, 20 January 1993.
16. Interview, Jeremy Cronin, 13 November 1992. Leaders had to negotiate around the accord because it provided for ways of regulating mass mobilisation.
17. *Negotiations: A Strategic Perspective*, document adopted by the national executive committee of the ANC, 25 November 1992.
18. Interview, Frederik Van Zyl Slabbert, 20 January 1993.
19. Interview, Joel Netshitenze (Peter Mayibuye), 15 December 1992.
20. At the conference on federalism mentioned in the previous section.
21. See *SA Barometer*, vol 7 no 2, 29 January 1993.
22. A government/PAC meeting in Botswana in March deadlocked when the PAC refused to suspend hostilities. *Sowetan*, 3/3/93.
23. Only the Azanian People's Organisation and extra-parliamentary right-wing groups remained outside the talks.
24. Interview, Gustav von Bratt, 3 March 1993.
25. *Business Day*, 11/2/1993, quoted 'parliamentary sources' claiming that the NP wanted an interim government to include only itself, the ANC and NP. Allister Sparks, 'Elections will show who is pretending', *Daily Dispatch*,

24/2/1993, claimed that the NP wanted to set the threshold at 15 per cent, which could exclude the IFP as well; the ANC wanted 5 per cent, which could produce a five-party government. This development is consistent with the comment of a senior government negotiator who suggested, even before Codesa began, that the NP would abandon its concern for 'minority rights' if it secured power sharing. See Friedman, *The Shapers of Things to Come?* Centre for Policy Studies, op cit.

26. *Rapport*, 21/2/1993 reported dissent within the NP on this issue.
27. Deputy Constitutional Development minister Fanus Schoeman. See *Business Day*, 15/2/1993, *Sunday Times*, 21/2/1993.
28. *Business Day*, 19/2/1993.
29. Land in the 'homelands' has traditionally been owned by the tribe. In KwaZulu particularly, the chief, as head of the tribe, has the power to allocate land. Legislation passed in KwaZulu in 1991 allowed for private land ownership, but only if the chief agreed to this.
30. Interview, Frederik Van Zyl Slabbert, 20 January 1993. At its Kabwe conference, the ANC adopted a strategy which made black incumbents of homeland governments and black local authorities targets for guerrilla activity and mass mobilisation.
31. Interview, Natal political analyst, December 1992. Buthelezi refused to join constitutional negotiations during the 1980s state of emergency, insisting that banned leaders and organisations should participate.
32. Interview, Joe Thloloe, 16 February 1993. Thloloe suggests that Buthelezi might then have joined the ANC, which seems to overstate the point.
33. *Business Day*, 12/3/1993.
34. *Business Day*, 15/1/1993.
35. Interview, Lawrie Schlemmer, 2 December 1992.
36. Friedman, Steven, in *Journal of Democracy*, forthcoming.
37. Friedman, Steven, in *Journal of Democracy*, forthcoming.
38. Friedman, Steven, *The Shapers of Things to Come?*, op cit.
39. Interview, Desmond Lockey, 18 November 1992.
40. See, for example, remarks by Thloloe in Rantete, *Liberation and Negotiation*, op cit.
41. Interview, Jeremy Cronin, 13 November 1992.
42. Lawrence Schlemmer, 'The Scenario of Scenarios', briefing, Centre for Policy Studies, 2/3/1993.
43. Van Zyl Slabbert, Frederik, *Quest for Democracy*, Penguin, 1992.
44. Interview, Lawrie Schlemmer, 2 December 1992.
45. Interview, Paul Zulu, 9 December 1992.
46. Interview, Gustav von Bratt, 3 March, 1993.
47. Interview, Oscar Dhlomo, 7 December 1992.
48. Informal interview with Natal politician, Pretoria, March 1993.
49. Interview, Oscar Dhlomo, 7 December 1992.
50. Interview, Lawrie Schlemmer, 2 December 1992.
51. Schlemmer briefing, op cit.
52. According to a survey by Market and Opinion Research (Pty) Ltd in 1989, only one in five whites supported racial partition; a 1985 survey found that 41 per cent of CP supporters believed negotiated power sharing to be inevitable. See Giliomee, Hermann and Schlemmer, Lawrence, *From Apartheid to Nation-Building*, Cape Town, Oxford University Press, 1990, pp 153, 157.
53. Rustow, Dankwart A, 'Transitions to Democracy: Towards a Dynamic Model', in *Comparative Politics*, April 1970.
54. See, for example, Shain, Yossi and Linz, Juan, 'Interim Governments', in *Journal of Democracy*, vol 3 no 1, January 1992.